THE ARCTIC PROMISE:
LEGAL AND POLITICAL AUTONOMY OF GREENLAND AND NUNAVUT

In Canada's Eastern Arctic and Greenland, the Inuit have been the majority for centuries. In recent years, they have been given a promise from Canadian and Danish governments that offers them more responsibility for their lands and thus control over their lives without fear of being outnumbered by outsiders. *The Arctic Promise* looks at how much the Inuit vision of self-governance relates to the existing public governance systems of Greenland and Nunavut, and how much autonomy there can be for territories that remain subordinate units of larger states.

By means of a bottom-up approach involving cultural immersion, contextual, jurisprudential, and historical legal comparisons of Greenland and Nunavut, *The Arctic Promise* examines the forms, evolution, and scope of the right to autonomy in these Arctic jurisdictions. Loukacheva argues that the right to autonomy should encompass or protect Inuit jurisdiction in legal systems and the administration of justice, and should allow the Inuit direct participation in international affairs where issues that affect their homelands are concerned. *The Arctic Promise* deals with areas of comparative constitutional law, international law, Aboriginal law, legal anthropology, political science, and international relations, using each to contribute to the understanding of the right to indigenous autonomy.

NATALIA LOUKACHEVA is a post-doctoral fellow at the Munk Centre for International Studies at the University of Toronto.

NATALIA LOUKACHEVA

The Arctic Promise

Legal and Political Autonomy of Greenland and Nunavut

UNIVERSITY OF TORONTO PRESS
Toronto Buffalo London

© University of Toronto Press Incorporated 2007
Toronto Buffalo London
Printed in Canada

ISBN 978-0-8020-9295-3 (cloth)
ISBN 978-0-8020-9486-5 (paper)

∞

Printed on acid-free paper

Library and Archives Canada Cataloguing in Publication

Loukacheva, Natalia, 1973–
    The Arctic promise : legal and political autonomy of Greenland and
Nunavut / Natalia Loukacheva.

    Includes bibliographical references and index.
    ISBN 978-0-8020-9295-3 (bound)
    ISBN 978-0-8020-9486-5 (pbk.)

    1. Constitutional law – Nunavut – Textbooks.   2. Constitutional
law – Greenland – Textbooks.   3. Nunavut – Politics and government –
Textbooks.   4. Greenland – Politics and government – Textbooks.   5. Inuit –
Politics and government – Textbooks.   6. Comparative government –
Textbooks.   I. Title.

    KEN8454.L68 2007   342.9719'50872   C2007-901650-2
    KF4482.L68 2007

This book has been published with the help of a grant from the Canadian
 Federation for the Humanities and Social Sciences, through the Aid to
Scholarly Publications Programme, using funds provided by the Social
Sciences and Humanities Research Council of Canada.

University of Toronto Press acknowledges the financial assistance to its
publishing program of the Canada Council for the Arts and the Ontario
Arts Council.

University of Toronto Press acknowledges the financial support for its
publishing activities of the Government of Canada through the Book
 Publishing Industry Development Program (BPIDP).

Contents

Acknowledgments   vii

Abbreviations   xi

Maps   xiii

Introduction   3

1 The Inuit of Greenland and Nunavut: From Subjugation to Self-Government?   17

2 The Constitutional Dimensions of the Governance of Nunavut and Greenland   33

3 Territorial Government versus Home Rule: The Structure of Nunavut's and Greenland's Institutions   53

4 The Jurisdiction of Greenland and Nunavut   73

5 Greenland and Nunavut in International Affairs   103

Conclusion   145

Notes   153

Bibliography   217

Index   249

Acknowledgments

This manuscript has benefited from the expertise and wisdom of many people. I would like to thank the residents of Nunavut and Greenland who participated in the interviews and shared their insights on the vision of governance in the Arctic. I am especially indebted in this respect to Jack Hicks, whose invaluable comments on early drafts, generosity in sharing research resources, and enormous support for this project made my field work in Nunavut and Greenland possible. I am grateful to Hugh Lloyd, Letia Obed, Nora Sanders, Sheila Watt-Cloutier, Paul Quassa, Simon Awa, Paul Okalik, Robert Carson, Jim Bell, Kenn Harper, Sandra Inutiq, Aaju Peter, David Omilgoitok, Beverly Browne, Cathy Towtongie, Claude Beauchamp, John Bainbridge, John Lamb, Kelly Gallagher-Mackay, David Akeeagok, Lynda Gunn, Tagak Curley, Jack Anawak, Jimi Onalik, Anne Crawford, Marianne Demmer, Nicole Arnatsiaq, and Rita Anilniliak in Nunavut; and to Mikaela Engell, Birger Poppel, Alfred Jacobssen, Peter Bertrand, Marianne Lykke Thomsen, and Paul Knudsen in Greenland. I also wish to express my special thanks to John Merritt in Ottawa and to Peter Hopkins of the European Commission.

I am deeply grateful to my former supervisors (2001–4) at the Faculty of Law, University of Toronto, Patrick Macklem and Lorne Sossin, for supporting me throughout my work and for their comments. I owe a special debt of appreciation to Peter H. Russell for patiently reading numerous drafts and providing constructive criticism of my work. This book substantially benefited from his wisdom. I wish to thank Peter Jull, whose numerous brilliant publications on subjects relevant to this book, which I have been reading for years, helped broaden my understanding and vision of the situation in Greenland and Nunavut. Special thanks also go to Darlene Johnston, for valuable suggestions on this manuscript, Franklyn Griffiths for commenting on drafts of chapter 5, Karen Knop for commenting on the first draft, and Martin Scheinin, director of the Institute for Human Rights, Åbo Akademi University, Finland, for taking his time to comment on this work. I am also grateful to Pierre Rousseau for his constructive suggestions on chapter 4 and to Ulrik Pram Gad for comments on various parts of this manuscript. I wish to thank Guðmundur S. Alfreðsson, Jens Dahl, and Rasmus Ole Rasmussen, for sharing information on developments in Greenland, John Borrows for sharing his experiences about Nunavut, and Albert Berry for his comments and suggestions on various parts of this book. I am especially grateful to reviewers of the University of Toronto Press for their valuable comments and careful examination of this book.

This book has been prepared during my term holding a postdoctoral scholar's award within the Major Collaborative Research Initiative on 'Globalization and Autonomy' sponsored by the Social Sciences and Humanities Research Council of Canada. I wish to thank the director of the project, William D. Coleman. I owe a special debt to my immediate mentor, Louis W. Pauly, director of the Centre for International Studies, Munk Centre, University of Toronto. This book would not be possible without his enormous support and encouragement. I am also thankful to Steven F. Bernstein.

This manuscript could not have been completed without the financial support of the Faculty of Law at the University of Toronto, the travel grants from the School of Graduate Studies and the Mary Beatty Scholarship at the University of Toronto, the Social Sciences and Humanities Research Council of Canada, and the Northern Studies Training Program (NSTP) INAC–Ottawa, and the Centre for International Studies, Munk Centre, University of Toronto.

I would like to thank the librarians at the Bora Laskin Law Library, particularly Karen Trevon and Esmé Saulig, for assistance with interlibrary loans; Michael Plaxton, Rachel Applebaum, and Janet Hyer for editorial assistance; Barbara Tessman for diligently editing the final version of the manuscript, and Tina Lagopolous at the Centre for International Studies, Munk Centre, University of Toronto, for technical assistance. I wish to express my appreciation to Virgil Duff and Anne Laughlin of the University of Toronto Press for supporting the book through to publication. I owe my greatest thanks to Matthew D. Garfield for reading and proofreading the manuscript at the early stages, for providing technical support and encouragement, and for his invaluable comments and insights. I am also grateful to my former mentor (1992–9) at the Urals State Law Academy, Yekaterinburg, the Russian Federation, Dr Peter Savitskiy, who guided my life-long interest in the field of comparative law and politics. Finally, I would like to express my gratitude to my parents for their moral support and care, and to my grandparents, the late Dr Aleksei Mezentsev and Dr Zoya Mezentseva, whose life-long commitment to medical science and passion for cures and research will always serve as an inspiration to me in my more modest endeavours.

Abbreviations

AEPS	Arctic Environmental Protection Strategy
BDM	ballistic missile defence
CARC	Canadian Arctic Resources Committee
DEW Line	Distant Early Warning Line
DIAND	Department of Indian Affairs and Northern Development
ECOSOC	Economic and Social Council (UN)
EDF	European Development Fund
EEC	European Economic Community
EU	European Union
HBC	Hudson's Bay Company
IA	Inuit Ataqatigiit Party
IASC	International Arctic Science Committee
ICC	Inuit Circumpolar Conference (from 2006, Inuit Circumpolar Council)
ILO	International Labour Organization
INAC	Indian and Northern Affairs Canada
IPS	Indigenous Peoples Secretariat
IQ	*Inuit Qaujimajatuqangit* (Inuit traditional knowledge and values)
MOU	memorandum of understanding
NATO	North Atlantic Treaty Organization
NGO	non-governmental organization
NLCA	Nunavut Land Claims Agreement
NORAD	North American Air Defence Command (from 1991, North American Aerospace Defence Command)
NTI	Nunavut Tunngavik Incorporated

NWMP	North-West Mounted Police
NWT	North-West Territories (to 1905); Northwest Territories
OCT	overseas country and territory
RCMP	Royal Canadian Mounted Police
RMWMP	Royal North West Mounted Police
TFN	Tungavik Federation of Nunavut
WTO	World Trade Organization

Map 1. Greenland and Arctic Region. Courtesy of the University of Texas Libraries, The University of Texas at Austin.

Map 2. Nunavut and surrounding Canadian provinces and territories. Courtesy of Listings Canada: http://listingsca.com/maps.asp

THE ARCTIC PROMISE:
LEGAL AND POLITICAL AUTONOMY OF
GREENLAND AND NUNAVUT

Introduction

Nunavut (meaning 'our land'), which was carved out of the Northwest Territories (NWT) of Canada in 1999, and Greenland (Kalaallit Nunaat, meaning 'the country of Greenlanders'), which obtained home rule status within Denmark in 1979, are in the process of attaining more autonomy – Nunavut within the framework of the territorial governance system in Canada's Eastern Arctic, and Greenland by anticipated extension of self-government within the Danish realm. This process of increasing autonomy is a result of a combination of factors. These include not only the development of Inuit political consciousness in both jurisdictions and consequent demands for self-determination, but also political compromises surrounding the accommodation of the Nunavut Inuit within a multi-ethnic Canadian polity, nation-building developments in Greenland, and the gradual devolution of powers from both Denmark and Canada. I argue that, with the evolution of Greenlandic and Nunavut governance systems, these Arctic jurisdictions are displaying a new form of autonomy that is not addressed adequately by international or comparative constitutional law. Further, there is no legal definition for this form of autonomy, and it can best be understood if we look at de facto developments that gradually shape the juridical scope and content of this autonomy.

Much scholarly writing on the issue of autonomy and indigenous self-governance demonstrates confusion with regard to legal concepts of autonomy. These concepts can be rendered clearer by a comparative constitutional analysis of measures that secure autonomy in Arctic areas where indigenous Inuit peoples are the majority. In Canada's Eastern Arctic and Greenland, the Inuit have been the majority population for centuries. As a result of gradual constitutional developments, they received promises from both the Canadian and Danish governments that encouraged them to assume more responsibility for their lands in order to regain control of their lives. This book evaluates how the Inuit vision of self-governance relates to the public governance systems of Greenland and Nunavut, which are based on non-indigenous institutions and norms, and how much autonomy there can be for territories that remain subordinate units of larger states.

In this study, I present a comparative empirical and normative survey of territorial governance in Nunavut and the home rule system in Greenland. I explore different legal arrangements for Nunavut and Greenland that secure a measure of legal and political autonomy for their indigenous peoples, and analyse the rapidly evolving governance systems of these Arctic jurisdictions. By addressing the question of whether there is an emerging right to indigenous autonomy, I hope to reveal the ambiguity surrounding the right to autonomy under international law. I argue that, although this right is housed in the concept of self-determination, its content and scope may vary from jurisdiction to jurisdiction and should be understood in the context of each particular situation. An empirical analysis of Greenland's and Nunavut's governance systems shows that autonomy is not a static phenomenon. It is a dynamic concept, constantly developing and evolving towards greater recognition at the de jure level.

The ways in which the right to autonomy is exercised in the two jurisdictions have been heavily influenced by the interaction between Inuit forms of social organization and the opposing legal and political regimes introduced by colonial and contemporary authorities. The dramatic differences in outlook and way of life between Inuit and non-Inuit populations require approaches to the development of autonomy in the Arctic that take into account indigenous values and knowledge. By means of a bottom-up approach – including contextual, jurisprudential, textualist, and historical legal comparisons of Greenland and Nunavut – this book will examine the forms and evolution of the right to autonomy among the Inuit. Governmental authorities should pay due respect to indigenous peoples' expectations for expanding their legal capability to exercise jurisdiction in areas traditionally non-transferable to subnational regions. Accordingly, the right to autonomy should encompass or protect Inuit jurisdiction in legal systems and the administration of justice. It should allow the Inuit direct participation in international affairs where their homelands are concerned and in security issues relevant to the development of their lands.

The subject of this study – the governance concepts of Greenland and Nunavut – was inspired by the unique legal position of the Inuit in these regions and by the remarkable changes that have taken place in recent decades in these Northern lands. This study examines the extent to which, within the framework of territorial public governance and home rule structures, the Inuit have been able to secure their interests and needs without de jure indigenous self-governance. At the same time, these subnational Arctic regions are constitutional hybrids with some jurisdiction comparable to provinces in Canada. Regardless of the profound differences between Canada as a federal state and Denmark as a unitary state, the two countries have strikingly similar policies towards, and relationships with, the Inuit peoples. In both jurisdictions the Inuit peoples, notwithstanding their geographical remoteness, are one people[1] with similar roots, needs, and aspirations for greater political autonomy.

There have been considerable efforts in recent years to promote different autonomous arrangements for indigenous peoples of the North. However, it is not clear within legal and political science scholarship whether the right to indigenous autonomy exists in international or domestic law, and, if so, how it can help indigenous peoples to preserve their livelihood, traditional culture, and values. By illuminating the legal position of the indigenous Inuit of Greenland and Nunavut, I will consider to what extent constitutional arrangements can be infused with indigenous values and perspectives, allowing these arrangements to attain greater legitimacy among those governed by their terms. The scope of this book is dictated by the geographical dispersion of the Inuit people and by their stage of development towards self-governance. I have chosen to examine the Inuit in Greenland and the Canadian Eastern Arctic because of the former's advanced state with respect to self-governance and the achievements of the latter in that direction. Despite the focus on these two regions, there are lessons to be learned from the experience of the Inuit of Chukotka, Alaska, and of other Canadian regions outside of Nunavut, as well as from other indigenous peoples of the Arctic. It should be noted, too, that the legal status of the Inuit of Labrador, Northern Quebec, and the Western Arctic remains a subject for further research.

A few qualifications are in order. In this book the term 'Nunavummiut' includes all citizens of Nunavut – Inuit and non-Inuit. Those Inuit who are the beneficiaries of the Nunavut Land Claims Agreement (NLCA) have their rights and obligations protected, and currently there is little confusion over who to consider a 'beneficiary.' In the National Registry in Greenland, the population is divided for statistical purposes into those 'born in Greenland' and those 'born outside Greenland.' Children who were born in Greenland but whose parents are not Greenlandic-born fit into the category 'born in Greenland,' whereas offspring of Greenlanders who, for example, had their children while studying in Denmark would be registered as 'born outside Greenland' when the parents move back to Greenland.[2] Although the term 'Greenlanders' can be applied to all residents of Greenland – including all linguistic groups among the Inuit population, Danes, and representatives of other nationalities who were born and live in Greenland – in this study, the term 'Greenlanders' often refers to indigenous residents, who identify themselves as Greenlanders and represent Greenland as a nation of Greenlanders.

'Autonomy' is a vague concept subject to multiple interpretations by different scholars and different groups, both Inuit and non-Inuit. For the purposes of this study, I define autonomy as being equivalent to self-government in the context of an internal right to self-determination. I do not explore the right to external self-determination, including secession, as an attribute of autonomy. Further, this study uses the concept of autonomy in constitutional legal terms, rather than in the context of local self-administration or municipal levels of government.[3] This narrows the scope of this book to autonomous entities in the Arctic with constitutional powers transferred from unitary or federal state authorities to the institutions of territorial or regional public governance. The book does not explore in detail issues of economic sustainability, political economy, fiscal autonomy, intergovernmental relations, language, or social policies in Greenland or Nunavut. Rather, it looks at the legal scope of political autonomy in the Arctic, with the main emphasis being on the areas of non-transferable jurisdiction of Greenlandic and Nunavut authorities – namely, the administration of justice, international affairs, defence, and security. In light of probable changes in the status of Greenlandic home rule, these non-transferable areas arguably raise the most challenging theoretical and practical questions surrounding frameworks of political autonomy and governance in the Arctic.

In 1999 the home rule government of Greenland set up a Commission on Self-Governance. The commission delivered its report in 2003 with recommendations for a draft partnership agreement between Greenland and Denmark with regard to Greenland's right to self-governance.[4] The commission's recommendations call for expansion of

Greenland's autonomy in a number of areas. Following negotiations between Danish and Greenlandic authorities, in 2004 a Danish-Greenlandic Parliamentary Self-Governance Commission was appointed with equal representation from Denmark and Greenland. The commission's mandate is 'with reference to Greenland's constitutional position and in conformity with the Greenlandic peoples' right of self-determination in accordance to international law [to] consider and suggest ways by which the Greenlandic authorities can assume further control where this is constitutionally possible.'[5] The commission aims to develop a plan for increased Greenlandic self-government within Denmark. Greenlanders hope that a partnership agreement will establish Greenland and Denmark as equal partners within the kingdom.[6] However, the mandate of the commission also notes that, according to the agreement between the Danish and Greenlandic governments, the people of Greenland shall decide whether they want independence.[7] Ongoing Danish-Greenlandic negotiations and anticipated changes in the constitutional status of Greenland by 2008, along with the possible introduction by the Danish and Greenland parliaments of the partnership agreement on self-governance and Greenland's probable focus on independence, have limited the present research to legislation and materials available up to February 2007. Despite existing limitations, I consider the Home Rule Act of 1978 as an important legal basis for understanding Greenland's present constitutional place within the Kingdom of Denmark.

This book covers areas of international law, comparative constitutional law, Aboriginal law, legal anthropology, history, political science, and international relations, and contributes to the literature on legal theory by deepening the understanding of the right to autonomy. It aims to fill the gap in current scholarship on the concepts of governance and autonomy in the Arctic. In terms of methodology, this study represents one of the first efforts to compare Inuit peoples' quest for self-governance in two jurisdictions. With regard to institutions, this study offers consideration of the concept of governance in the Arctic and information on current problems, prospects, mechanisms of dispute resolution, and structures of governance. Thus, it may be useful for indigenous groups of the North who are bringing forward self-government arrangements.

In chapter 1, 'The Inuit of Greenland and Nunavut: From Subjugation to Self-Government?,' I compare Greenland and Nunavut in terms of the historical, political, social, economic, and legal conditions that have affected these Arctic jurisdictions in their transition to modern

governance structures. I argue that the Inuit quest for political autonomy in these two jurisdictions has similar origins. I will show that there
are also striking similarities in the political, legal, cultural, economic,
and social development of Inuit governance and in the policies of Denmark and Canada towards the Inuit.

In chapter 2, 'The Constitutional Dimensions of the Governance of
Nunavut and Greenland,' I examine the constitutional significance of
Greenland's and Nunavut's governance arrangements. This analysis
shows that, although the Greenland Home Rule Act, the Nunavut Act,
and the NLCA do not explicitly envisage Inuit self-government, and
some features of 'colonial legacy' are retained in these documents, self-
government is not a legal fiction in either jurisdiction. Home rule in
Greenland has evolved to meet the Inuit's needs at a functional rather
than juridical level. In Nunavut, the combination of decision-making
powers and institutions created under the system of public governance
provides valuable instruments for Inuit self-governance.

Chapter 3, 'Territorial Government versus Home Rule: The Structure
of Nunavut's and Greenland's Institutions,' provides an overview on the
effectiveness of Inuit self-governance through the lens of Inuit participation in Greenland and Nunavut politics, political systems, and institutions of governance. It shows how the Inuit in both jurisdictions are
being challenged by the transition and adjustment to the non-Inuit values of other societies and how they risk being overwhelmed by Western
concepts of governance. The study then turns to an examination of
legal autonomy in the Arctic and explores the jurisdiction of Greenland
and Nunavut in non-transferable areas as an important indicator of the
evolution of the concept of autonomy for Northern lands.

Chapters 4 and 5, which examine the jurisdictional authorities of
Greenland and Nunavut, draw on the aspirations of Inuit authorities to
take over responsibilities in the non-transferable areas of judicial/legal
systems and international relations, including defence/security, as a
means of promoting their autonomy. Potential sources of legal authority
for these areas are examined. Chapter 4, 'The Jurisdiction of Greenland
and Nunavut,' explores the possibility of Inuit legal institutions and judicial powers within the scope of the home rule and public governance
arrangements. I argue that there is no formal legal obstacle to the creation of a more or less independent justice system in Greenland and an
Inuit judiciary within Nunavut. However, social, political, economic, and
technical difficulties do not favour these developments. Chapter 5,
'Greenland and Nunavut in International Affairs,' first assesses the legiti-

macy, perspectives, and outcomes of international af-fairs involving Greenland and Nunavut. It also examines Inuit forms of international cooperation. This chapter further considers the transferability of security jurisdiction to Greenland and Nunavut in the framework of the both regions' legitimate interests. It addresses the question of whether citizens of subnational entities like Greenland and Nunavut should have some legal capacity on questions of defence or homeland security policies that concern or affect their lands.

Although this book examines the general framework of constitutional and political autonomy in Arctic regions where indigenous peoples are the majority, I do not mean to suggest that internal self-government is a panacea or the ideal solution for realizing their right to self-determination. Instead, I argue that existing forms of public governance may be effective in meeting indigenous peoples' needs without the enactment of special forms of indigenous autonomy. The 'Arctic promise' means that there might be room for a unique vision of governance in the North inclusive of Southern modes of governance, indigenous knowledge and values, and flexible legal imagination on the scope of autonomy. This book leaves open the question of whether autonomy is a temporary stage on the road to independence (one of Greenland's options) or an 'artificial' construct that can coexist in the framework of financial dependence and neo-colonial paternalism of national states. Despite the political significance of existing constitutional arrangements to the Inuit of Greenland and Nunavut, I do not suggest that their models of governance are applicable to all Arctic areas where indigenous peoples are the majority. I argue that forms of autonomy in the North vary and should be understood in the context of each particular situation. Finally, it should be noted that I do not speak for the Inuit of Greenland or Nunavut. The views presented in this study solely reflect my understanding of the issues of governance in the Arctic from an outsider's perspective.

Why the Inuit of Greenland and Nunavut?

Resemblances are the shadows of differences. Different people see different similarities and similar differences.

Vladimir Nabokov

Although there are differences in the legal status of Greenland and Nunavut, geographical, demographic, cultural, political, economic, and historical similarities predominate and make these jurisdictions good candidates for comparison. An analysis of these commonalities is required for our understanding of the roots of Nunavut's and Greenland's governance arrangements.

Greenland (see map 1, p. xiii) is the largest island in the world, encompassing an area of 2,166,086 million square kilometres, of which 410,449 square kilometres are ice-free.[8] Nunavut, covering more than 2.1 million square kilometres, is the largest territorial unit in the Canadian federation (see map 2, p. xiv). Both entities belong geographically to the North American continent. Both Greenland and a major part of Nunavut are isolated from the mainland, have a similar Arctic climate, and lie above the treeline, with the exception of Greenland's southwest forest, where the ice cap is absent.

In terms of demographics, both entities are sparsely populated: Nunavut has one city and twenty-four hamlets, while Greenland, until an expected merger in 2009, has eighteen municipalities.[9] Inuit are a clear majority of the population in both: of Greenland's 56,969 inhabitants, about 88 per cent are Natives; similarly, approximately 85 per cent of Nunavut's 2006 population of 30,245 is Inuit.[10] Culturally, the Inuit of Nunavut and Greenland have shared a 'nomadic' lifestyle, a common mode of hunting, fishing, and gathering, and similar methods of making snow houses, clothing, and drums. They share similar traditional values and belong to the same language group, though speak different dialects.

Historically, the Inuit in both countries were confronted with some similar methods of colonization, from relocation to assimilation, although neither group was subject to a reservation system. With regard to politics, many Inuit of both entities consider themselves as one people. They have gone through similar experiences of political awakening and self-identification in their struggle for self-determination and self-governance. They share the same political goals and promote international collaboration with Inuit of the Russian Federation, the United States, and other regions of Canada (Labrador, Northern Quebec, and the Western Arctic). Both Greenland and Nunavut face transition from traditional to modern sustainable societies, resulting in the same type of social, health, and education problems that challenge the stability of their governments. Economically speaking, both entities aspire to sustainability, self-reliance, and self-accountability, but in the meantime they accept substantial financial support from Denmark and Canada.[11] In legal terms, public governance based on the territorial principle functions in both territories and applies to both Native and non-Native residents. Finally, the strategic location of Greenland and Nunavut in the Arctic requires special legal guarantees for their demilitarization and encourages Arctic cooperation.[12]

Although there are striking similarities between Greenland and Nunavut, there are some notable differences. The Nunavut Act ensured the creation of the new territory of Nunavut in 1999 as a result of the division of the Northwest Territories of Canada. In 1993 the Inuit also negotiated the Nunavut Land Claims Agreement. Nunavut's present boundaries do not cover all of the traditional territory of the Inuit-used lands in the Canadian North, and the Inuit of Nunatsiavut (Newfoundland and Labrador) and Nunavik (Northern Quebec) as well as the Inuvialuit of the Western Arctic (NWT) live beyond its borders. Greenland was a part of Denmark, which at the time of introduction of Greenland's home rule placed little emphasis on the interests of the Inuit as an indigenous people.[13] In contrast, Nunavut is an example of 'distinctiveness' in the multicultural and multinational Canadian federation. There also exists a difference between Canadian and Danish approaches to the concepts of indigenous rights, which have affected the establishment of Greenland home rule and the territory of Nunavut. The creation of Nunavut was negotiated as an integral part of the Nunavut land claims settlement, whereas the home rule system is not rooted in indigenous use or occupation of the land.

Generally, Danish policies of colonization regarding the Inuit of Greenland were somewhat less intrusive than those imposed on the Canadian Inuit. The former underwent more gradual stages of colonization and did not experience residential schools or the controversial practice of the numbered identification disk system, a tracking system used by the NWT authorities from 1941 until the early 1970s to facilitate the maintenance of government and administrative records on the Inuit. The preservation of the Greenlandic language, the establishment in the 1850s of a printing house (which in 1861 started to publish the *Atuagagdliutit* national newspaper), and the development of Greenlandic literature played key roles in the development of Greenlandic national identity.[14] Finally, while Greenlanders created a unified nation with a political system based on a number of political parties, Nunavut's system of governance is non-partisan. Political goals are achieved by the active role of Inuit organizations.

These distinctions may partially explain the differences in the Inuit people's relationships with the Danish and Canadian states. They also help to elucidate the divergence in the stages of colonization, decoloni-

zation, and modern approaches to governance in Greenland and
Nunavut.

Approach of This Study

The notion of autonomy in legal and political science theory is subject
to much confusion. At the same time, there is an evolving understanding of the right to autonomy in law. Depending on the methodological
grounds, there are several ways to approach the legal concept of autonomy.[15] To date the right to autonomy has a stronger basis for its legal justification in the sphere of the right of indigenous peoples to autonomy.

I hope to reduce the ambiguities surrounding the right to autonomy
in areas where indigenous peoples are the majority by exploring empiri-
cally and through some elements of normative analysis how the right to
autonomy is emerging and how its legal scope is evolving in Greenland
and Nunavut. In so doing, I follow a non-traditional way of studying the
concept of autonomy: I focus on a bottom-up approach, revealing how
empirical or de facto comprehension of the right to autonomy is evolving towards greater recognition on a de jure level and thereby advancing our legal understanding of autonomy. This method is blended into
the methodology of interdisciplinary research and employs a variety of
investigatory approaches for analysing a number of theoretical and
practical questions. Each chapter addresses a distinct topic, but my
methods of research remain consistent. These include cultural immersion and comparative legal and historical analyses with the main emphasis on contextual, textualist, and jurisprudential interpretation.

Despite profound differences between the historical, political, and
legal backgrounds of Canada and Denmark, the policies pursued by
these states towards the Inuit people, and their consequences for the
Inuit's present legal status and political development, have been similar.
Both countries applied comparable methods of colonization, including
the banning of traditional Inuit practices, like shamanism and dances;
the imposition of the colonizers' religions; the use of similar policies of
assimilation, relocation, and integration of the Inuit with the larger,
dominant societies; the devaluation of unique Inuit culture and needs;
and the stalling of the Inuit people's quest for self-determination and
greater political autonomy.

How could the experiences of Inuit people in such different countries and legal contexts have been so similar? What is the basis for a legal
comparison within these different legal systems? Denmark is a member

of the continental legal family. Nordic law, to which Denmark sub-scribes, is 'considered to constitute its own legal family, though it is also often seen as a part of the Continental Roman-German legal family.'[16] However, some Nordic scholars view the Danish legal system as being closer to common law, 'since the judges do not view themselves so strongly, only as mere executors of codified legal rules.'[17] The Canadian system of law strives to find a balance between a common law and civil law tradition. One must also factor in the influence of European, inter-national, and common law practices in both countries, and the increas-ing importance of supranational law presenting challenges to the comparison of different legal systems.

Alongside all of these influences, Inuit customary law and perceptions have to be considered. This process raises many questions. How does indigenous peoples' law fit into the process of legal transformation? Legal transformations in other countries involved a significant level of institutional emulation and adaptation.[18] This was not the case with respect to indigenous peoples' ideas or legal systems, which the colon-izers did not consider valuable and which have had little impact on mainstream legal developments in Canada or Denmark.[19] Against this history, how do we define the line between the 'legal' paradigms of the modern Canadian or Danish state and 'non-legal' traditional Inuit cus-tomary practices? To what extent does the traditional culture of the Inuit possess normative significance? Governance in the Arctic is regu-lated by many factors, including law. What is the law's role in the man-agement of Northern governments, and are there any efforts to recognize elements of Inuit legal systems in contemporary constitu-tional arrangements?

These are difficult questions that cannot be adequately addressed only through existing approaches to Aboriginal law and politics. Full answers require a comparative approach, but such a methodology brings with it a unique set of challenges. A basic difficulty lies in the vagueness of the comparative method generally and its application to this particular type of legal scholarship. Unfortunately, an analysis of the literature on comparative law methodology does not yield a clear method of legal comparison. Many scholars argue about how and why comparison should be done but do not provide a clear definition of a proper method of legal comparison.[20]

In conducting this research and recognizing the multiplicity of approaches to comparative law, I have incorporated Vivian G. Curran's suggestions on cultural immersion comparison.[21] Thus, in order to collect information first-hand and generate original research, I conducted field studies in Iqaluit (Nunavut) and Nuuk (Greenland) in the fall of 2002. Interviews in the form of open conversation were conducted with selected Inuit leaders, activists, governmental officials, lawyers, and Northern residents who were willing to express their views on governance and political issues regarding their communities and to explain their expectations and concerns about the process of autonomy building. All participants in the study were asked a similar set of open-ended questions formulated in accordance with their competence or expertise, which allowed them to freely express their own views on the issues. Anonymity and confidentiality of the information were guaranteed, as requested.

The comparative method applied in this book consists of three related approaches: contextualist, textualist, and jurisprudential. A *contextualist approach*, which focuses on 'law in action,'[22] situates the analysis of the Inuit's legal status in the two countries within the context of social changes. It regards the legal situation of the Inuit in both countries as strongly affected by the surrounding society. Moreover, specific geographic, economic, political, and cultural factors related to the Inuit's way of life in the Arctic influence legislation in a number of ways. In many cases, existing conditions require special regulations, applicable only to Northern or cultural Inuit settings. A *textualist approach*, which targets 'law in books,'[23] focuses on the interpretation of texts and statutes. In this instance it examines the concept of autonomy and its relevance to the Inuit people's rights in the juridical literature and legislation of the two countries as well as in international documents. A *jurisprudential approach*, focusing on 'law in minds,' or a style of conscious thought,[24] includes an understanding and comparison of ideas of legislators and indigenous activists about the essence of autonomy for the Inuit people.

I adapt several comparative approaches not just to find reasons for differences and similarities among the Inuit of the two countries, but to attempt to provide a comprehensive assessment of the quest for autonomy by the Inuit. This macro-comparative study is possible because of the striking similarities between national policies towards the Inuit in the two countries.

Despite the value in the approaches I have outlined above, the application of non-Native methods of study to the interpretation of Inuit views on self-governance has its limits. It is difficult to realize indigenous government within the existing institutional and legal structures of the

Canadian and Danish states. Because they are alien to the Inuit culture, it is also difficult to apply common methods of legal study to the legal systems in question, which are imposed upon the Inuit by the dominant states. Using the experiences of the Inuit in Greenland and Nunavut, I will show that certain legal definitions and concepts – for example, 'human rights' and 'mainstream domestic law' – are 'unknown' and confusing to some Inuit. How does one incorporate existing methods or principles of the dominant society (for example, the rule of law) to Inuit governance? The challenge is how to apply non-Native approaches to research on Inuit perceptions on governance when, on the one hand, despite the evolution of the modern Inuit language, it still has no precise definition of the notion of autonomy and there is no unanimity among the Inuit regarding what this notion means. There is also no authentic translation for this notion in legal terms. On the other hand, there is no precise definition or understanding of the concept of autonomy or self-governance in the legal doctrines of Canada or Denmark.

Another limitation for this study results from the lack of complex comparative legal studies on issues of Inuit governance. There are some notable comparative studies on Aboriginal self-government in general and on the rights of Arctic indigenous peoples,[25] but they are not specific enough to enhance our understanding of the legal situation of the Inuit of Greenland and Nunavut. The scope of existing legal research on Inuit issues is limited, as it usually consists of a single country or case study of Inuit communities. Also, with some exceptions, this project is mostly restricted to the analysis of English-language literature on the autonomy of Greenland and Nunavut, with the inclusion of many publications by Danish and Greenlandic scholars.

From what angle does one examine the issue of autonomy in Greenland and Nunavut if, on the one hand, Canadian and Danish legal systems were imposed on the Inuit, and, on the other, the Inuit had their own methods for resolving social problems and exercised what is called in the dominant societies a system of customary law? Some elements of customary law practices were partially incorporated in the Greenland Criminal Code of 1954, and the process of further consideration and inclusion of Inuit legal practices in the modern justice system is currently taking place in Nunavut. For the purposes of this study, should the Inuit people in the two countries be regarded from the point of view of the legal systems of the dominant societies? Or should there be some recognition that they possess their own 'legal' system and structures of governance?

Kelly Gallagher-Mackay suggests that a legal study of the Inuit of Nunavut should be conducted in a way that considers their cultural system and partially deconstructs the key political and legal institutional context in which the cultural elements are working.[26] Greg Poelzer argues that such an analysis should be focused on Aboriginal collectivities, which should be treated as separate political communities, distinct from the societies that dominate them.[27] His argument raises the question of whether the Inuit people of Canada and Denmark consider themselves part of Canadian and Danish societies and should therefore be treated as such, or whether they should be treated separately.

I employ a blended approach, examining the Inuit people in Nunavut and Greenland as both separate communities and as part of the broader, dominant societies. Recent developments in Nunavut have shown that its political trajectory of development is different from that of Greenland. The Inuit of Nunavut see themselves as a part of Canada and are interested in further devolution of powers and in stronger cooperation and partnership with the wide spectrum of Canadian federal structures. The fact that Greenland is functioning within the institutional, legal, and political settings of a unitary state does not make a significant difference to its citizens' political choices regarding their country's future and expansion of autonomy in partnership with Denmark.

The nation of Greenlanders is looking for greater autonomy within the Danish kingdom based on a new partnership agreement on self-governance, with the ultimate goal of economic and possibly political independence in the future. The Greenlanders' desire for increased self-government is linked to the necessity of economic sustainability and the realization of their right to self-determination. In the meantime, this dynamic process of obtaining increased autonomy is based on mutual respect, equal partnership, and consideration of existing close ties with the Danish state. The case of Greenland is of great learning importance for Nunavut, and vice versa. At the same time, the Inuit of both Nunavut and Greenland have historical, cultural, economic, and geopolitical relationships with the broader societies in which they are located. Finding the points of convergence and divergence among views held by Southerners and Northerners is crucial to this study.

1 The Inuit of Greenland and Nunavut: From Subjugation to Self-Government?

Before European Contact

According to some scholars, the Inuit of Greenland and Nunavut were self-governing people prior to colonization.[1] In both Greenland and Nunavut the extended family provided the social structure of Inuit society.[2] The extended family coordinated its members and made decisions about where to set up camp and about hunting and gathering activities. Overall leadership of each group rested with the oldest male.[3] The Inuit 'lived in numerous, dispersed clusters of small hunting camps ... Individual camps within each group tended to be made up of interrelated extended families, living together by common agreement.'[4] The Inuit had a flexible system of governance based on consensus and making decisions through discussion.[5]

Accordingly, the pre-colonial Inuit had no permanent administration or centralized political organization in the form of territorial government. The modern state system necessitated modifications to traditional Inuit social organization. However, the extended family structure and informal self-regulation that existed prior to European contact influenced both the administrative forms established by the Danish and Canadian colonizers as well as the eventual form of home rule and Nunavut public governance. Despite their informal, traditional social organization, the Inuit were able to adjust rapidly to formal, non-indigenous institutions and practices. How did they adapt so quickly to the new governmental systems?

The Impact of Colonization on the Inuit of Greenland and Nunavut

The Inuit of Greenland and Nunavut share a common history of colonization, albeit with an approximately 150-year time difference between them.[6] Both Canada and Denmark legitimated their sovereignty over Inuit territories using similar methods – missions and religious proselytizing, trade activity, and establishment of administrative systems. Although there were many similarities in the colonial experience of the two regions, there were differences as well. In contrast to Greenland, the Northwest Territories (NWT) did not face the 'frontier phase' of conquest, which according to Jette E. Ashlee, dated from 1721 to 1776, and was marked by competition between Denmark and other European countries for control over the island.[7] There was no conquest of the Inuit of Nunavut, and British imperial rule 'over the area was established long before the Arctic was adequately charted.'[8] British sovereignty over the territory occupied by the Inuit was partially established by Martin Frobisher in 1576 but was not formally asserted until 2 May 1670, when King Charles II of England granted what was then called Rupert's Land – an enormous tract comprising the lands in the entire watershed of Hudson Bay – to 'The Governor and Company of Adventurers of England trading into Hudson's Bay.' The validity of the Royal Charter and the extent of the granted territories were questioned until 1870. The British North America Act, 1867 (s. 146) provided for and stipulated conditions for admission of these territories to the Dominion of Canada. One year later the British Parliament passed an Act for enabling her Majesty to accept a Surrender upon Terms of the Lands, Privileges, and Rights of 'The Governor and Company of Adventurers of England trading into Hudson's Bay,' and for admitting the same into the Dominion of Canada (Rupert's Land Act, 1868). Such a surrender took place in 1869. Sovereignty of what was known as Rupert's Land and the North-Western Territory was transferred peacefully to the Dominion of Canada in 1870. Upon the admission of these regions to the dominion, the province of Manitoba was established out of a portion of their territory. The remaining territory was united and named the North-West Territories. Ten years later Canada's northern boundaries were changed with the transfer from Britain of jurisdiction over all Arctic islands.[9]

With re-colonization of West Greenland on a permanent basis in 1721 after the arrival of Pastor Hans Egede and the Bergen Trading Company, the conversion of the Inuit population to Christianity gradually led to the demise of their traditional beliefs, social organization, and political system. The Inuit were becoming wards of the Norwegian-Danish Crown and were administered by traders and missionaries.[10] Danish sovereignty over Greenland was vested through the creation of the Royal Greenland Trading Company (KGH). In 1776 Denmark declared paramount control over trade in Greenland and promulgated a Royal Declaration entitled 'A Revised Royal Ordinance and Prohibition against Unjustified Trade with Greenland,' which provided an exclusive Danish monopoly of trade and travel to Greenland.[11]

Europeans colonized the Inuit of Greenland and Nunavut by trade and settlement, which was largely in the form of missions and trading posts.[12] Gradually, the Inuit were put under alien authority by the activity of the KGH in Denmark and the Hudson's Bay Company (HBC) in Canada. These companies, however, played different roles. Ashlee writes that 'the KGH was an agent of state; as a result it constituted a full body politic in Greenland, whereas the HBC was chiefly concerned with trade.'[13] It is revealing that, in seeking to establish their sovereignty over these areas, neither Denmark, Great Britain, nor, later, Canada saw the necessity of concluding treaties with the Inuit themselves. Some argue that this lack of treaties shows that the colonizers did not recognize the Inuit as sovereign people.[14]

Canada and Denmark each had difficulties in justifying their sovereignty over their Arctic possessions. Denmark's claim of sovereignty over Greenland in 1776 was based on the 'right of discovery.' Thus, the Danish title to Greenland was recognized by other sovereign European countries. Yet Denmark had to compete with some rivals, particularly Norway, which considered the uncolonized part of the east coast of Greenland as a *terra nullius* and claimed the right to it.[15] Consequently, Denmark faced challenges to its assertion of sovereignty over the island.[16] The Dominion of Canada, which had obtained Hudson's Bay Company territories through transfer of title from Great Britain, had to seek international recognition of its sovereignty by 'effective occupation.'[17] The dominion's title was not recognized in international law, which asserted at the end of the nineteenth century that 'mere discovery, which was the basis of British sovereignty and Canadian title to the Inuit homelands, was insufficient to maintain territorial rights over an area in perpetuity.'[18]

Neither Denmark nor Canada fully recognized the Inuit as legal persons or saw much need for legislation to recognize or regulate their legal status. The Danish Instructions of 1782 – 'the Instrux' – contained some form of recognition and has even been described by some as 'a genuine Magna Carta or Bill of Rights for the island's Eskimos.'[19] However, this document was mostly concerned with trade and wage regulations. Furthermore, there was no mention of Greenland Inuit in the

Constitution of the Kingdom of Denmark of 1849 and consequent constitutional amendments simply because they did not exist in the eyes of legislators.

Similarly to the Instrux, the British Royal Proclamation of 1763 has been called by some the Indian Bill of Rights.[20] Yet while the Crown recognized Indian nations or tribes, and acknowledged that they continue to possess traditional territories until they are 'ceded' to or purchased by the Crown, it did not specifically refer to the existence or rights of the Inuit. It is debatable whether the proclamation applied to Rupert's Land. Indeed, 'the second paragraph of the part relating to Indians, which reserved certain lands for their use, expressly excluded "the Territory granted to the Hudson's Bay Company."'[21] However, it is argued by some scholars that other paragraphs of the proclamation that deal with Indian lands apply to Rupert's Land.[22]

Furthermore, notwithstanding that some legal documents dealing with the admission of Rupert's Land and the North-Western Territory to the Dominion of Canada refer to 'Indians' and compensation for their 'lands required for purposes of settlement,' thus recognizing some legal rights for Natives, the Inuit were not specifically mentioned in these documents and were not explicitly referred to in the Indian Act of 1876.[23] Importantly, the Inuit were eventually treated as subjects of law with the implementation of a British-based criminal justice system in Canada in the 1920s. However, it was only in 1939 that the Supreme Court of Canada decided that the term 'Indians' included Inuit.[24]

It is an open question whether Canada would have prevented challenges by foreign states to its sovereignty in the North had it recognized the Inuit as citizens. That such a step was not taken reveals the depth of the colonial mentality that governed Ottawa's relationship with the North and its indigenous peoples. This mentality, however, was not unique to Canada but was common among colonizers. Thus, to Denmark Greenland was just a colony with an inferior vassal population.

If the broad perspectives of both Canada and Denmark vis-à-vis the Inuit were similar, their colonial policy differed. Part of the difference was dictated by geography. Anthropologist Jens Dahl notes that the Danish administration of Greenland had an external character, whereas the Inuit of Nunavut were the subject of internal colonialism. The geographical separation of Greenland from Denmark by several thousand kilometres and the lack of permanent Danish settlers meant that Greenlanders were not as influenced by outsiders. Consequently, their demands for decolonization have been much more radical than those put forth by Inuit in Canada or Alaska. The lands of Canadian Inuit, while remote, were directly connected to the rest of the country, and their indigenous occupants were more directly influenced by non-Aboriginal migrants. Consequently, it was more difficult for the Inuit of Nunavut to develop either a political elite or political unity.[25]

The Danish assertion of sovereignty over Greenland was more active than Canada's over Nunavut. A political system based on Western concepts of law, religion, and property ownership was intended to replace the existing Inuit social order and was backed by Danish absolute authority. The Instrux of 1782 established rules for wages and codes of behaviour for Inuit and Danish merchants, divided Greenland's population into social categories, set forth heavy penalties for 'corrupting' the Inuit with alcohol and other things that might jeopardize their livelihood and health, prohibited marriages between Europeans and 'pure' Greenlanders, and closed Greenland to outsiders by permitting only the king's officials to have contact with Greenlanders.[26]

This document gave expression to the Danish principle of keeping the Inuit away from the corrupting influences of the Europeans. The Danish government assumed that protecting Greenland from outsiders and exploiting the resources of the island themselves would result in profits that would defray business and administrative expenses. Thus, every trader was supposed to become a mentor and protector of the Inuit involved in trade, and the Inuit's welfare had to '*receive the highest possible consideration, even override when necessary the interests of trade itself.*'[27] This policy of making an 'arctic colony a Garden of Eden where happiness would come through isolation and paternal rule'[28] both protected Greenlanders from outside influences and made them dependent on Danish tutelage. The idea was to 'civilize' Greenlanders and to keep them as junior Danish partners without pushing for any development of the Inuit population or putting extra money into improving their living conditions.

In contrast to Denmark, which protected its trade interests by economic paternalism towards the Inuit population and used the profits to modify the Inuit social system with mercantile principles, Canada pursued a 'passive' approach to colonization. It adopted a laissez-faire policy towards the Inuit, who 'were to be left as little disturbed as possible, provided that peace prevailed.'[29] Several researchers have emphasized that Canada was a reluctant guardian of the Inuit.[30] In comparison to Denmark, Canada did not take notice of the 'lords of the North' or acknowledge any responsibility for their fate until circumstances forced it to do so. It was motivated to take action partially by the challenges to Canadian sovereignty in the Arctic by foreign states, which prompted the establishment of permanent posts of the North-West Mounted Police in the region in the early 1900s.[31]

Several factors account for this reluctance. First, Canada obtained its title to the North via a peaceful transfer rather than by any rivalry for the new territories. Second, as a recent British colony, the Dominion of Canada acquired responsibility for territories that were at the time of little importance to the national policy. Third, organized as a federal state, Canada had a different pattern of nation building than unitary Denmark, which tried to 'civilize' Greenlanders by promoting a centralized, collective cultural identity. Finally, partially because of geographical remoteness, the Inuit were legally 'unknown,' and they had little contact with Europeans until the nineteenth century.[32]

Because of their isolation, the Inuit in both regions were less affected by European colonizers than were other Aboriginal peoples, and colonial practices were relatively benign because of the lack of oppression by force.[33] According to Robert Petersen, the Danish colonization had a peaceful character because 'the Greenlandic community had no organization above the household level, and thus lacked anyone who might be interested in defending his power.'[34] This observation can also be applied to the Canadian Eastern Arctic. There were similar, though slightly different, reasons why both territories were not subject to forcible oppression. Greenland was isolated by Danish protectionism and its geographical location, whereas the Canadian North had little communication with dominion powers because of its remoteness and Ottawa's indifference.

The spread of liberal ideas in Denmark in the nineteenth century resulted in a reorganization of Greenland's social life. In 1871 Greenlandic language was standardized, and the gap between a literate Inuit minority (the future elite) and uneducated hunters increased social stratification.[35] The administration of Greenland was rationalized by the creation in the second part of the nineteenth century of local administrative bodies, the Boards of Guardians, which served the function of a municipal council. In response to criticism that they were undemocratic and too heavily composed of Danish officials, the boards were replaced by new municipal councils in 1908. Danish legislation was frequently updated to accommodate the island's social conditions.[36] An important change was undertaken by the separation of trade and administration, and by the creation for the first time in 1911 of two provincial councils of Northern and Southern Greenland, with Greenlanders' exclusive participation.[37] In the opinion of Dahl, these were key steps towards political unity and the formation of a true Greenlandic nation, which was in sharp contrast to the fragmentation that characterized the Inuit of Canada and Alaska. These developments were also important for shaping a political infrastructure that included Greenlanders' participation in the political process and for the emergence of a class of indigenous leaders.[38] In 1910 Greenland's elite founded a nationalist movement with the motto 'forward and upward' and was talking about Greenland as a nation.[39] Further realization by the educated Greenlandic elite that Greenlanders were second-class citizens because of their lower social status and education, and of the necessity to be able to compete with Danes for jobs, led to a political philosophy shaped by 'the need for making the society as Danish (European) as possible and as Greenlandic as necessary.'[40] It also encouraged Greenlanders to learn Danish, which became more widespread in Greenland after the Second World War.[41]

Paternalistic policies, based on the assumption of Inuit inferiority and centralized control and domination of the Inuit political and social systems, caused economic dependency on Denmark and escalated the conflict between the Greenlandic elite and the Danes. At the same time, the colonial administration was based on an indirect form of government with Greenlandic and Danish participation. According to Dahl, in order to achieve better results, the Danish administration looked to Greenland's precolonial form of societal organization.[42] This outlook affected the structure and scope of the Greenlandic home rule system and stands in sharp contrast to the Nunavut case.

Canadian administration in the North was ad hoc, shaped by the separate activities of missionaries, traders, and police, and was based on the government structures in Ottawa, with minimal interest or intervention by the dominion.[43] There was no active coordination of these activities. The Inuit of Canada's Eastern Arctic did not have an opportunity to participate in the administration of their area, as did Greenlanders. Except for some experiments, Canada ignored the Inuit's existence and abandoned any responsibility for their welfare.[44] British/Canadian legislation was not updated for Northerners' social needs. In the early 1920s criminal law was extended to Canada's Eastern Arctic because of 'a cry' in the South demanding that the Inuit be subject to 'white men's' justice. This 'cry' was precipitated by a series of murders of non-Inuit in the North.[45]

Although Canadian and Danish policies and perspectives with regard to treatment of the Inuit differed in some ways, in many respects the outcomes were much the same. The result was a path that brought enormous changes to the Inuit's lives, including the spread of diseases (particularly tuberculosis and smallpox), dependency on European technologies such as firearms, loss of indigenous belief systems to Christianity, the change of subsistence patterns of livelihood, and replacement of indigenous leaders by outsiders.[46] The longer period of colonization in Greenland, cultural factors, the distinct Danish policy towards Greenlanders, and the beginning of the formation of the Greenlandic nation caused faster social stratification in Greenlandic society and led to the emergence of a new elite characterized by growing dissatisfaction with the privileged Danes. This phenomenon did not occur in Nunavut because of the different relationship between the Inuit and the Canadian government.

Decolonization and the Road to Self-Governance

The current governance arrangements in Greenland and Nunavut were influenced by factors preceding the creation of the Nunavut territory and Greenlandic home rule. These factors, which dated from the end of the Second World War to the early 1980s, included the end of colonization and the legal recognition of the Inuit by their respective states; the increased exploitation and extraction of natural resources; military activity and challenges to Arctic sovereignty; social and economic changes brought about by the modernization of Inuit societies; and the Inuit's political mobilization and move towards self-determination and autonomy.

The Second World War and the postwar years brought enormous changes to the lives of the Inuit in Greenland and Canada. In both countries isolation was broken by increased military activity, which raised the issue of Greenland's status within the Danish kingdom and brought new challenges to Canada's sovereignty in the North. Germany's invasion of Denmark in 1940 brought Allied forces to Greenlandic shores to protect the Danes' overseas territory, which they were unable to do themselves. This situation heightened Greenlanders' awareness of the need for radical change. Moreover, after 1941 U.S. military bases were established in Greenland. When the war ended, Denmark wanted to demolish them, but the United States prolonged the negotiations until the bases came under the authority of the North Atlantic Treaty Organization (NATO) in 1949.[47] Meanwhile, in 1942–3 and between 1952 and 1957, a U.S. Air Force base was built at Frobisher Bay (now Iqaluit) in Canada's Eastern Arctic, and the U.S.-Canadian Distant Early Warning (DEW) Line was established from Alaska to the east coast of Baffin Island in response to the threat of Soviet missiles.[48]

The strategic importance of the Canadian Arctic and quasi-permanent American presence in the region threatened Canadian sovereignty and forced the Canadian government to look more closely at its Northern territories. One result was the creation in 1953 of the Department of Northern Affairs and National Resources.[49] Moreover, the increased scrutiny brought about by the war had shown that there was a huge disparity in the living conditions of the Inuit and the rest of the population. In the words of Peter Jull, 'the country had been forced to "discover" Inuit and other Northern peoples through War and Cold War.'[50]

In 1945 the Greenlandic provincial councils expressed their wish to seek an equal footing with the Danes.[51] In 1948 the Danish prime minister, Hans Hedtoft, appointed a Royal Commission on Greenland (G-50) to look into the situation on the island. The commission's report, which was published in 1950, formed the basis for a 'new order' plan oriented on the modernization and transformation of Greenland from a Danish colony to an industrial society within the Danish kingdom.[52]

In contrast to Denmark, Canada had no clear plan for dealing with its Inuit population. Since the early postwar years, the Arctic had been flooded 'with white administrators, school-teachers, doctors, nurses and welfare officers, all committed to raise the Eskimos' cultural level and improve their standard of living; but progress [was] disturbingly slow' because there was no clear policy for organizing the endeavours of all these well-meaning individuals or any effort to coordinate the numerous programs.[53]

In the postwar period Canada and Denmark took different approaches to the well-being of the Inuit. They also took different directions on other issues regarding further development of their Arctic territories. One such issue was resource extraction and the dimensions of industrial policy. Under the new order of 1950, Greenland proceeded with modernization and industrialization simultaneously. This was followed by the G-60 plan in the 1960s, which led to further increases in investment in Greenland but failed to facilitate the training and education of Greenlanders to take on jobs that were carried out mostly by skilled Danes.[54] There were no resources in the Canadian North that could provide an effective economic base for the modernization of Inuit economies. However, the thinking of policymakers and administrators was that the Inuit of the NWT would become a modern workforce for a resource economy through education and 'acculturation.'[55] With Ottawa's desire to extend the standards of the Canadian welfare state to the Inuit, and with its need to indicate to the international community its commitment to the provisions of the UN Charter, 'quasi-modernization programmes were introduced long before an adequate wage economy was founded for the area.'[56]

The changed international climate, including Canada's and Denmark's adherence to the principles of the UN Charter, led to the realization in both countries that changes had to be made in the legal and social status of Greenlanders and the Canadian Inuit. From 1946 to 1954 Denmark in its report to the UN listed Greenland as a non-self-governing territory under Chapter XI of the UN Charter, thus confirming the colonial nature of its administration on the island.[57] However, in the general atmosphere of criticism of colonialism and the Greenlanders' expressed desire for decentralization, 'Danish authorities, who were eager to eliminate the supervision by the United Nations and other international scrutiny of the conditions in their possession, seized the initiative and transformed the requests of the natives into integration.'[58]

Consequently, the Constitution of 1953 ended Greenland's colonial status by integrating the island into the Kingdom of Denmark.[59] However, it is not clear to what extent the colonial mentality towards Greenlanders and the ability of the latter to exercise direct influence and control of their own affairs remained unchanged between this move and the introduction of home rule on 1 May 1979.[60] While Greenland was placed on an equal footing with the rest of the Danish kingdom and obtained the right to send two representatives to the Danish Parliament (the Folketing), there was no real equality between Greenlanders and their Danish counterparts. Living standards in Greenland were much lower than in Denmark. Furthermore, a 'colonial' relationship actually intensified, with the immigration to Greenland of a significant number of Danes and the continuation of a neo-colonial economic policy.[61] Moreover, as Guðmundur Alfreðsson notes, Greenland was not given a choice other than to opt for integration with Denmark. Greenlanders had not participated in the enactment of the new constitution, either through elections or a referendum. However, Danish lawyers have argued that Greenlanders raised no objections to integration with Denmark.[62] Indeed, the new arrangements raised high hopes among Greenlanders for increased management of their own affairs and for greater economic prosperity, but in some ways the practices of the former colonial relationship remained unchanged.

As in Greenland, the quality of life for the Inuit in the Canadian Arctic remained far behind that of the majority population. Furthermore, 'equality was interpreted as uniformity,' as the Inuit children read books full of pictures and stories about trees and pet dogs and cats. The scattered Inuit camps were gathered into central villages near trading posts, nursing clinics, schools, and mission churches. Inuit elders were replaced by white administrators who were to supervise 'an acculturation.'[63] Contact with the rest of the country was infrequent, and the only Inuit to experience life outside their communities were tuberculosis patients sent to recuperate in the South.[64] The Canadian Citizenship Act 1947 designated the Inuit as Canadian citizens. Citizenship might imply a vague equality among Canadians, but it did not result in sudden improvements in living conditions, economic status, or in the poor level of formal education among the Inuit. Nor did citizenship confer automatic realization of voting rights by the Inuit and other residents of the NWT, who were unable to vote in federal elections until 1962.[65] This delay was mainly (though not entirely) logistical, as holding elections in the Canadian Arctic was nearly impossible. By comparison, Greenlanders, who had a higher level of literacy and formal education than the Canadian Inuit, were familiar with forms of electoral democracy at an earlier time than their Canadian counterparts and were able to raise their voice through their representatives in the national legislature.[66]

Canada and Denmark employed similar welfare state methods in their Northern lands. Attempts to improve the standard of living for the Inuit by means of employment, income assistance, health, housing, and education programs met with limited success. In Greenland industrialization and the extension of social welfare required the movement of the population to urban districts. In the words of Mark Nuttall, 'people were "encouraged" to migrate from outlying areas to west coast towns by the closing down of what the Danish authorities regarded [as] "unprofitable" settlements.'[67] This policy transformed Greenlanders into wage-earning urban workers and widened the income gap between the Danish and Greenlandic labour force, as Greenlanders received lower salaries than their Danish colleagues.[68] Furthermore, as Nuttall states, 'movement to the towns led to the fragmentation of kin-based groups and individuals now experienced alienation, social and economic marginality and discrimination, accentuated by ethnic divisions between Inuit and Danes.' One unintended result of this policy was an emerging Inuit political awareness.[69]

In Canada's Arctic, the Inuit were concentrated in their communities, as government schemes of relocation to major industrial urban centres in the South were not considered a priority. In the 1950s Ottawa introduced a highly controversial relocation plan in the High Arctic, affecting the Inuit of Inukjuak (Northern Quebec) and Pond Inlet (now Nunavut). Although the federal government argued otherwise, the Inuit claimed that they were being used as pawns to bolster Canada's sovereignty in the area. In some ways this experience is similar to the relocation of the Inuit of Greenland in 1925, which was done to establish Danish sovereignty over Northeast Greenland, and the relocation of the Inuit of Greenland in 1953, which occurred to make way for a U.S. military base in the Thule area.[70] Despite some changes, Canada's Arctic remained a northern frontier characterized by isolation and infrequent contact with the rest of Canada.

The political mobilization of Greenlanders, which had begun in the early 1900s, reached its peak in the 1970s. It produced a new generation of young (mostly Denmark-educated) Greenlandic politicians as well as the formation of 'Inuit parties.' The impetus for self-determination and political autonomy came from the activities of these groups. Greenlandic politicians, frustrated by increasing Danish dominance and the failure to achieve equal status with Danes, advocated 'a more Greenlandic Greenland, i.e. a society as Greenlandic as possible and as Danish as necessary.'[71] Influenced by growing talk of decolonization for the Fourth World, they demanded to have a greater say in their own country.[72] Formed in the 1970s, Greenlandic parties put forward a wide spectrum of political platforms, from separation from Denmark to further integration with the kingdom. As will be discussed in chapter 3, they made a valuable contribution to the radical shifts in the Greenlandic-Danish relationship.

In Canada, the formation of Inuit political associations in the 1970s was stimulated by several factors, including the failure of the 1969 White Paper on Native policy, the discovery of oil fields in Alaska, the impact of the Supreme Court of Canada's *Calder* decision, which revived the recognition of a common law Native title, and the signing of the James Bay and Northern Quebec Agreement.[73] In 1976 the Inuit Tapirisat of Canada (ITC) proposed to the federal government to create Nunavut as a part of a comprehensive settlement of Inuit land claims in the Northwest Territories.[74] Unlike in Greenland, where the Inuit were the island's sole Aboriginal group, the NWT contained several Native groups with distinct interests and claims. Thus, the Inuvialuit of the

Western Arctic, who were originally covered by the ITC's Nunavut proposal, negotiated a separate land claims agreement in 1984.[75]

Unlike in Greenland, where the process towards self-government was a process of nation building, 'the regionalism of Canadian Inuit politics was further nourished by the division of the process of negotiating self-government.'[76] That was part of the reason why it took so many years for the Inuit of Canada's Eastern Arctic to make their dream of the creation of Nunavut come true.[77] The process of establishing Nunavut had many stages, culminating in the combination of a 1993 land claims agreement and the creation of the new territory and government on 1 April 1999.[78] The Nunavut success story is testimony to the decades of persistent work and patient strategy of Inuit organizations and their leaders.

In contrast to the situation in Greenland, an Inuit elite did not exist in Canada when Inuit organizations were first created. In Greenland by the 1970s the internal political course was driven by a bilingual Greenlandic elite disappointed with continuing oppression and broken promises of equality with the Danes.[79] Thus, a so-called Greenlandic intelligentsia with well-formed political goals led the 1970s movement for home rule. But in Canada in the 1970s a Western-educated Inuit intelligentsia was still emerging.

In both regions, the quest for self-determination and autonomy was a product of nationalism and a unique Inuit identity. Elana Wilson argues that in Nunavut 'much of the call for self-government was rooted in the idea that the Inuit identity was challenged and subverted by their participation in essentially foreign governance structures ... The Inuit autonomy movement adopted and internalised the rhetoric of nationalism, particularly in the discourses of land, tradition, and institution building.'[80] The creation of Nunavut can be seen as the result of an indigenous nationalist movement. In Greenland, the struggle for autonomy was validated by the image of a Greenlandic nation and a Greenlandic elite that 'when demanding self-government, spoke on behalf of *all* Greenlanders.'[81] Therefore 'the process of negotiating and establishing self-government was a process of nation building, a gradual process transforming an ethnic identity to national cultural and political identities.'[82] By contrast, in Canada, the claims process 'was a process towards strengthening ethnic identity – a process in which new identities were asserted.'[83] Nonetheless, the seizing of the political momentum played a crucial role in negotiating the Greenland home rule and Nunavut governance arrangements. As Jose Kusugak has noted, outside events, like upcoming federal election in 1993, the tragic events at Oka, Quebec, and the breakdown in a single comprehensive land claims agreement in the Mackenzie valley prompted the final negotiations of the Nunavut agreement and helped to realize the creation of Nunavut.[84]

Greenland's membership in the European Economic Community (EEC) was a decisive impetus towards autonomy. Although the majority of Greenlanders voted against entry during the 1972 referendum on Danish membership in the EEC, Greenland became a member of the EEC along with Denmark.[85] This event led the provincial council to submit a proposal to the Danish government in 1972 requesting that local authorities be granted wider jurisdiction over Greenlandic matters.[86] This proposal resulted in the establishment of the Home Rule Committee, whose partial report led to the creation in 1975 of the Danish-Greenlandic Home Rule Commission.[87] The commission's report developed the basis for the Greenland Home Rule Act of 1978, which came into force on 1 May 1979.[88]

Greenland's home rule and the creation of Nunavut became possible partly because of the idealism within the dominant societies regarding the Inuit. In the process of its creation, Nunavut experienced 'the enormous advantages that follow from finding support in non-aboriginal society.'[89] As Jull states, 'Canadian idealism and romance about Inuit and the Arctic has included readiness to accept high costs.' Thus, 'for Inuit, Nunavut is an astonishing achievement; for other Canadians, it is a monument to national idealism and goodwill.' [90] Idealism also existed in Danish society with regard to Greenlanders.

In both regions, the Inuit succeeded in overcoming their subjugation by using the methods and the 'language' of their colonizers.[91] In Dahl's opinion, the fact that Greenlanders 'fought the colonial power-holders with their own [Danish] weapons ... was the major organizational reason behind the successful process that resulted in Home Rule.'[92] Similarly, the Inuit's use of language and tactics acceptable to the federal and NWT governments may explain their success during negotiations. At the same time, the creation of Nunavut paralleled the reform of Canada's Constitution and was influenced by existing political culture. The Inuit were negotiating their cultural and political autonomy and their water and land rights in the framework of de facto citizenship and constitutional processes.[93] As Jull stresses, 'the Nunavut self-government and claims teams maintained high moral and intellectual ground in constitutional, cross-cultural, and environmental matters, e.g., parading the quest for a Nunavut territory as Canada's first "made in Canada" constitutional reform process since white settlement.'[94] Thus, the Inuit 'won over enough Canadians and white *élites* to establish themselves as full Canadians, but a new kind of Canadian, with Nunavut a new kind of Canada.'[95]

Despite differences in their organization, home rule in Greenland and public governance in Nunavut were shaped by similar experiences that propelled these regions towards self-determination and autonomy. As the Inuit both in Canada and Greenland had their traditional way of life supplanted by social, economic, political, and legal structures imposed on them by the Canadian and Danish governments, they became dependent on their colonizers for financial support and other forms of social welfare. This situation seriously eroded Inuit economic and ecological sustainability and established solid grounds for continuing voluntary colonialism, which put the future of Inuit self-governance and self-determination in question.

As the Inuit became dependent on state welfare, their capacity for traditional independent subsistence was largely extinguished. Hugh Brody describes the experience of Pond Inlet (now in Nunavut): white men (that is, police, missionaries, and traders) had come 'with many powers and purposes ... Under their supervision, the "old days" changed. A mix began to take shape, with life on the land yielding to various forms of modern poverty. Inuit women became servants in the white officials' homes; men had opportunities for occasional wage labour. This was work that yielded small amounts of money or credit at the store. It also meant a shift towards store-bought food and clothes, and some degree of dependence on newcomers who were anything but generous.'[96]

The road to self-governance did not end with the introduction of home rule in 1979 or the creation of the territory of Nunavut in 1999 and the signing by the Inuit of the NLCA in 1993. Because of the continuous evolution of Greenland's system of governance and fulfilment of all legal and political possibilities embedded in the Greenland Home Rule Act of 1978, the reform of Greenland's legal status within the Danish realm was necessary. This led to the creation in 1999 by the Greenland Government of the Commission on Self-Governance, which in 2003 released its report offering recommendations for expansion of Greenland's autonomy in a number of areas. In 2004 a Danish-Greenlandic Self-Governance Commission was created to develop a plan for increasing Greenland's autonomy within Denmark. It is expected that ongoing Danish-Greenlandic negotiations on Greenland's constitutional status will lead to the signing by 2008 of a new partnership agreement on self-governance that will provide Greenlandic authorities with possibilities of greater autonomy. In Nunavut we also witness political and legal evolution of governance. Even though the Nunavut system of public governance was created with active Inuit participation, it is not clear yet whether it is going to develop towards any form of self-governance for all residents of Nunavut or towards Inuit autonomy, or if Nunavut will eventually become a province of Canada. In the near future Nunavut is expected to reach a devolution agreement with the federal government, which may transfer more province-like powers from Ottawa to the territory. Thus, both Greenland and Nunavut are looking forward to a greater measure of autonomy in regaining control over their affairs.

2 The Constitutional Dimensions of the Governance of Nunavut and Greenland

Inuit Perspectives on Self-Governance and the Governance Systems of Greenland and Nunavut

Are Greenland and Nunavut examples of real autonomy for the Inuit or are they legal fictions, indulgences granted by Denmark and Canada? The legal understanding of the constitutional arrangements in Greenland and Nunavut cannot be explored without consideration of Inuit perspectives on autonomy. Canadian and Danish political, social, economic, and legal institutions were imposed on the Inuit. Colonial and modern state practices eroded traditional Inuit systems of self-regulation. Thus, the Inuit had to live under the alien structures of colonizers, who were not always inclined to accept indigenous institutions.

Published materials and interviews with the Inuit show that they consider themselves to have been a self-governing people.[1] The Inuit perceptions of governance are closely connected with their perceptions of their rights. However, discussing the concept of rights among the Inuit is complicated. As Inuit representatives state, 'there is no concept of rights in Inuit tradition but they were always there, part of our mentality even though they were never written.'[2] Thus, from their own perspective, the Inuit were self-governing prior to European contact, notwithstanding the fact that there were no formal concepts of governance and its constituent elements in Inuit tradition and practice.[3]

This discussion highlights the problem of the compatibility of Western notions of governance with Inuit values. If formal doctrines of autonomy and rights are not inherent to the Inuit tradition, how could the Inuit have been expected to comprehend and apply these concepts when state institutions, including law, were imposed on them?[4] For many years, the dominant society told the Inuit what to do without special accommodation for their traditional values, and the Inuit have adapted accordingly. But with the rise of Inuit political consciousness, it became necessary for the Inuit not only to understand such rules but to be able to use them to justify their own political aspirations. This becomes evident in remarks by the late Inuit leader Mark R. Gordon, who stated that 'the concepts of land claims and Aboriginal rights were introduced by non-Inuit lawyers and were "a tool not of our invention" but were used by Inuit "with the intention to run our own lives."'[5] The Inuit Tapirisat of Canada agrees with Gordon, but indicates how difficult this process could be.[6]

> At the political level, the uneven power relationship between aboriginal peoples and non-aboriginal decision-makers has provided little opportunity for aboriginal peoples to shift discussion from conceptual frameworks rooted in western legal traditions towards some more neutral ground. The decision to work within a common law framework, a human rights framework or some other conceptual framework to articulate Inuit self-government rights is a strategic decision influenced by a range of complex political, legal and other factors. Needless to say, Inuit are placed at some disadvantage in attempting to express Inuit perspectives of Inuit rights through an alien legal system.[7]

Currently, there is no common view on self-governance among Aboriginal peoples, among the Inuit of the different regions of the Canadian Arctic, and particularly between the Inuit of Nunavut and Greenland.[8] During interviews, many of the Inuit respondents emphasized the importance of developing economic opportunities, self-sufficiency, and partnership with the criminal justice system as the best means for dealing with social issues and promoting human development. As expressed by a senior official of the Inuit Circumpolar Conference (ICC; renamed the Inuit Circumpolar Council in 2006), self-government begins when people have the ability to be a part of the governance structures. Self-government has to reflect the Inuit culture, values, and principles. 'It has to be completely in a way where we have been part of that process from the bottom up. And so, the self-government, self-governance ... must reflect the actual empowerment of the individual, the family, the community, and the nations as a whole to be real.'[9] Genuine self-government starts with people's ability to realize themselves and to promote their values and beliefs within governmental structures. The success of current governance systems in Nunavut and Greenland depends not just on the development of the institutionalized structures but also on people's active participation in processes, initiatives, and contributions in making different levels of their governance machinery efficient and responsive to its citizens' needs and expectations. Furthermore, in both Greenland and Nunavut, Inuit values should form the basis for self-government or at least be reflected in the administration of governance institutions.[10]

The home rule process is evolving towards greater autonomy for the Greenlandic nation, whereas in Nunavut the focus is on nation building. In contrast to Nunavut, Greenland is a unified nation. The Inuit of Greenland act as national representatives of the country of Greenlanders. Thus, the existing home rule system and anticipated legislation on Greenland's expanded self-governance do not put special emphasis on promotion of ethnic rights of the Inuit. Furthermore, after more than two decades of home rule, the system in Greenland has evolved to a more advanced level of governance and nation building compared to that in Nunavut, where the process is still rooted in Inuit nationalism and regionalism. Along with settlement of the Nunavut Land Claims Agreement (NLCA), which guaranteed the Inuit a variety of rights and benefits, the Inuit of Nunavut chose the form of public government for their territory. However, despite the fact that this created system of public governance applies to all Nunavummiut – that is, citizens of Nunavut – it gives special priority to the accommodation of the Inuit interests and protection of their rights. Thus, a dual political culture and a hybrid system of governance policies have developed in Nunavut. On the one hand, there is a legal regime and polices intended for the beneficiaries of the NLCA, who represent the majority of Nunavut's population. On the other hand, there is public government for all Nunavummiut, which gives special consideration to Inuit values and concerns.

In the political discourse within Greenland, many rights are claimed for the Inuit. However, for several reasons, every demand for rights put in ethnic terms has been transformed and interpreted into rights for the territorially defined population of the island. Consequently, de jure rights are not conferred on anyone for being an indigenous person.[11] Thus, in Canada and Denmark there are different approaches to the ethnic rights of the Inuit citizens of Nunavut and Greenland. This is partially because of the history of colonization, differences in Canadian and Danish legal and political perceptions of indigenous rights, and uncertainty regarding availability of mineral resources in Greenland.[12] Thus, the concept of an inherent Aboriginal right of self-government or negotiations of a land claim agreement with Greenlanders has never been at issue in Denmark. Unlike their Canadian counterparts, the Inuit of Greenland are the only indigenous group of the Danish realm occupying a distinct territory, and they did not face rivalry with other Aboriginal peoples in asserting their political aspirations. Finally, because of fluid ethnic boundaries in Greenland (the result of hundreds of years of intermarriage) and because of the reluctance of Danish authorities to apply ethnic criteria, the legal definition of who is a Greenlander includes every Danish citizen living on the island.[13] In sharp contrast to Nunavut, ethnicity was not the basis for Greenlandic identity, and there was no need to decide whom to consider Inuk or non-Inuk in terms of rights and access to benefits.[14] Despite the prevalence of intermarriage between Inuit and non-Inuit in the Canadian North, the special protection of Inuit residents, and especially those who qualify as beneficiaries of the NLCA, has been a matter of vital importance in Nunavut.[15]

The question of the Canadian Inuit's right to self-government requires some further attention because of its theoretical complexity arising from political and constitutional practices that affect the relationship between the Inuit and the state of Canada. The Inuit of Canada view their right to self-government as part of the right to internal self-determination and as an inherent, fundamental human and Aboriginal right. Thus, if the ancestors of the Inuit of modern Nunavut were self-governing prior to colonization, then an Inuit right to autonomy, being inherent, continues to exist notwithstanding any governance structures created by Canada (for the Northwest Territories [NWT] or Nunavut). Consequently, the Inuit could choose to establish a system of indigenous autonomy with all the necessary components based on their traditional beliefs. In the Inuit view, 'Aboriginal self-government is not an abstract concept which needs definition; it is the means by which Inuit can regain control over their lives.'[16] Thus, the Inuit Tapirisat of Canada emphasizes that 'Inuit believe that the Canadian Constitution and Canadian aboriginal rights doctrine should be interpreted and developed in a manner that recognizes individual and collective rights as integral parts of a comprehensive human rights regime. For example, the inherent right of self-government is an aspect of our right to self-determination and therefore has the character of a fundamental human right.'[17]

As summarized by Rosemarie Kuptana, the Inuit Tapirisat of Canada has elaborated several elements of the right to self-government:

It is a pre-existing and fundamental human right and therefore not subject to extinguishment (inherent); the inherent right of self-government exists independent of any self-government agreement (non-contingent); governments established by aboriginal peoples in exercise of the inherent right constitute an order of government with constitutional status (aboriginal peoples' governments are one of the three orders of government in Canada that are sovereign within their spheres of jurisdiction); the consent of aboriginal peoples is necessary in defining the relationship between aboriginal peoples' governments and federal and provincial governments (consent requirement); the inherent right of self-government does not prescribe any particular form of government and therefore encompasses ethnic and non-ethnic forms of government (Inuit are not restricted to traditional forms of government or from joining with others in the exercise of their inherent right of self-government).[18]

A 1987 position paper by the Inuit Committee on National Issues mapped the general terms of what Canadian Inuit are seeking from self-government. Canadian Inuit favour a territorial base for their institutions of self-government but 'do not claim absolute sovereignty in the areas in which they live.' Further, 'Inuit seek legislative authority and other powers necessary for raising their own revenues.' They stress that 'self-government means full authority over most local and regional matters, and concurrent jurisdiction with federal or provincial governments over matters of common concern.' The Inuit also have emphasized an importance of having a constitutional protection for self-government.[19]

In Canada, the 'Inuit maintain that the federal Crown has a specific relationship with Inuit as a people and a fiduciary duty to Inuit.' This fiduciary duty includes the obligation of the federal government 'to respect the fundamental human rights of Inuit, including the right of self-determination,' which encompasses self-government.[20] As noted by Jull, '*Self-determination* refers to the right of a culture, society or region to decide for itself whether its future will be as an independent sovereign entity in the world, or whether, like Nunavut, its people accept association with or an integration in an existing national constitutional order.'[21] The Inuit perception of self-government needs to be viewed through the Inuit's special relationship with the Canadian and Danish states. How is this relationship reflected in the governance arrangements for Greenland and Nunavut?

Legal and Political Nature of Greenland's and Nunavut's Governance Arrangements

The key to sustained and effective Inuit participation in politics does not lie in further elaboration and consolidation of existing structures, nor in tinkering with existing mechanisms for decision-making. It lies in the formal constitutional recognition of the Inuit's right to determine their own future and to develop the institutions and procedures most appropriate to the expression of their deepest concerns.

Peter Ittinuar, Inuit leader

The legal and political foundations of the Greenland Home Rule Act, the Nunavut Land Claims Agreement, and the Nunavut Act constitute the basis of the governance systems of these two jurisdictions. Consequently, the following questions have to be considered: What are the main legal features and principles of these documents? Are they results of the Inuit right to self-government/self-determination or the outcomes of political necessity? Do they actually provide the Inuit with effective self-government?

It is important to note that both jurisdictions are based on the territorial principle, with some differences in the intent of the legislators in the elaboration of the Home Rule Act, the NLCA, and the Nunavut Act.[22] Some authorities maintain that 'the Inuit of Greenland became the first population of Inuit to achieve a degree of self-government over a large region of the High Arctic.'[23] They also state that under the structure that established the system of Greenland home rule, an emphasis was placed on 'the definition of indigenous peoples as collective entities, being the first inhabitants of part or all of the country.'[24] Although these statements are technically correct, in reality, home rule status was given to all residents of Greenland, including non-Inuit. As a former premier of Greenland, Lars Emil Johansen, noted, 'The Home Rule agreement is not an agreement honouring or even referring to the collective rights of the Inuit population, but rather a law concerning everyone living permanently within the geographical entity of 840 000 square miles known as Greenland ... From a legal point of view, the rights and powers of the Home Rule Agreement were not granted to us as a people or ethnic group, but as the inhabitants of a certain landmass.'[25] Before the introduction of home rule in 1979 there were arguments among the political parties of Greenland on this very issue. For example, the Inuit Ataqatigiit Party claimed that 'Home Rule does not acknowledge the title to land of the aboriginal people.'[26] In the same vein, Hans C. Gulløv noted that, in its work, 'the Commission on Home Rule has not used the aboriginal right to sovereignty of the Greenland Nation as a basis.'[27] These statements indicate that the Home Rule Act of 1978 was not designed as a special form of self-government for the Inuit people of Greenland but applied to all inhabitants of the island. The Home Rule Act is a classic example of a statute based on territorial autonomy. However, over time, the system of governance created by the act has evolved into one that, at a functional rather than a juridical level, goes far towards meeting the interests of the Inuit, who represent the majority of the population.[28]

In contrast, negotiations around the creation of Nunavut were at the very beginning oriented towards some form of self-government for the Inuit, but in the end Inuit leaders chose the form of public government. The creation of the new territory of Nunavut was ensured by the Nunavut Act, and by a Nunavut Political Accord concluded by negotiators for the Tungavik Federation of Nunavut, the government of Canada, and the government of the Northwest Territories.[29] At the same time, this political settlement, which was a part of the negotiation of the Nunavut Land Claims Agreement, was explicitly included in the NLCA.[30]

Nunavut's system, like that of Greenland, is an example of public territorial governance for all inhabitants of the area. The Greenlandic model of governance was based on already existing legal concepts (e.g., the Faroese Home Rule Act of 1948).[31] In Nunavut this choice was a pragmatic political move consistent with the patience and determination of the Inuit in pursuing their goal of regaining control over their lands. They recognized that the model of public government was more palatable than Inuit self-government to the federal government and Canadians in general.[32] John Amagoalik, often called the father of Nunavut, has noted that Nunavut is 'not purely Aboriginal self-government because, right from the beginning, we have proposed that Nunavut be a public government where everyone has the same rights and responsibilities.'[33]

Inuit leaders accepted that Nunavut was not formally recognized as an instance of Inuit self-government. At the same time, they pragmatically pointed to the de facto consequences of adopting the public government model in a territory with a clear Inuit majority. In the words of the Inuit leader Jose Kusugak, 'the creation of a new territory with a government representing all its residents is a workable and attractive form of empowering the Inuit of Nunavut. This is entirely a function of our demographics – unlike aboriginal people in other parts of Canada, we have never been a minority in our homeland.'[34] A senior official with the government of Nunavut further notes that:

It is a public government, because anybody in Nunavut, who is a resident, can run for an office, like the Legislative Assembly. But at the same time, if we look at the population ratio, and the control of the government, we can look at it as an Inuit government because Inuit are majority right now. Inuit control the government. At the same time, when we were establishing the Nunavut government, we did not want to see an aboriginal self-government, as in the other parts of the country. We wanted to have a public government to be established in Nunavut.[35]

As in Greenland, the Inuit majority in Nunavut transformed formal territorial autonomy into de facto Inuit governance: it is a 'Public Government with an Inuit Face.'[36] As Amagoalik has stated, 'No other land claim has involved creating a new territory with our own government. It is a victory. We've achieved what other aboriginal people can only dream about.'[37] The question becomes whether territorial autonomy alone can protect the rights of indigenous peoples or whether there is a need for a special type of indigenous autonomy for the Inuit living in Greenland or Nunavut. The Greenland and Nunavut cases prove that there is not. The Inuit majorities in Nunavut and Greenland in practice are turning de jure territorial forms of governance into de facto indigenous ones.

Some Differences in the Greenland Home Rule Act, the NLCA, and the Nunavut Act

Although both Greenland and Nunavut are genuine homelands for the Inuit, there are significant differences in the Home Rule Act, the NLCA, and the Nunavut Act. The major distinction is that home rule in Greenland is regulated by a single act of the Folketing (Danish Parliament), which treats Greenland as a distinct community within the kingdom with limited self-governing powers exercised within the framework of public administration. Two acts pursuing different goals regulate the legal status of Nunavut. Similar to the Greenland Home Rule Act, the Nunavut Act of 1993 is a creature of the Canadian Parliament; at the same time it ensured the creation of a new unit in the Canadian federation, which was created as a result of division of the NWT. A territory of Nunavut came into being in 1999 with the form of public government. Importantly, the proposal for legislation establishing Nunavut and the recommendation and timing of the Nunavut Act were included in a political accord that was itself the result of long-term Inuit struggle for control over their homeland. Furthermore, the Inuit of Nunavut negotiated the NLCA, passed by the federal Parliament in 1993, which ensured, among other things, Inuit title to approximately 350,000 square kilometres of land, of which 35,257 square kilometres include mineral rights (the rest of the land in Nunavut is Crown land). From the beginning, the NLCA, as an Inuit achievement, intended to embrace all possible Inuit interests. Its premise was that the Inuit should regain control of their lands and their lives. As Inuit leader Jack Anawak has stressed, 'What we have been seeking throughout the years is the acknowledgment by the Canadian government that this was, and is, our land and that we have the right to control what happens to that land, our homeland.'[38]

The NLCA is the largest comprehensive land claims settlement in Canada that is constitutionally recognized. Through the NLCA the Inuit received defined rights and benefits in exchange for surrender of any claims, rights, title, and interests based on their assertion of an Aboriginal title anywhere within Canada.[39] Arguably, this controversial 'extinguishment' provision of the NLCA brings some features of colonial legacy to the agreement. To some extent, features of the colonial legacy can also be observed in the Home Rule Act, the content and even the title of which highlights the continuation of voluntary colonialism. During the interviews I conducted, many of the Inuit respondents considered the 'extinguishment' clause to be a weakness of the NLCA and an indicator of a continuing colonial mentality. As one of the key negotiators of the NLCA noted, it was hard for the Inuit to accept this clause. 'It is colonial legacy when you have to give up a certain thing in order to get something. This is not the Inuit way. That certainly is from another form, because the federal government adopted that policy, because that mentality of colonialism is always there. We had to accept it, but in return we said: "give us Nunavut government," "give us Nunavut territory."'[40]

When the Home Rule Act was introduced in Greenland, the Inuit greeted it enthusiastically and with high expectations. Notwithstanding the limited nature of the proposed home rule arrangement and its basis in Danish legal and political paradigms, Greenlanders were reluctant to reject it. As Lars Emil Johansen, then the member for Greenland in the Danish Parliament, said in the first reading of the Greenland Home Rule Act in 1978, 'The people of Greenland have not been given many such possibilities, and we cannot afford to say "no".'[41]

The Greenland Home Rule Act is less comprehensive than the NLCA and the Nunavut Act. It contains twenty sections with narrow and sometimes vague provisions.[42] If the Home Rule Act is ambiguous partially as a result of its brevity, the Nunavut documents, despite their length and comprehensiveness, are also subject to problems of interpretation, largely because of their complexity.[43]

In many ways the NLCA has failed to meet the expectations of the Inuit. It has been criticized for being a male-biased document that does not pay enough attention to women's rights; nor does it sufficiently take into consideration socio-economic rights and guarantees, or provide an adequate base for dealing with modern challenges of globalization or economic self-sustainability[44] Critics are also concerned that via the NLCA the Inuit surrendered too much of their land in exchange for cash payments rather than negotiating a more solid block of Inuit ownership rights. There were also problems with providing an authentic translation of the NLCA into Inuktitut, a language that does not always have words to express some Western legal and political concepts. Consequently, it is a challenge for unilingual Inuktitut-speaking beneficiaries of the agreement to understand its provisions. This situation is exacerbated by the absence of a unanimous interpretation of the NLCA by Nunavut's various governmental institutions.[45] Other irritants include the lack of a mechanism to make a 'reluctant' federal government fulfil its obligations, the continued dependence on Ottawa for economic support, and the existence of a federal ministerial veto over the decisions of Nunavut co-management bodies (often referred to as institutions of public government). In December 2006 a dispute that had been ongoing since 2001 between the Nunavut Tunngavik Incorporated (NTI), the government of Nunavut, and the government of Canada regarding the update of the implementation contract for the NLCA led to the $1 billion lawsuit against the federal government for breach of contract. In its lawsuit the NTI pointed out that the NLCA have been breached in a number of areas including inadequate funding for the Nunavut co-management bodies and for hunters' and trappers' organizations; failure by the Crown to provide funding for implementing the NLCA after the initial ten-year period following its coming into force; non-conclusion of Inuit Impact and Benefit Agreements and lack of funding required for their realization; non-implementation of a general monitoring plan (article 12, part 7, s.12.7.6 of the NLCA) and of Inuit employment obligations (article 23 of the NLCA). Clearly, the agreement and its implementation is a work in progress and a lot of effort will be required to bring it to fruition.[46]

To more fully answer the question of the extent to which the Greenland Home Rule Act and the NLCA and Nunavut Act have resulted in effective self-government, it is important to examine the underlying principles of these documents.

The Constitutional Place of Greenland in Denmark and Nunavut in Canada

Continuous evolution of Greenland's home rule system since its introduction in 1979 and the increase in political aspirations among Greenlanders towards obtaining greater independence in managing their own affairs have outstripped the provisions of the Greenland Home Rule Act of 1978. Greenland's development and, to some extent, its jurisdictional capabilities went far beyond what was imagined to be possible within the home rule arrangement and even the Danish constitution, as they were generally interpreted in the late 1970s. Currently, the recommendations of Greenland's Commission on Self-Governance for a partnership agreement between Greenland and Denmark with regard to Greenland's right to self-government point to the need to expand autonomy of the island.[47] Nonetheless, there will still be continuity between the new partnership agreement and the principles of the Home Rule Act.

The work of the Commission on Home Rule for Greenland (1975–8) was influenced by three major considerations. First, a political solution was required that would strengthen the ties and relations between Greenland and Denmark. Second, the solution chosen had to be one that could be implemented easily by Greenlandic authorities, given the shortage of qualified Greenlandic manpower. Finally, all the arrangements arrived at had to conform to the Danish constitution.[48] For these reasons, among others, the commission envisioned that preserving the principle of the unity of the realm should be the core element of the introduction of home rule.[49] Consequently, chapter 1, section 1(1) of the Greenland Home Rule Act reads: 'Greenland is a distinct community within the Kingdom of Denmark. Within the framework of the unity of the Realm, the Greenland home rule authorities shall conduct Greenland affairs in accordance with the provisions laid down in this Act.'[50] Under home rule, Greenland had to remain a part of the Kingdom of Denmark, and sovereignty belonged exclusively to the Danish authorities. The latter delegated to the home rule authorities part of their jurisdiction in those areas that relate exclusively to Greenlandic matters.[51] Thus, the Greenland Home Rule Act was limited by the principle of national unity: the act reflected a respect for the interests and solidarity of all parts of Denmark as a unitary state.[52] This principle was designed to prevent the establishment of a Danish federation or the transformation of home rule to the independent state of Greenland.

Despite this principle, some commentators consider Denmark as a federation or a special legal construction. In the opinion of Bogi Eliasen, Denmark today is not a unitary state 'but a structure with some federative elements of divided power.'[53] This assessment is based on the divided Danish kingdom's membership in the European Union (Greenland and the Faroe Islands have chosen to exclude themselves from the EU) and Denmark's partial vesting of its sovereignty in that organization. Other factors contributing to the characterization of the Danish kingdom as a federation are a result of the legislative powers of the parliaments of Greenland and the Faroe Islands, and Denmark's inability to independently fulfil international obligations in spheres that are in the home rule authorities' jurisdiction. Frederik Harhoff states that Denmark 'is neither a federation (since it lacks a treaty to this effect), nor it is a confederation.'[54] But, in his words, home rule of Greenland and the Faroe Islands has made an illusion of the unitary state. Denmark today is a *Rigsfællesskabet*, or a form of commonwealth. It is 'a tripartite community of separate and autonomous parts, each with their own original powers, but with Continental Denmark as the hegemonial part with residual authority.'[55] J. Berglund Nielsen claims that 'the present Greenland Home Rule should be developed into something which could be labeled as Extended or Sovereign Home Rule with a new relation to the Danish Realm, based on principles of commonwealth or unionism.'[56]

These varied opinions raise the issue of the status of Greenland's home rule within Denmark. Is Greenland just an integral part of the unitary state, following the Danish Constitution, or is it an autonomous entity that has altered the 'unitary' nature of the Danish state? Breinholt-Larsen argues that 'the Greenlanders became a self-governing nation within a *de facto* federal government.'[57] If that is true, Greenland should have a status generally comparable to the subjects of federal states. Jull notes that 'the home rule government ... has wider governing power than an Australian state or Canadian province.'[58] However, this is not evident from the legal framework of the Home Rule Act. Clearly, it is hard to classify Greenland's status within Denmark. Formally, it is an integral part of a unitary state with autonomous authority in a limited number of areas. Greenland's enigmatic constitutional status may be clarified with the introduction of a new partnership agreement on the island's self-governance, as it would move towards an extended form of political autonomy. Possibly on the basis of legal options available in the framework of this new partnership, Greenland eventually might even opt for independence.

Clarity on the legal status of subnational entities within a unitary or federal state is crucial for the scope of powers to be delegated to those entities. Unlike Greenland's 'enigmatic' position within Denmark, Nunavut received the defined status of a territory.[59] This means, among other things, that it is a distinct member of the Canadian federation. This fact is important for understanding Nunavut's legal status. There are significant differences between the powers exercised by a province and those exercised by a territorial government. Provinces derive their power from section 92 of the Constitution Act, 1867, while territories receive theirs from specific federal statutes. This situation is analogous to that of Greenland, which is subject to centralized Danish legislation. However, 'much of the power they [the territories] wield is not provided for by statute, but is in place due to discussions between political leaders in the North and the federal minister. In some cases, this is given formal recognition in Letters of Instruction, while in others it is instituted through unwritten understandings between the federal and territorial governments.'[60] This is in contrast to the Danish practice, according to which statutory regulation is formally required, but sometimes the regulation simply recognizes a practice that had already been introduced by Greenlandic authorities.

In the meantime, the Nunavut position as a new territory in the Canadian state is unique. Thomas Isaac argues that, 'Nunavut represents something more than a traditional territory (like the Yukon) and something less than a province.'[61] This is analogous to Greenland's status within Denmark: it exercises more powers than other administrative units of the Danish realm but has less jurisdiction than most subjects of federal states.[62] Without a doubt, Greenland and Nunavut are distinct societies within Denmark and Canada. This distinctiveness was incorporated into legal and political governance arrangements for both societies.

The Legal Status of Arrangements for Greenland and Nunavut

What is the legal status of the territory of Nunavut and Greenlandic home rule? There is no easy answer to that question: the Nunavut Land Claims Agreement is constitutionally recognized, whereas the constitutional status of the Nunavut Act and the Greenland Home Rule Act is marked by ambiguities. Both systems of governance are based on the delegation of 'secondary' powers from the state to the authorities in Greenland and Nunavut partially with the purpose of alleviating central or federal responsibilities for remote lands.[63]

Greenland home rule was created on the Commission on Home Rule's 'assumption that an irreversible division of the constitutional powers would be incompatible with the unity of the Danish Realm. A truly independent legislative or executive power for Greenland, therefore, could not exist within the framework of the Danish Constitution of 1953.'[64] Following the principle of national unity, home rule of Greenland could not be based on an international treaty or amendment to the constitution. As Lise Lyck concludes, home rule is a 'cooperation model' – in other words, autonomy is 'not given by constitution or by international agreement.'[65]

The Greenland Home Rule Act is an ordinary statute of the Folketing that formally can be amended by unilateral action of that body. As Harhoff states, 'from a strict constitutional legal point of view, all legislative and administrative (executive) powers are still vested *solely* in the Danish Parliament and the Danish Government, the theory being that powers have been only *delegated* to the two Home Rule authorities subject to unilateral withdrawal by Denmark at any time.'[66] Similarly, the Nunavut Act, as a federal statute, is subject to the direct jurisdiction of the federal Parliament: Nunavut does not have the authority to amend the provisions of this act. Laureen Nowlan-Card notes that, 'as a delegated authority, the Nunavut Territorial government only derives those powers which the federal government chooses to delegate to it. The federal government retains the ultimate authority to rescind the delegation or to alter the powers.'[67] Furthermore, according to section 28 of the Nunavut Act, the governor in council (the cabinet) can override Nunavut's legislation.[68] It is also questionable whether the two Greenland members in the Folketing and the two representatives from Nunavut in the Canadian Parliament would be able to exert much influence over the legislatures' decisions.[69] However, there is a remote possibility that the Danish and Canadian governments might be tempted to restrict unilaterally the Greenland Home Rule Act and the Nunavut Act.[70]

Although the Nunavut Act is not a mini-constitution of Nunavut, the territory itself attracts constitutional protection because Nunavut was created as an integral part of the Nunavut land claim settlement (NLCA, art. 4), which is constitutionally recognized. As is the case for other comprehensive land claims agreements (known as 'modern treaties') in

Canada, the NLCA is entrenched in the constitution under section 35 of the Constitution Act, 1982.[71] This section recognizes and affirms existing Aboriginal and treaty rights of Aboriginal peoples in Canada and by '"treaty rights" includes rights that now exist by the way of land claims agreements or may be so acquired.'[72]

Analysing the Nunavut Agreement-in-Principle (1990), Isaac points out that 'the Inuit have held consistently that the creation of a Nunavut territory is "the core demand for the Inuit agenda, with the claim as a means of attaining it." Therefore, because the creation of the territory is an integral part of the agreement, the territory itself will become constitutionalized ... Once Nunavut is created, it could not be dismantled unilaterally by the federal government.'[73] Gallagher-Mackay discussed several options for constitutional recognition of Nunavut. She suggested, among other possibilities, that 'Nunavut is entitled to constitutional protection' because of 'the status of both the Land Claims Agreement *and* the Political Accord as treaties between the Crown and the Inuit acting collectively as a people.'[74] The arguments of both Isaac and Gallagher-Mackay ultimately sanction the constitutionalization of the Nunavut territory. Furthermore, as Kevin Gray argues, 'the creation of a new political entity lessens the importance of entrenching the Nunavut government into the *Constitution*.'[75]

In Greenland's case, there are various opinions on the necessity of amendments to the Danish constitution and directions for possible constitutional reforms dealing with Greenlanders' rights and status of their home rule. As Mininnguaq Kleist suggests, there might be an option of solving the problem of repealing the Greenland Home Rule Act by taking the matter to the Danish Supreme Court. Another option is that Greenlanders demand that Denmark acknowledge constitutionally their right to nullification, which would allow home rule authorities to nullify laws and orders issued by the Folketing and the Danish government. They could also demand constitutional acknowledgment of Greenland's right to veto laws proposed by Denmark that cover the whole Danish commonwealth. Demanding these rights would require changing the Danish constitution, which is theoretically possible.[76]

Some observers argue that the Greenland Home Rule Act does, in fact, get constitutional recognition. Thus, Harhoff stresses that, despite the fact that

Home Rule is not mentioned in the Danish Constitution Act ... Faeroese Home Rule, which preceded the current constitution of 1953, was believed to be in conformity with the old constitution of 1915, and this view was also taken when Greenland achieved Home Rule in 1978. Thus, the Home Rule Act serves partly as a constitution for Greenland, although some parts of the Danish constitution, notably those relevant to the Danish currency, the Monarch, and rights and freedoms, are still common to the entire Danish realm and are therefore in force in Greenland.[77]

Harhoff notes that the Greenland Home Rule Act is believed to alter the Danish constitution by customary practice and, thus, 'the Home Rule Act has the status of a constitutional appendix that is superior to ordinary Danish legislation but remains under the Danish constitution.'[78] If one accepts Harhoff's argument that the Home Rule Act is 'customarily entrenched' and by itself the act is valued as a constitutional appendix, then there is no need for amendment of the Danish constitution. As Harhoff has noted, home rule authorities perceive their autonomy as a permanent and irrevocable institution.[79]

In contrast, in the opinion of J.B. Nielsen, the Danish constitution needs to be revised because a new relationship between Greenland and Denmark has to be developed.[80] Elaine Ward states that there is a need for some reform of the Danish constitution in order to entrench the Inuit's special rights. She further notes that 'there is also need for a separate constitution for Kalaallit Nunaat enacted and passed by the Greenland Home Rule Authorities, and officially recognized by the Danish Government.'[81] This constitution (or act, or code of conduct) could begin with a bill of rights section, which could be a model constitutional document for other indigenous groups around the world who wish to exercise self-government short of complete political independence from a larger nation-state.[82] Ward's ideas have merit, but it can be argued that although the constitutional inclusion of indigenous rights may strengthen the legal position of the indigenous group, even constitutional provisions could be amended. The functionality of Greenland's system and protection of Inuit rights in several international documents ratified by Denmark mitigate the necessity for development of a separate bill of rights for the Inuit.

The development of home rule transcended the enigmatic constitutional status of the island, the assumptions of the Home Rule Commission, and the limited legal scope of the Greenland Home Rule Act of 1978. Thus, in its recommendations the recent Commission on Self-Governance focused on the development of possibilities for the new partnership between Greenland and Denmark in conformity with existing legal options, constitutional principles, and limits of the present constitution.[83]

As mentioned above, the NLCA as a 'modern treaty' is constitutionally protected. However, the question remains whether the Nunavut Act and the NLCA provide the Inuit with effective self-government. Nunavut has a public government, but to a certain degree it also reflects Inuit self-government where the Inuit culture, traditions, and language are supported by existing governmental institutions.[84] However, various commentators and interviews with Nunavummiut indicate that there is no unanimous view on the nature of Nunavut governance today. Some scholars believe that, 'despite some weaknesses, the new Nunavut government will mean de facto self-government for the Inuit.'[85] At the same time, as one Akitsiraq Law School student has noted, because of the shortage of skilled Inuit in the top bureaucratic positions, Nunavut does not mean self-governance for the Inuit.[86] Provisions of the NLCA or Nunavut Act per se do not identify the Nunavut Settlement Area or created territorial public government as self-government. By the terms of the settlement of the NLCA, the Inuit surrendered only their Aboriginal title to land and waters anywhere within Canada and adjacent offshore areas. In the NLCA there is no explicit reference to the right of self-government, and so this right must be assumed to continue. Under current federal policy, the Inuit could negotiate a self-government arrangement separate from the NLCA.[87] However, the Inuit chose to negotiate the NLCA and the form of public government as distinct from Aboriginal self-government. The Inuit chose the public governance model because it leaves them room to negotiate a separate self-government arrangement in the future if demographic or economic circumstances not in the Inuit's favour should arise. As a senior official with the government of Nunavut notes, 'This is a public government, which gives us a role in overall administration of governance of Nunavut, but there is no guarantee that Inuit are always going to be a majority, so we retain our right to self-government.'[88]

There is no ultimate answer to the question whether the current system of governance in Nunavut, which at many levels is interlinked with the land claims settlement, has led to the realization by the Inuit of their internal right to self-determination. During interviews, many Nunavut residents regarded the NLCA and the Nunavut Act as the results of political necessity and, partially, the Inuit right to self-determination. In other words, it is debatable whether the settlement of the land claim and the creation of the territory and government of Nunavut have led to de facto or de jure expression of Inuit self-government.[89] As Isaac points out, the fact that the territory of Nunavut does not have its own constitution and is ultimately subject to federal jurisdiction makes the prospects for Inuit aspirations of self-government rather grim.[90]

The question of a separate Inuit self-government arrangement is not on the agenda of Nunavut today. The system of public government takes into consideration Inuit culture and values. However, Nunavut governance is a dynamic concept that might some day lead towards Inuit autonomy. Similar to the experience of Greenlanders, the self-governance of Nunavut's Inuit will be shaped by the development of their homeland. As Gray puts it, 'Any notion of self-government or self-realization for the Inuit ultimately relies not on the present wording in the *Agreement*, but on participation at the community level as well as higher regional levels.'[91]

An examination of the legal status of the Greenland Home Rule Act, the NLCA, and the Nunavut Act reveals that these documents have different legal characteristics that result from distinct Danish and Canadian legal traditions and approaches to indigenous people's rights and policies towards the Inuit. The different government systems in Greenland and Nunavut result from the fact that the creation of the territory of Nunavut was a basic precondition to the settlement of the NLCA; such was not the case in Greenland. Thus, in Nunavut, a dual system of governance policies has developed: one is for the Inuit beneficiaries of the NLCA; the other is for all Nunavummiut but with clear consideration of Inuit values and interests in the framework of public governance. The Inuit of Greenland represent the nation of Greenlanders, and thus the system of home rule governance is not oriented towards special endorsement of the Inuit's indigenous rights. At the same time, the Greenland Home Rule Act, the NLCA, and the Nunavut Act share some similarities stemming from legal perceptions, influenced historically by colonial mentalities in the Danish and Canadian constitutional systems, including the imposition of foreign, positivist notions of governance and constitutional principles on the Inuit.

Although none of the acts examined in this chapter explicitly guarantee Inuit autonomy per se, Greenland and Nunavut have a 'virtual' form of 'self-governance' based on the de facto development of home rule and the public government systems, rather than on the juridical provisions of the Greenland Home Rule Act, the NLCA, and the Nunavut Act. The development of Greenland's home rule since its introduction in 1979 has proved that this virtual autonomy is rather effective. However, forthcoming changes to home rule show that legal recognition of self-government is crucial for defining an equal partnership with Denmark and the ability to exercise a higher level of autonomy. It is too early to assess the effectiveness of the Nunavut public governance as 'virtual self-governance.'[92]

There is an undeniable element of paternalism in Canadian and Danish policies towards the Inuit of Nunavut and Greenlanders, though how much is a matter of opinion. Charles J. Marecic states that 'federal restrictions create a significantly modified version of *self*-government. The paternalism (or is it colonialism?) bleeds through.'[93] Some critics have characterized Greenland's home rule as 'overdeveloped,' a product of Danish colonial presence on the island.[94] Greenlander Aviâja Egede Lynge notes that Greenland did not go through a process of decolonization, even mental decolonization. She claims that her people were thankful to be colonized and were taught that they are the best colony in the world. Thus, despite more than two decades of home rule, the system is still characterized as the outcome of the Danish presence in Greenland since 1721, and Greenlanders still feel overshadowed by the Danes.[95]

In many ways, the functioning of the Greenland Home Rule Act, the NLCA, and the Nunavut Act is shaped by Danish and Canadian legal cultures. However, these documents should not be regarded as legal fictions in the alien clothes of Danish and Canadian jurisdictions because of their positivist and 'unknown' (to the Inuit) features. Greenland's and Nunavut's governance systems are dynamic entities evolving towards greater Inuit involvement in the management of their affairs, despite the legal frameworks of the Greenland Home Rule Act, the NLCA, and the Nunavut Act. Another important factor is that Inuit values and traditional ways of life are changing over time and intersecting with the perceptions of other societies. However, incorporation of indigenous traditional knowledge and concepts into Western-based legal formulas and legislation remains a challenge. Furthermore, for the Inuit of Greenland the Home Rule Act is a political compromise between Danes and Greenlanders. Similarly, the Inuit of Nunavut had to compromise with the federal government and the Canadian public in political and practical terms. Therefore, the NLCA was divorced from the quest for self-government, and the Inuit accepted the concept of public territorial governance as more palatable to the Canadian system. The provisions of the Greenland Home Rule Act, the NLCA, and the Nunavut Act reflect the compromises that underpin these documents.

Finally, some may argue that Nunavut and Greenland continue to display voluntary colonialism because of acceptance of paternal practices and Inuit dependency on the dominant societies. I have argued that the Greenland Home Rule Act, the NLCA, and the Nunavut Act retain some features of colonial policies. However, the Inuit need time to regain control of their lands and their lives. In this context, the Greenland Home Rule Act, the NLCA, and the Nunavut Act are good starting points towards Inuit self-determination: they are tools whereby the Inuit can take matters into their own hands and create their futures.[96] It is debatable, however, whether these documents should be interpreted as a realization of this goal.[97] They are an expression of the Inuit peoples' right to internal self-determination and show that constitutional protection of autonomy, though important, is not a precondition for its effectiveness. Regardless of the limited powers entrenched in the Greenland Home Rule Act, and the comprehensive provisions of the NLCA and the Nunavut Act, the success of autonomy will depend on its progress in practice.

Because of the dynamic development of the governance system in Nunavut and expected devolution deal with the federal government, there might be a shift towards more political autonomy of the territory – just as has happened in Greenland, where steps in the development of extended self-governance have already been taken. This self-governance does not stem only from the fact that the Inuit are a majority of the population in Greenland and Nunavut, as some authors claim,[98] but derives significantly from active Inuit participation in the political life of their territories and the work of home rule and public governance bodies.

3 Territorial Government versus Home Rule: The Structure of Nunavut's and Greenland's Institutions

When we can make our own laws, we will be able to do things to make our lives better ... We'll be able to communicate with the government in Inuktitut. I think the Nunavut government will be there to deal with issues that Inuit feel are important ... As long as we hold tight to what we believe and as long as the Nunavut government responds to the needs of the people, Inuit will be a lot stronger.

John Amagoalik, Inuit leader

The Greenland Home Rule Act, the Nunavut Land Claims Agreement (NLCA), and the Nunavut Act provide the legal frameworks of governance, but the normative dimensions of these documents are not sufficient for understanding the internal developments and political institutions of Greenland's home rule and Nunavut's government. The effectiveness of Nunavut and Greenland governance systems and their institutions stems largely from thoughtful and active Inuit participation in politics. The autonomy of Greenland and Nunavut should be viewed through the policies of Greenlandic parties and Nunavut Inuit organizations. In this chapter I will examine the example of Greenlanders' democratic participation in the formation of home rule institutions and the processes used by the Inuit of Nunavut for building their governance institutions. In both cases, I consider the pillars of Greenland and Nunavut political organization to be a driving force behind the normative and functional exercise of autonomy. Political factors are shaping the nature of Inuit governance and internal politics and are affecting the Nunavut and Greenland legislatures and their legislation.

Political Organizations, Parliaments, and Governments of Greenland and Nunavut

The Nunavut system of public governance is distinguishable in many ways from that of Greenland. Nunavut has a non-partisan system in which political parties are absent during territorial electoral campaigns, whereas Greenland's system is rooted in party activities. The operations of Nunavut's and Greenland's institutions are grounded in the Canadian and Danish parliamentary systems, but their respective institutional practices are different, and this affects the composition and activity of the legislative and executive branches. There is also a difference between the decentralization efforts of Nunavut's governance and Greenland's centralization priorities. Finally, the details of Nunavut's system of governance have been crystallized in the numerous reports of the Nunavut Implementation Commission (NIC).[1] Although the four-volume report of the Home Rule Commission on Greenland was ambiguous on the subject, the *Report from the Commission on Self-Governance* paid special attention to the restructuring of public administration and the structure of Greenland's internal administration.[2]

I will address some of the particularities of Greenland's party system and Nunavut's non-partisan system in forming and operating the legislative and executive branches of governance. The Greenland Home Rule Act of 1978 created a quasi-parliamentary system, consisting of 'an assembly elected in Greenland, to be called the Landsting, and an administration headed by a Landsstyre (Executive).'[3] In a similar vein, Nunavut has a legislative assembly and an executive council (cabinet).[4]

Greenland's political parties play a key role in the composition of the legislative and executive institutions of home rule. They emerged before the enactment of the Greenland Home Rule Act and became significant during the first election to the Landsting in 1979.[5] The leading social democratic party, Siumut (Forward), which since 1975 had developed into a broad political movement with a common ideology and strong support among hunters, workers, and fishermen in the majority of villages and towns, influenced the course of development of home rule and its institutions.[6] As Dahl notes, the Siumut Party dominated the home rule process, formulated the political demands on the Home Rule Commission, and became the most powerful social force in Greenland, especially after winning the first election, in 1979, and gaining the majority of seats in the Landsting.[7] Siumut was originally 'united under slogans such as: "The new policy," "Development in Greenland on Greenlandic terms" and "Greenlandization."'[8] Its ideology is based on moderate socialism combined with nationalism, and its political goals include 'the creation of a Greenlandic society with equal rights and opportunities for all, the creation of an educational system of international standard, the protection of the environment and a sustainable exploitation of the living resources, and the continuation and strengthening of an open democratic leadership of the country.'[9] Siumut favours independence from Denmark, but only on the condition of economic sustainability.[10]

Although Siumut was and remains the dominant party in Greenland, other parties developed as well. Chief among them was the Atássut (Solidarity) Party, which arose from the moderate liberal political movement of the same name.[11] Oriented towards interdependence and strengthening the solidarity between Greenland and Denmark, the Atássut Party supports home rule for Greenland within the framework of the realm. It believes in increasing independence for Greenland without complete severance from Denmark.[12] Finally, the socialist Inuit Ataqatigiit (IA, Inuit Community) Party has to be mentioned. Shifting from opposing home rule to accepting it, the party today stands for the values of Greenlandic ethnicity and promotes the process of developing Greenlandic autonomy (i.e., a better-developed Greenland with looser ties to Denmark).[13] In 2002 Greenland's political landscape changed with the creation of a new centre-right party called the Democrats.[14] In addition to the existing parties, a new self-government network group, Inussuk, was launched on 1 May 2006 to facilitate cooperation among national organizations and Greenlandic parties in strengthening the independence movement.[15]

In Nunavut political parties are not prohibited as such, and to some extent they are relevant to Nunavut's politics, especially during federal elections.[16] In other words, 'political parties are not completely absent from territorial politics, but they are not the main method of organization in territorial election campaigns,'[17] where candidates contest seats as independents. The lack of a party system works in Nunavut's small, geographically remote communities.[18] Although Greenland's conditions are similar to those in Nunavut, its population has embraced the political party system. The practice of party politics in Greenland is common for municipal and parliamentary elections.[19] As Dahl has commented, 'it is difficult to imagine how Greenland's parliament and government would have handled the many complicated issues if each member had only been elected on the basis of his personal character and local status.'[20]

The greater role of party politics in Greenland compared to that in

Nunavut can be explained by different levels of development of political systems and varying levels of political consciousness among the Inuit. Historically, the Inuit of Canada's Eastern Arctic had a less developed political system that of Greenlanders.[21] As Graham White and Jack Hicks point out, only thirty years before the Nunavut Implementation Commission presented its recommendations on a political system for Nunavut, the federal government introduced an oversimplified notion of democracy to the Inuit:

> Several men in the community will have been nominated to each position on the Council. In order to decide which of the men should have those positions, an election was held. Each person was probably asked to write, on a slip of paper, the name of the man he or she wished to have on the Council. When the voting was completed, the votes were counted and the man who received the highest number of votes was declared elected. It is unlikely that everyone voted for the man who was elected. People do not all think the same way so they are not likely at all to want the same man in office. The man who won the election was elected by the majority of the voters. The minority of the voters had to accept the decision of the majority. This is what democracy means.[22]

In contrast, Greenland's political system emerged long before the introduction of home rule.[23] Ultimately, a well-educated Greenlandic political elite arose that was eager to use the party system to take power from the Danes. In the opinion of André Legaré, the Inuit of Nunavut have traditionally opposed the introduction of the party system because of their preference for expressing their opinions individually instead of subordinating themselves to party discipline.[24] As White, analysing the case of the Northwest Territories (NWT), has noted:

> Idealism and pragmatism both play a role in the rejection of parties. Political parties are rooted in, perpetuate and accentuate social divisions, and many in the NWT wish to avoid what they see as the harmful, artificial divisions that parties would engender. Those who believe in the superiority of the NWT's 'consensus government' recognize that it would not survive the arrival of political parties. On a more pragmatic level, native leaders believe that the introduction of parties could imperil native unity and deflect attention and energy from the attainment of their primary political goals in the realm of land claims and self-government ... In interviews, several indicated distaste for the structures of conventional party discipline; oth-

ers, citing the Yukon experience, argued that in a small legislature a party system would mean the exclusion of too many of the best members from the cabinet.[25]

White's observations are true for the governance of Nunavut, which, though distinct from that of the Northwest Territories, of which it had been a part, in many ways follows the practices and traditions of that administration.

The institutions of Nunavut and Greenland are rooted in different types of parliamentarism. Nunavut has a structure similar to the institutions of the other Canadian territories and has adopted a model of British parliamentarism modified to Northern realities. Greenland's quasi-parliamentary system stems from Danish parliamentarism and party politics.[26] As Greenlander Finn Lynge notes, in Greenland 'traditionally, people vote for the person, not for an ideology. The Danish pattern, however, of voting for a party programme, has clearly gained ground. Thus, one can well maintain that political behaviour in Greenland is becoming less and less Greenlandic, and more and more Danish.'[27] Although the Greenlandic members of the Folketing (Danish Parliament) have traditionally joined with Danish parties that are ideologically familiar, the two present Greenlandic members of the Folketing have formed a new 'separatist' group with Faroese politicians in the Danish Parliament.[28]

The parliamentary systems of Nunavut and Greenland are particularly influenced by the electoral structure. All residents of Greenland eighteen and older are eligible to vote.[29] Usually the Parliament is elected for a four-year term.[30] At the time of writing, the most recent election had been held on 15 November 2005. Table 3.1 compares election results from 1979 to 2005. The data show that the social democratic Siumut, which has governed alone or in a coalition for the period in question, has held a stable leading position.[31] Inuit Ataqatigiit is also stable, but Atássut's support has decreased. The Democrats party has seen its popularity rise with the most recent election. As Dahl states, the political picture in Greenland has changed. It is a mistake to rely just on the party labels. Now 'much depends upon the person in charge of the political party or fraction thereof.'[32] This is evident from the success of the Democrats, 'which has profiled itself on a conservative status quo policy that is more often characterized as being populist.'[33]

The 2002 election was a turning point for Greenland, bringing significant challenges to the stability of Greenland's political system.[34] Siumut

Table 3.1
Election results in Greenland, 1979–2005

Party	1979	1983	1984	1987	1991	1995	1999	2002	2005
Siumut	13	12	11	11	11	12	11	10	10
Atássut	8	12	11	11	8	10	8	7	6
Inuit Ataqatigiit	–	2	3	4	5	6	7	8	7
Akulliit (Centre Party)	–	–	–	–	2	2[a]	–	–	–
Issittup Party (Polar Party)	–	–	–	1	1	–	–	–	–
Others[b]	–	–	–	–	–	1	5	1	1
Democrats	–	–	–	–	–	–	–	5	7
Women's Party	–	–	–	–	–	–	–	–	–

[a]In 1995 one Akulliit Party member of the Landsting left the party to join the Siumut Party.
[b]'Others' include independent candidates or alliances of candidates.
Source: Results for 1979–91 are from Petersson (1994:64); results for 1995–2005 were obtained from www.nanoq.gl.

formed a new government in coalition with Inuit Ataqatigiit.[35] However, the coalition did not last. One major disagreement between the two parties concerned Siumut leader Hans Enoksen's recruitment of political friends for positions without following the required procedures.[36] One such recruit was Jens Lyberth, a top civil servant, who set off another controversy when he hired an Inuit healer to cleanse the government offices of evil spirits. He also urged the six hundred bureaucrats under his control to use methods similar to his to improve the strained relations between Greenlanders and the Danes.[37] As a result of this political crisis, a new coalition government was formed on 17 January 2003, between Siumut and Atássut.[38] This partnership did not last either. Siumut broke the coalition because the leader of Atássut, who was the minister of finance, refused to resign over a budget miscalculation of approximately US$16 million.[39] On 13 September 2003 Siumut and Inuit Ataqatigiit again formed a coalition government.[40] Further wrangling followed in September 2005, when an audit commissioned by the premier reported that two members of the Landsting were freely using public money to cover entertainment expenses for themselves and their family and friends.[41] According to the official statements, the premier called an election because Siumut could not come to terms with its coalition partner on a new child benefit program, but in reality the split had its roots in the expenses scandal.[42] Following the 2005 election, 'no two parties could team up and have a majority of seats in the Landsting.'

Thus, Siumut formed a new three-party 'Northern Lights coalition' with the Inuit Ataqatigiit and Atássut.[43] As Dahl states, all the initiatives from the coalition partners are focused on the process of stronger Greenland self-government. They aim to create the basis for increased societal equality, economic and political self-reliance, environmental sustainability, and greater Greenlanders' influence at various levels of society.[44]

Since 1999, elections have been conducted under a new electoral system. Greenland was turned into one electoral district, instead of being divided into eight ridings, as was formerly the case.[45] This system was introduced to deal with the regional approach of many members of the Landsting, who were often also mayors of their electoral districts. Turning Greenland into one electoral district allowed voters to evaluate politicians on the basis of their national political accomplishments, rather than judging their roles in local communities.[46] Reformers hope that this system will strengthen Greenland's nation-building process and that the country will become a unified entity.[47] At the same time, this electoral system is criticized for being unfair to rural areas, which, because they are less populated than urban centres, may get fewer seats in the Landsting.[48] In order to provide representation for all regions in the Landsting, the Commission on Self-Governance recommended the introduction of an arrangement whereby the most distant districts with small populations be allowed to become individual constituencies, while the rest of Greenland is kept as one constituency.[49]

Greenlandic political parties have been instrumental in shaping the institutions of home rule and further developing self-governance. Despite some political cataclysms in Greenland, they have created an enduring political system that works well for the realization of Inuit interests. Although the Greenland Home Rule Act was not framed as a special form of autonomy for the Inuit population, the political parties make up for this deficiency by promoting a truly Greenlandic agenda.

In Nunavut, several Inuit organizations, including Nunavut Tunngavik Incorporated (NTI), the Qikiqtani Inuit Association, the Kivalliq Inuit Association, and the Kitikmeot Inuit Association, safeguard and advance the rights of the Inuit in the three regions of the territory.[50] These groups are important political actors and have wide responsibilities under the NLCA and participatory powers in the bodies of public government. One of the most powerful organizations is the NTI, which, in dealing with the implementation of the NLCA, represents and protects the interests and rights of the Inuit of Nunavut.[51] The NTI is the main channel for communication between the regional Inuit associations and the government of Nunavut. It is a watchdog for the implementation of obligations by all the parties under the NLCA. Due in part to the NTI's powerful position, its relationship with other decision makers 'has been worn thin,' and tensions have arisen between it and the government of Nunavut.[52] Because of its mandate and 100 per cent Inuit representation, the NTI creates a 'second level of governance' in Nunavut, a corporate governance along with the public one. This phenomenon does not exist in Greenland.

Acting on behalf of the Inuit majority with a broad mandate, Nunavut regional organizations and the NTI are a powerful political force.[53] Considering the small size of communities and the familiarity of the population with potential members of the government and the MLAs, the indirect role of these organizations in forming public opinion is as important as party agitation is in Greenland. The parallels with Greenland on this point are telling: despite the absence of political parties in Nunavut, the influence of Inuit organizations has had a role similar to party politics in Greenland. In both jurisdictions, the Inuit majority in the legislative and executive bodies hold Inuit interests paramount.

In contrast to the Landsting's four-year term, the Nunavut Legislative Assembly has a term of no longer than five years.[54] After much debate, Nunavut leaders decided that the territory would consist of nineteen single-member electoral constituencies.[55] Nunavut's first election took place on 15 February 1999, the second on 16 February 2004.[56] Candidates put their names forward for the nineteen seats, running as independents. The operation of the Nunavut legislature is akin to that of the Legislative Assembly of the NWT, which functions according to a consensus model.[57] It includes some uniquely northern modifications to the standard Westminster parliamentary system.[58] Political parties are absent in the Legislative Assembly of Nunavut, which allows each MLA to vote according to his or her wishes. However, approval of each decision requires consent by the majority of the MLAs. After a general election, MLAs choose from among themselves the speaker, the premier, and the cabinet (executive council). The premier of Nunavut is the head of the executive government.[59]

In Greenland members of the Landsting elect the cabinet, which is headed by the premier (the chair of the Landsstyre).[60] To be elected, the premier and cabinet ministers need a simple majority in the Landsting. Since the introduction of the home rule arrangement it has so far always been the leader of the party with the largest number of seats who becomes the premier after closing a formal or informal agreement with one or more parties with whom the leader can form a majority. In Nunavut the cabinet is drawn from the members of the legislature; in Greenland most of the members of the cabinet are members of the Landsting, although this double role is required only for the premier. In this sense the legislative and executive branches overlap. Furthermore, in both jurisdictions, the cabinet and the premier, who assigns the ministerial portfolios, play the most important roles.

Significantly, in Nunavut there is hardly any ideological divergence among members of the Legislative Assembly along party lines. By contrast, members of Greenland's parliament can be placed along two continua. One is the more or less traditional left/right split with regard to economic policy. On this continuum, the Atássut has been to the right, Siumut just left of the centre, and Inuit Ataqatigiit (IA) to the left. In the past decade positions have become more complex: IA has moved to the right on issues such as privatization and market orientation but kept to the left on redistribution. Atássut has (in most cases) moved to the left; they compete with Siumut in relation to protecting subsidized 'private' business in the primary sector. The second continuum concerns relations with Denmark and the Danes. Here the position of the traditionally pro-Danish Atássut has been taken over by the Democrats. The IA is at the nationalistic end of the continuum; it has legitimized its movements along the left-right continuum under the slogan 'we need to get competitive to gain independence.' Nunavut's and Greenland's parliamentarians are not divided along structural lines, as members of the legislatures almost always form the cabinet. Finally, there are few cultural demarcations in these institutions because of the small number of non-Inuit representatives.[61]

Unlike the situation in the NWT and Greenland, the Nunavut Implementation Commission recommendations considered the possibility of directly electing the Nunavut premier.[62] That would have added a new element to the Westminster system of parliamentary government, but it did not materialize in the first and second territorial elections. However, during the 2006 Nunavut Leadership Forum, the question of direct election of the premier was raised by several MLAs, and Iqaluit city council passed a resolution in its support.[63]

It is questionable to what extent Nunavut's governmental institutions are adapted to Inuit culture or *Inuit Qaujimajatuqangit* (IQ), Inuit traditional knowledge and values. The MLA from Uqqummiut, David Iqaqrialu, commenting on the first election in Nunavut, noted that 'although elections were not part of *Inuit Qaujimajatuqangit*, Inuit have embraced elections as a measure of public support throughout the land·claims process and the steps leading to the creation of the new territory. Elections allow us the means to govern ourselves.'[64] Elections, though unknown in traditional Inuit life, are now recognized as an important part of modern Inuit society.

Compared to that of he Landsting, the representation of women in Nunavut's Legislative Assembly is low.[65] The issue of gender parity in the Nunavut legislature has been a matter of much academic and public discussion and many NIC recommendations.[66] The NIC suggested legally guaranteeing an equal number of male and female members. Such a step would have made the Nunavut legislature the first parliament in the world with guaranteed gender parity, but voters rejected this proposal in a referendum.[67] Greenland's experience shows that a significant representation of women in politics is possible without a legislative requirement. It is probable that over time women will form half of the Landsting's members. Despite the failure of the Women's Party to win any seats during the election of December 2002, and the party's dissolution in 2004, there is general acknowledgment that Greenlandic women are assuming political positions previously occupied by men. Moreover women are becoming more outspoken in political debates and decision-making forums.[68] Current successes are the result of a long process of recognition, marked by a struggle against male-dominated traditions inherent in the system, and hampered by numerous obstacles.[69] In Canada Inuit women actively participate in Inuit organizations such as the Inuit Circumpolar Council (ICC), Pauktuutit, and the NTI, but that participation has not yet translated into substantial representation in the legislature.[70]

There is a significant difference in the number of members in the Landsting of Greenland (thirty-one) and the Nunavut Legislative Assembly (nineteen). This difference stems from the fact that Greenland's population is greater than Nunavut's. However, in 2006 a report of the Nunavut Electoral Boundaries Commission, created by the Nunavut Legislative Assembly, proposed the redrawing and adjusting of the boundaries of several electoral districts in the territory to better reflect the interests of Nunavut communities. The commission's considerations were based on a number of factors. One was 'to create equitable representation for all Nunavummiut' and especially to accommodate concerns of small communities that share the MLA with a larger community and thus often feel under-represented in the territorial legislature. The commission proposed to 'increase the total number of electoral districts to 23.' The Legislative Assembly of Nunavut will make final decision on this matter, with implementation of the change being probable.[71]

Both Nunavut's and Greenland's legislatures are unicameral, which is typical for the parliaments of small entities. Presiding over the legislatures is a chairperson of the Landsting in Greenland and a speaker in Nunavut.[72] The Legislative Assembly of Nunavut sits at least once every twelve months. Meetings of the Landsting are normally held twice during the parliamentary year, once in the spring and once in the autumn.[73]

In designing the future Nunavut government, the Nunavut Implementation Commission underlined its essential principle – decentralization. This was dictated by several realities, including the availability in the villages of employable people (often women) for clerical work and the fact that life in Iqaluit was seen by some as unhealthy compared to that in the settlements because of social problems (e.g., substance abuse, domestic violence, etc.).[74] Decentralization has been implemented gradually in Nunavut over the past few years with the expectation that it will yield benefits in the long term. According to evaluations, residents of Nunavut 'saw decentralization as "*a more IQ form of government*" ..., and as expen-sive but necessary for Nunavut.'[75] Although it is questionable whether decentralization itself is an Inuit value, an attempt to incorporate IQ into the government of Nunavut on a decentralized basis is in keeping with the approaches of indigenous culture, which is more receptive to decentralized power.[76] No plans were undertaken to introduce Inuit traditional knowledge into the administration of home rule.

Greenland's system was originally centralized, with the major administrative powers concentrated in the capital, Nuuk. This led to a further increase in centralization and intensification of communications by Greenlandic politicians with their Danish and foreign counterparts. Greenlandic senior officials were criticized for spending too much time outside Greenland, which resulted in less attention being paid to the internal political structures of Greenland.[77] It also was the reason for the further alienation of elitist Greenlandic politicians from populations in the settlements.

The government of Nunavut's dispersion in major Nunavut communities, instead of being concentrated entirely in the capital of Iqaluit, was a cornerstone of the NIC policies, which recommended that

the size of the headquarters staff in the capital of Nunavut be kept to a min-

imum to allow for the sharing of government employment opportunities
with as many communities as reasonably possible; the community that is
selected to be the capital should not continue to be a regional centre as
well; regional offices located in that community should move out to other
communities in that region; and, a high level of program, financial and
personnel authority and accountability should be delegated to managers
and officers at the regional and community level.[78]

Despite such efforts, the administrative power of the government of
Nunavut has become de facto recentralized in Iqaluit, where major decisions are made.[79] Moreover, some observers have questioned the benefits of decentralization policy.[80]

Political parties shaped the structure and priorities of the legislative
and executive powers of the home rule government and influenced the
movement of Greenland towards extended autonomy. Regardless of the
existence of an effective system of 'Inuit parties' in Greenland, and the
lack of such a system in Nunavut, the institutions of home rule and public governance are characterized by the Inuit majority and oriented
towards the expression of Inuit needs and concerns. At the same time,
the institutional and structural elements of Greenland's and Nunavut's
legislatures and executive derive from a 'foreign' neo-colonial authority,
which raises the issue of their legitimacy among the Inuit. Can structures created under neo-colonial power facilitate the development of
autonomy or self-government among the Inuit?

The 'Inuit' and Other Institutions of Governance in Greenland and Nunavut

Although Greenlandic 'politicians and cabinet ministers ... were the titular
heads of government ... if you peeled back that layer, they were all blonde blue-
eyed Danes running the new home rule government.'

Dennis Patterson

Initially, enthusiasm for home rule was 'somewhat dampened' by a recognition of the dominance of Danes in the new government. 'Now, hap-
pily, the Greenlandic involvement can boast more depth. But, this
cosmetic autonomy speaks to the fears of Inuit leaders who are determined, sooner rather than later, to fill the depth charts of their own
public sector.'[81]

The people of Nunavut and Greenland were given political power over their affairs by way of democratic representation in the Western pattern of legislative and executive institutions. Consequently, the main elements of the legislative assemblies and executive bodies of Nunavut and Greenland mimic Canadian and Danish institutions of governance, which contradict Inuit traditions.[82] That raises the question of whether Inuit representation and participation in these institutions in itself transforms these institutions into agents of 'genuine' Inuit self-governance. Interviews with residents of Greenland and Nunavut show that traditional Inuit structures, values, or ways of decision making have had minimal effect on modern institutions of governance.[83]

The government of Nunavut has been following what is known as the Bathurst Mandate or '*Pinasuaqtavut* – that which we've set out to do, our hopes and plans for Nunavut' – a five-year plan developed by the first government in 1999. This document emphasized the importance of the introduction of the *Inuit Qaujimajatuqangit* in public administration for developing responsive, open, and accountable government.[84] In the updated version of *Pinasuaqtavut (2004–2009)*, the government of Nunavut reconfirmed that IQ is essential to the management of local affairs and elaborated that Inuit societal values are particularly relevant for the conduct of affairs of the government. These values include the following:

> *Inuuqatigiitsiarniq* – respecting others, relationships, and caring for people …
>
> *Tunnganarniq* – fostering good spirit by being open, welcoming, and inclusive …
>
> *Pijitsirniq* – serving and providing for family and/or community …
>
> *Aajiiqatigiinniq* – decision making through discussion and consensus …
>
> *Pilimmaksarniq/Pijariuqsarniq* – development of skills through practice, effort, and action …
>
> *Piliriqatigiinniq/Ikajuqtigiinniq* – working together for a common cause …
>
> *Qanuqtuurniq* – being innovative and resourceful … and
>
> *Avatittinnik Kamatsiarniq* – respect and care for the land, animals, and the environment …[85]

Although these values serve as guiding principles for delivering programs and services by the government of Nunavut and they are incorporated into policy documents of the territorial government's departments, it is hard to evaluate their implementation in practice. Most of the interviewees in Nunavut (where, unlike Greenland, significant attempts are taken to bring the IQ to life) were not able to identify which Inuit values form the basis of the modern administration of their government. In 2003 an elders' advisory council, Katimajiit, was created to provide advice to the government on how to use the IQ and how to incorporate Inuit language and culture into its operations.[86] In 2005 the government appointed a second Katimajiit to advise departments on their efforts to incorporate traditional Inuit values into their daily operations.[87] There are numerous discussions and studies on making the IQ the 'living policy' of Nunavut governance.[88] Of importance in this respect is an innovative Wildlife Act containing a set of IQ principles to guide wildlife management in the territory.[89] Despite these developments, the question of how to incorporate IQ into the institutional governance culture of Nunavut and how to make it workable within various governmental departments is a challenging one.[90]

The Inuit of Greenland and Nunavut do not share or show cultural affinity for the institutions that have been imposed upon them. This reduces the legitimacy of these structures among the Inuit. Not accidentally, in 2001, ten MLAs on the midterm leadership review of the Legislative Assembly of Nunavut stated: 'The government system is not our traditional Inuit way of life. If we had governed in an Inuit way, we would not be judging whether our leaders are good or not, as we are doing in this review. But, although we have agreed to use the parliamentary system, we still want to be incorporating *Inuit Qaujimajatuqangit* within the system. We are using a system that contradicts our way of life, because we have to abide by legislation now. But we want to get our values back into government.'[91] Although in both jurisdictions the Inuit constitute a majority of parliamentarians, and this should guarantee the priority of Inuit interests and direct the policies of these institutions towards Inuit needs, from a legal standpoint Nunavut's and Greenland's legislative and executive bodies are non-indigenous structures. It is hoped, however, that 'indigenous' elements will constantly be incorporated into these institutions by the pervasiveness of Inuit culture at a functional level. Ideally, the fact that Inuit representatives, who are known to the Inuit communities, form these bodies should increase their legitimacy among the Inuit population. There is the threat that the significance of these bodies will be undermined by growing class stratification of Nunavut society, a situation paralleled by the clash between the Greenlandic elite and the unskilled working classes.

At the beginning, home rule was based on the Danish model with excessive paternalistic control. As the system evolved, it incorporated more Greenlandic elements, including Greenlandic politicians. In Nunavut, notwithstanding that the adopted system of public government has had to follow and operate within Canadian principles of parliamentary democracy, there are attempts to blend Western traditions with indigenous values. However, similar to the situation in Greenland, which relies heavily on the Danes for assistance, the newly created territory of Nunavut had to accept help from mostly non-Inuit Canadians. In both jurisdictions, presence of indigenous elements in governance structures is not sufficient, despite the Inuit majority. The adjustment to the patterns of Western modes of governance puts genuine Inuit self-governance, in the form of public governance, in question. The incorporation of traditional Inuit knowledge, values, and decision-making practices at the juridical level could make a difference in the status of the legislative, executive, and other institutions in Greenland and Nunavut.

The Greenland Home Rule Act and the Nunavut Act do not stipulate Inuit institutions of governance. However, the establishment under the NLCA of several regulatory tribunals and co-management agencies with equal federal government and Inuit participation brings some indigenous element to Nunavut's wildlife, fishery, land, and water resource management.[92] In legal terms, these agencies, often referred to as institutions of public government, provide comprehensive co-management regimes and do not substitute for Inuit self-governance institutions.[93] Moreover, since these agencies' mandate is mostly advisory, and they share joint decision-making powers with federal representatives, their capacity for autonomy is limited.[94] Currently the land and its resource management is one focal point of the Inuit political agenda. Thus, according to Jack Anawak, even negotiations on the NLCA were seen by the Inuit primarily 'as the means to preserve our relationship with the land and ensure our survival as a people in the larger society surrounding us. Therefore, we are also taking economic and political means to control what happens on our lands.'[95] Some Inuit of Nunavut view their responsibility for the management of their lands as self-governance. Thus, Paul Quassa, the Tungavik Federation of Nunavut's chief negotiator, stressed that 'what we wanted all along and what we negotiated is a series of management regimes that will eventually give us self-governance.'[96]

Non-Aboriginal scholars maintain different views on this issue. White suggests that 'by allocating important government functions in the realm of land and resources to public governments, it could be argued

that the boards derogate from the possibility of full-fledged self-government ... They constitute a new genus of institution within Canada's federal system, existing at the intersection of the three orders of
government.'[97] Gurston Dacks states that these agencies 'represent the
fullest measure of self-determination and political control over important aspects of their [Inuit] lives' and, because they are created within
the NLCA, these agencies 'are protected under section 35 of the *Constitution Act, 1982.'*[98] Nonetheless, the constitutional protection of the
above-noted boards, and Inuit participation in their management, does
not make them Inuit institutions of self-governance or provide for 'the
fullest measure of self-determination.' Thierry Rodon, in his analysis of
these agencies, states that their powers 'are more akin to self-manage-
ment than to self-determination.' Thus, such co-management can be
seen as essentially a process of co-optation because it allows Inuit participation only in accordance with Western standards.[99] Similarly, Gallagher-Mackay finds that co-management boards in many respects
resemble Southern technocratic institutions; aside from providing translations of their documents into Inuktitut and a high level of civility, they
hardly can be distinguished from other boards working in the North.[100]

So far, the main goal of co-management boards – to incorporate traditional Inuit ecological knowledge into administration and policy decision making – has not been sufficiently met. Formed on the basis of
Western legal structures, these agencies of public government are foreign to Inuit institutions. At a functional level, despite Inuit participation these bodies operate within the bureaucratic frameworks of the
Canadian state.[101]

Nunavut's and Greenland's bodies of public governance include
other agencies, the evaluation of which might shed some light on the
nature of autonomy. In order to provide a link between the central state
and the Inuit homelands, the former is represented by the commissioner in Nunavut and the Rigsombudsmand (high commissioner) in
Greenland. The Rigsombudsmand is the chief of the Danish administration in Greenland. The position's functions include control over local
legislation and matters concerning family law; reporting to the Danish
Prime Minister's Office; planning and organizing meetings between
home rule and Danish authorities; overseeing referendums on Danish–
Greenlandic relations; organizing visits in Greenland by the royal family; and recommendations for royal distinctions (orders of chivalry and
medals). The Rigsombudsmand is also in charge of elections in Greenland to the Folketing.[102] The commissioner for Nunavut, appointed by

the governor in council (i.e., the federal cabinet), acts in accordance with any written instructions given to him or her by the latter or by the minister of Indian Affairs and Northern Development.[103] The role is similar to that of a provincial lieutenant-governor. There is no clause mandating that either the commissioner or Rigsombudsmand should be Inuk.[104] Whereas in Greenland the high commissioner is usually a Dane, in Nunavut, according to the existing practice, the commissioner is Inuk.[105] As in Greenland, the commissioner's role is mostly ceremonial; the commissioner does not interfere in the running of the Legislative Assembly. Other offices of state in Greenland and Nunavut include the police and court systems and various committees in Greenland representing the Danish administration.[106]

Since 1995 there has been a Greenlandic ombudsman, known as the parliamentary commissioner for administration.[107] The ombudsman hears complaints about administrative actions as part of the task of creating more openness in public administration.[108] He or she also submits an annual report on the office's activities to the Landsting.[109] However, since the office of parliamentary commissioner was inspired by the Danish ombudsman institution and was created following Western tradition, it is seen by the Inuit as alien to their tradition.[110]

The degree of autonomy and effectiveness of Greenlandic and Nunavut institutions is in part determined by the competence of administrative personnel. Since its introduction, the administration of Greenland has overcome enormous challenges, including adapting to the modified Danish model and dependency on Danish civil servants and know-how.[111] Because of the ambitions of Greenland's political elite, home rule authorities took over powers that they could not effectively wield without qualified Danish manpower. Though a new generation of Greenlanders is replacing Danish personnel, the administration of Greenland still has to deal with frequent exchange of employees, insufficient and unclear political goals, and ethnic differences.[112] Underdeveloped infrastructure, financial dependency on Denmark, insufficient economic resources, the significant size of the public sector (which is a strain on the Greenlandic economy), a shortage of skilled and educated workers, and social problems all hamper the administration's functioning.[113] As well, there is a gap between younger educated Greenlanders and 'uneducated,' 'unskilled' workers and hunters who would prefer to follow the traditional ways of life; to this are added the ambitions of the Greenlandic elite to manage in the context of modernization and globalization.[114] To reduce the size of the public sector, the Commission on Self-Governance suggested regionalization: redistribution of jurisdiction and responsibility to the regions; restructuring of cooperation with the home rule authorities; reform of the administration of municipalities, including the introduction of consolidated frame work legislation and incorporation of a 'proximity principle,' which would bring performance of public tasks and the public authority closer to Greenlanders.[115]

At the time of writing, Nunavut is encountering many similar problems. The government of Nunavut is better staffed now than it was at its inception, 'but it's clear that many employees still don't know what they're doing, and that some departments are still suffering from the effects of decentralization.'[116] The Nunavummiut are facing the challenge of building up a cohort of Inuit civil servants. Potential employees come from a generation of Inuit who often lack the required qualifications and are ill-prepared to work for the government.[117] During the early days of Nunavut, the shortage of trained Inuit to staff government positions led to the recruitment of Qallunaat (whites).[118] To increase the Inuit labour force within the government and improve Inuit training, an affirmative action clause was included in the NLCA. Article 23 of that agreement requires that the level of Inuit employment within the government of Nunavut be increased and maintained at a 'representative level' – that is, that the level of Inuit employees within the government should reflect the ratio of Inuit to the total population in the Nunavut Settlement Area (the area to which the terms of the NLCA apply, as designated in art. 3 part 1, s. 3.1.1). Thus, about 85 per cent of government personnel should, in time, be Inuit.[119] The extent of the challenge is revealed by the fact that the government hopes to have 56 per cent Inuit employment by 2010.[120] The government faces substantial difficulties in implementing article 23 because of the shortage in financing for Inuit employment and training programs. A long-running dispute between Nunavut Tunngavik Incorporated (NTI), the government of Nunavut, and the government of Canada over a new ten-year implementation contract for the NLCA has also hindered bringing the requirements of article 23 to fruition. In its December 2006 lawsuit against the federal government, the NTI emphasized that, as a result of the Crown's failure to develop Inuit employment plans and to fund not only initiatives to increase Inuit employment in the territory to a representative level but also measures that would provide a basis for realistic employment plans to guarantee Inuit employment in the federal and territorial public service, the Inuit have lost approximately $130 million per year in direct employment income.[121]

Affirmative action was not introduced as a legal measure in Greenland. Danes still hold some key governmental positions, and government services and written administrative tasks are carried out mostly in Danish.[122] There has been ongoing debate over the dominant use of the Danish language in public administration and the job promotion preference given to Danish-speaking experts compared to equally qualified Greenlanders.[123] There are also suggestions to use Greenlandic as the language of the home rule government, the Landsting, and municipalities.[124] Furthermore, Danes still dominate high-profile positions in business, education, and central and local administrations in Greenland.[125] Greenland faces the problem of attracting a large number of inexperienced Greenlandic and Danish specialists, who often do not know how to deal with internal issues. There are growing demands to hire more native Greenlandic-speaking representatives for leading positions to close the era of 'Danish bosses.'[126] In Nunavut, where the use of Inuktitut, Inuinnaqtun, English, and French is intended to reinforce the policy of multilingual administration, efforts have been made on the legislative level to protect both Inuit languages spoken in Nunavut. However, because Inuktitut is used by the majority of the Inuit of Nunavut and Inuit government employees, there are suggestions to introduce 'bureaucratic' Inuktitut as a working language among senior government officials by 2008.[127]

Expectations of 'perfect' Inuit self-governance are unrealistic for Greenland and Nunavut. Unique Northern and cultural circumstances and the borrowing of Western patterns of governance and administration throw into question the viability of Inuit autonomy. The issues of how to address cultural differences and entrench Inuit traditional values and methods of decision making into a developing Nunavut system of public governance and home rule in Greenland are of great concern. Notwithstanding more than two decades of home rule in Greenland, and approaching a decade of Nunavut governance, the Inuit in both regions are being challenged by the transition and adjustment to non-Inuit values of other societies and the risk of being overwhelmed by Western concepts of governance. Without further strengthening the role of Inuit in the public service and continuous incorporation of Inuit values and practices into Western forms of governmental institutions, these bodies will not be able to promote Inuit self-governance or maintain clear legitimacy among the Inuit population. The Inuit are developing their policies in the framework of Western institutionalism. This may work for cooperation with other levels of government and the international community, but it raises the question whether Inuit representation in the alien Western institutions of Nunavut and Greenland can mean true Inuit self-governance. Currently, the Inuit are repeating the schemes and stages of development of former colonial societies, with some cultural modifications. Nevertheless, because of the Inuit majority and active participation in regional policy making, Greenland and Nunavut governance systems are evolving towards a greater measure of Inuit autonomy.

4 The Jurisdiction of Greenland and Nunavut

The competence of Greenland and Nunavut in the justice system, international and foreign affairs, and security and defence policy is limited because these are areas where jurisdiction is traditionally non-transferable to subnational entities. Yet, the evolution of Greenland's system of governance shows that Greenlandic authorities aspire to acquire more responsibilities than those envisaged by the Home Rule Act. As was indicated by the Report from the Commission on Self-Governance, if the island is to expand its autonomy and conduct its own affairs on a more independent basis, jurisdiction in these spheres must be reconsidered. The report examines issues such as natural resources, the economy and business development, human resources, foreign policy, security, language, and the central internal administration of Greenland within the framework of a new partnership between the island and the Danish realm.[1]

A similar tendency can be seen in Nunavut, with the gradual devolution of powers from Ottawa to the territory and evolution of the public government system. Nunavut is expected to conclude a devolution agreement with the federal government by 2008, dealing with policy areas such as the environment, governance, social issues, economic development, Northern science, and Circumpolar affairs.[2] Of particular significance will be Ottawa's transfer to Nunavut of responsibility for the management of oil, gas, and mineral extraction on Crown lands and offshore. The further development of Nunavut as a political entity will likely mean that the territorial government will be drawn into taking over more responsibility in what are presently non-transferable areas of jurisdiction.

One could argue that, as a part of Canada, Nunavut should not be treated differently than other territories. If Nunavut is granted special autonomous status or rights, the other Northern territories may wish to pursue the same course. Nunavut has a stronger argument than other territories do for political autonomy (without secession) by virtue of the Inuit peoples' right to self-government under domestic law. The Inuit of Nunavut retain their inherent right to autonomy despite the establishment of a territory with public government and settlement of the Nunavut Land Claims Agreement (NLCA). Moreover, according to developments in international law and practice, the Nunavut Inuit's right to autonomy finds justification as an emerging right based on an outgrowth of the right to self-determination.[3]

The jurisdictional challenges of Nunavut are in some ways similar to those of the Northwest Territories (NWT) and the Yukon Territory because of the specifics of Arctic political geography. However, Nunavut has a unique governance system, the effective implementation of which requires more flexibility in the boundaries of its legal jurisdiction. In addition, Nunavut has a different legal status than the other territories. For example, as we have seen, the territory of Nunavut was created as an integral part of the NLCA settlement, which is constitutionally entrenched. Thus, the territory itself attracts constitutional protection, and in that respect it is different from other Canadian territories. If Nunavut is distinct from the other territories, it is also different from the ten provinces, some of which are seeking to expand their jurisdiction in non-transferable areas and may already have expanded this jurisdiction in practice. The concerns of Nunavut are unique. Most Canadian provinces and regions (except for the lands of the Inuit of Nunavik in Northern Quebec, the Nunatsiavut in Newfoundland and Labrador, and the Inuvialuit in the Northwest Territories) are not located in the High Arctic, and thus are not affected by such harsh climate conditions or issues arising from the assertion of Canada's sovereignty in the North. The way of life and cultural existence of most of the residents of the Canadian provinces are not so deeply and directly affected by issues such as global warming or pollution in the Arctic.

In contrast to Greenland, which is looking to expand its jurisdiction into traditionally non-transferable areas, Nunavut presently has other priorities. It has to deal with serious problems with regard to the process of institution building within its government. Proper implementation of the NLCA and exercise of existing jurisdictional capacity in areas such as education, social, linguistic, economic, and business development are currently more important than increasing capacity in the areas of non-transferable jurisdiction. The experience of Nunavut reveals the necessity of a pragmatic approach to the scope of jurisdictional opportunities.

One must ask whether there is a need for the formal legalization of Nunavut's or Greenland's jurisdiction over non-transferable spheres. There are, for example, informal methods of participation in international forums: problems may be addressed through meetings, conferences, the establishment of advisory councils, and so on. However, informal approaches are not always either sufficient or efficient. Thus, there is a need for some legal capacity of Nunavut and Greenland in traditionally non-transferable jurisdictions on matters that directly affect the development of these territories and the existence and livelihood of their citizens. This does not mean that Nunavut or Greenland should have an absolute say or veto in these areas. Control could, for instance, be exerted in specified spheres by means of an agreement with the federal or central government.

I am not suggesting that Nunavut or Greenland should receive preferential treatment and expand their jurisdiction simply because it is desired by their residents. More political autonomy is not necessarily the best solution. Moreover, most subnational entities with autonomous status enjoy no powers whatsoever over the justice system or foreign affairs, including security and defence policy. But it is important to be aware of the particular jurisdictional challenges that arise from Nunavut's and Greenland's unique situation and geopolitical position in the Arctic. Some legal capacity of Nunavut and Greenland in non-transferable areas would not threaten Canada's or Denmark's sovereignty in general. Thus, jurisdiction in these areas can be partially transferred to subnational entities in the process of devolution.

The scope of self-governing jurisdictions can vary, and may include competence in, among other things, social, educational, language, health, transportation, intergovernmental activity, mineral rights, resource management, environmental, and economic areas. The effectiveness of Nunavut public governance and Greenland home rule depends substantially on the breadth of powers delegated to them. The legal framework for home rule and Nunavut's jurisdiction is pulled in two directions – by Inuit peoples' aspirations and their expectations for effective governance, and by the realities of the isolated North and pragmatic expectations for future economic sustainability. Theoretically, both Nunavut's and Greenland's systems should become economically self-sufficient and responsible for managing their own affairs. Yet, this is hard to achieve in practice without significant financial assistance from the national authorities. The problem is that both Greenland and Nunavut were created without an adequate economic base. If there is no adequate economic development and no local financial base sufficient to fund all areas of Greenland's or Nunavut's jurisdiction, then how can the idea of expanded political autonomy, which means self-reliance, be reconciled with the need for substantial funding from the national governments? This economic reality throws into question the viability of home rule/self-governance in the Arctic and makes the concept of autonomy rather artificial. Continued financial dependency on Canada and Denmark is the key factor prohibiting true self-determination and self-governance in Nunavut and Greenland. Both regions are struggling to develop a self-sufficient economy, which would considerably reduce Danish block grants to Greenland and Ottawa's transfers to Nunavut. The Commission on Self-Governance considered the question of Greenland's self-sufficiency and mitigation of the island's dependence economy as a core prerequisite for effective autonomy.[4] In particular the commission outlined that foreign trade, restructuring of the public sector in correspondence with the economic capacity of the society, citizen-wide input into the economy, and developing a sustainable economy and businesses may allow Greenland to achieve economic independence and replace the block grant.[5]

Economic analyses of Greenland's dependency show that there are several obstacles to Greenland's economic self-sustainability and that the island continues to be highly dependent on Denmark in terms of financial transfers and the economic expertise of Danish advisers.[6] However, the Commission on Self-Governance is optimistic about a self-sufficient economic future for Greenland. High expectations for economic sustainability derive from wind, solar, oil, gas, and hydrogen energy production projects; the huge hydroelectric potential of Greenland and possible offshore reserves of oil can eventually make the island a major hydrogen and an oil producer.[7] This can boost economic progress and have long-term consequences for Greenland's future.[8]

Likewise, Nunavut's economic viability is vital for the success of the public government. According to the findings of reports on Nunavut's economic outlook by the Conference Board of Canada and the Nunavut Economic Forum, the key elements of Nunavut's economic future include a collective approach to socio-economic development and a focus on economic activities primarily at the community level; a move towards greater self-reliance and more Inuit political and economic control of Nunavut and its environment; integration of Inuit traditional knowledge and values (*Inuit Qaujimajatuqangit* [IQ]) in consultation and decision making; land-based economic activity; and sustainable development with equal importance given to the development of human and natural capital and a wage-based economy.[9] There are both obstacles to and opportunities for the long-term growth of Nunavut's economy, the major part of which is still government employment and government spending.[10] It is expected that, over the next five years, development of hydroelectric and wind energy projects and investment in the private sector, especially in mining, will increase. The building of a deepwater military/civilian port in Nunavut is also seen as an important step for the territory's economic development.[11] However, the participation of Nunavummiut, strong political leadership with clear government spending priorities, and dealing with disastrous infrastructure are key to Nunavut's sustainability.[12]

The government of Nunavut has taken some steps for economic development of the territory based on the priorities of sustainable development, youth training, education, application of new technologies, innovation and the new economy, investment, export development, and infrastructure.[13] The forecast for Nunavut in 2020, based on strategic directions for building a sustainable economy, strengthening self-reliance, and maintaining diversity, is for a place 'where Nunavummiut own and manage a strong mixed economy where residents have productive choices for economic participation.'[14] The major legal challenge is how to reconcile the idea of self-sustainability and liability with financial dependency on Ottawa. Nunavut hopes to boost its economy by concluding the devolution deal with the federal government, which could help to reduce Nunavut's dependency on Ottawa.[15]

In addition to these economic challenges, the legal authority of Nunavut and Greenland is limited by Canadian and Danish legal paradigms, which do not fully take into account the specific interests of the Inuit population. It is possible for the citizens of Nunavut and Greenland to shape their own policies of public/home rule governance, but they can expand their homelands' areas of jurisdiction to a very limited extent. Gradually this challenge can be addressed by the development of Greenlanders' and Nunavummiut political consciousness, public initiatives, increased economic sustainability, and socio-cultural predominance. Despite the limits of the competence of the Nunavut and Greenlandic authorities, the evolution of these governance systems inevitably will dictate greater local involvement and responsibility for matters not currently included by their jurisdictional frameworks. To date, the Inuit have used the methods and language of their ex-colonizers to overcome their subjugation. At the same time, they demonstrate how they value their own cultures by their aspirations for self-determination and autonomy. Arctic indigenous peoples may have an image of governance and its institutions that differs from that of their former colonizers. There is a need for greater flexibility and rethinking of the boundaries of the Danish-European/Anglo-Canadian legal imagination in order to adapt to Inuit realities and better serve the aspiration to self-governance.

Some Features of the Inuit Traditional Legal Order

We are run by coldness and our natural laws. When the white man's law comes to a cold place, it never works out. Because white men don't understand the Inuit, laws today aren't working out. People making laws throughout the North should have Inuit working at it too, not just Qallunaaq, so that it would be fair to both.

Unnamed Inuk

The trouble is that it's so different, it's so dangerous, it's so wrong to impose a foreign alien system on people in a totally different culture.

Hans Christian Raffnsoe, chief justice, High Court of Greenland

An examination of the role of the legal institutions of Greenland and Nunavut in developing the right to indigenous autonomy raises the question of whether Inuit societies should develop their own juridical bodies or use existing ones. Because Inuit legal institutions are not well understood, customary Inuit mechanisms of social regulation and control have to be considered in any possible reform in the field.

Can Inuit legal tradition sustain the institutions of an independent system of justice or one that is parallel to the mainstream system? Some argue that informal arrangements are the best way for introducing uniquely Inuit forms of social control and legal culture into Greenland's and Nunavut's contemporary legal systems. However, strictly informal approaches are not feasible, as they require a tremendous amount of government and human resources. Others believe the rule of law in Nunavut and Greenlandic societies should generally follow the legal order of their dominant states. For example, despite long debates over whether Nunavut's Human Rights Act was alien to Inuit values, it was passed by the Nunavut legislature because of the necessity and pressure to follow similar legislation in the rest of Canada.[16] However, this practice does not accommodate concerns of Inuit, who are eager to preserve their traditional ways of dealing with matters of legal significance. Thus, neither view on its own is persuasive. Furthermore, it can be argued that legal recognition of the Greenlandic justice system and Nunavut's Inuit judiciary or legal institutions is possible theoretically if, in practice, it finds strong support in contemporary Greenland and Nunavut societies, and if legal interpretation of the scope of the right to autonomy will encompass more or less independent justice systems for these subnational entities.

At the present time, despite their Inuit majorities, Greenland and Nunavut do not embrace separate indigenous justice systems. To understand the possibilities of legal reforms in contemporary Greenland and Nunavut societies, I explore the extent to which *lex loci* (customary law) can be adjusted to the system of Danish and Canadian laws and fulfil Inuit aspirations for governance.[17] Traditional Inuit society included a number of law-ways or legal ways – that is, methods of social-behavioural control and beliefs that functioned as laws and created a basis for Inuit 'customary,' 'informal,' 'folk,' or 'natural' norms of justice.[18] These norms flowed from unwritten rules applicable and transferable within Inuit communities and transmitted through generations. Presently, old Inuit systems of social control are underused or have disappeared because of colonial practices, exposure to Euro-Canadian culture, and changes in the Inuit's ways of life. Instead, Greenland and Nunavut often copy or adapt to imposed Danish-Canadian legislation. What should be done about the gap between Western and Inuit traditional systems of social control? What legal/judicial system would best suit the Inuit?

The legal ways of the Inuit are embedded in and dependent upon their culture. Community and independent households shaped the structure of traditional Greenlandic and Nunavut societies.[19] Any perception of Inuit traditional norms and order should be evaluated through the prism of Inuit understanding and their socio-cultural patterns of behaviour. But relatively few Inuit representatives have expressed their opinion on the subject.[20] Study of the Inuit's traditional legal concepts is also complicated by differences within Inuit groups inhabiting Greenland and Nunavut and is limited by the Euro-American literature's interpretation of these concepts.[21] It is possible to give only a general overview of the Inuit of Greenland's and Nunavut's customary practices that existed prior to the introduction of Western legal culture.

An analysis of existing scholarship shows striking differences between Inuit and Western legal beliefs.[22] It also points to the limitations of studying a non-Western social order on the basis of modern law concepts. In trying to apply Western legal categories to the Inuit social order, many scholars have questioned whether traditional Inuit forms of social control can be considered 'law' within the framework of Western legal thought. This questioning has led to different analyses of the existence of law among the Inuit and divergent views of the nature and concepts of their law-ways.[23] For example, according to Geert Van Den Steenhoven and E. Adamson Hoebel, traditional Inuit society exhibited minimal legal mechanisms and structures.[24] Others recognize adjudicative mechanisms and legal structures among the Inuit. Norbert Rouland, for example, concluded that traditional Inuit forms of social control had a legal nature and that legal structures were developed among the Inuit.[25] In his opinion, the failure by many observers to recognize that Inuit legal systems of social regulation, practices, and beliefs amounted to legal status reflected ethnocentric bigotry on the part of Western jurists and legal anthropologists.[26] Renée Fossett found that the Inuit created a highly complex and holistic system of law and justice.[27] In a similar vein, Norman Hallendy argued that a traditional system of justice once existed on southwest Baffin Island. He had been shown an *Akitsiraqvik* – a place with a structure made up of a circle of stones – by an elder from Cape Dorset (Nunavut). According to the elder, this was the place where the great council met and justice was exercised before the arrival of white people. The last known traditional trial in that area occurred in 1924.[28]

Inuit representatives claim that they had a system of law and justice prior to colonization. Susan Inuaraq notes that 'before the Europeans brought their system of law upon the Inuit they had a system of their own like most of societies ... The legends and the power of the elders and shamans were intertwined together to form a very unique system of justice.'[29] Similarly, Zebedee Nungak contests the claim that

Inuit did not possess any semblance of a justice system before contact with European civilization. That our people lead a nomadic existence in a harsh unforgiving Arctic environment may lead Qallunaat or others to conclude that Inuit did not have a sense of order, a sense of right and wrong and a way to deal with wrongdoers in their society. Inuit did possess this sense of order and right and wrong. The way it was practised and implemented may never have been compatible with European civilization's concepts of justice, but what worked for Inuit society in their environment was no less designed for conditions of life in the Arctic than that of Qallunaat was for conditions of their life.[30]

Those who claim that Inuit legal mechanisms and structures were underdeveloped generally approach the subject with the preconceptions of Western legal systems. For such observers, it is significant that, as Van den Steenhoven's linguistic analysis concluded, there were no words for 'crime,' 'justice,' and 'law' in the Inuit language.[31] Nelson Graburn suggests that different conclusions about the existence of Inuit legal practices stem from Inuit's variant behaviour in the field of law, and their preference for judging each situation of conflict in terms of the particular factors and the personalities of the people involved.[32]

Although it is difficult to conceptualize traditional Inuit law from a Euro-American perspective, I have attempted to identify some aspects of traditional Inuit justice and legal concepts by analysing sources on Inuit social order.[33] Inuit legal culture did not exist in written form; it was elaborated by oral traditions (stories, myths, tales, legends) planted in people's minds by elders and shamans and transmitted from one generation to another. According to Greenlander Robert Petersen, 'the relationship between different households and the relationship between people inside and outside the household structures were regulated by unwritten rules and a strong demand for self-control.'[34] As an elder from Rankin Inlet (Nunavut), Mariano Aupilaarjuk, puts it, 'The *maligait* [laws] of the Inuit are not on paper. They are inside people's heads and they will not disappear or to be torn to pieces ... It is part of a person. It is what makes a person strong.'[35] There was no codification of the Inuit laws as such.[36]

The Inuit's spiritual beliefs and rituals formed the basis of their society's moral code. One belief that underpins Inuit legal thought is animism. The Inuit view people and animals as equal creatures, and ascribe human characteristics to animals. They believe that both humans and animals have a soul (*inua*), character, and the capacity to think (*isuma*).[37] Consequently, 'every object, every rock, every animal indeed even conceptions such as sleep and food, are living.'[38] The paucity of legal rules in the traditional Inuit system was compensated for (and partially caused) by religious norms that controlled and directed the Inuit's social and economic life.[39] Taboos played the role of regulatory mechanism in Inuit daily life.[40] As E.A. Hoebel notes, legal action was rare, despite the fact that 'the consequences of sinful behavior may be believed to result in famine and starvation for the entire community.'[41]

In the traditional Inuit society, custom served as a source of law and rights. According to Rouland, law arose from such sources as the 'opinion communis' and the repetition of precedents. Customary rule protected the individual from 'the aggressive forces of the environment against the group.' Thus, custom was not a 'biological' or instinctive behaviour 'but was a result of empirical thinking initiated by the fear of anything the individual considered beyond him.'[42] The rights and duties that emerged had a collective-communal rather than an individualistic nature.[43] Public-communal opinion had great value in enforcing the law-ways, and no one was allowed to break the law without colliding with public opinion.[44] The definition of right and wrong is based on traditional behaviour codes, which were governed by 'common-sense, realism, self-criticism and a happy absence of righteousness.'[45] E.A. Hoebel shows how the postulates of jural significance in Inuit culture shaped such definitions of right and wrong. For example, he notes that, 'the third basic postulate (Life is hard) and its corollary (The unsupportability of unproductive members of society) are expressed not in the form of legal injunctions but, on the contrary, as privilege-rights. Infanticide, invalidicide, senilicide, and suicide are privileged acts: socially approved homicide.'[46] These forms of homicide were legally acceptable in traditional Inuit society and were not regarded as criminal acts.[47]

Traditional Inuit society lacked courts, police, penitentiaries, or any other forensic or law-enforcement institutions. The 'administration of justice' was exercised by the community (which often played an active part and mediated between the shaman and the guilty person), shamans, and headmen who often possessed quasi-legal powers.[48] For instance, by initiating 'legal action,' a reputable shaman could denounce a group member as guilty of an act repulsive to spirits or animals, and could command penance, which in its lightest form meant abstention from foods suggested by the shaman.[49] The Inuit traditional system of social control was marked by its flexibility in reaction to conflicts. Inuit laws were oriented towards restoring peace and communal conciliation, rather than exercising justice through punishment.[50] In sharp contrast to the Euro-Canadian definition, traditional Inuit sanctions sought to aid the offender instead of imposing a punishment. As Kaj Birket-Smith puts it:

In essence it is not the mission of the society to execute law and justice, but exclusively to restore peace, using this word in the medieval sense of the ordinary, regular course of life. On this basis the settlement may, for instance, combine in killing a man or a woman suspected of witchcraft, for such persons are a menace to the peace of the society. The killing is not, however, a *punishment* for the practising of witchcraft, for the society may in the same manner get rid of a man with a wild and brutal temperament, or of old or sick people who are a burden upon the settlement.[51]

The determination of guilt was measured, and 'decisions were reached individually on the basis of the offender's situation and *not* on the basis of the offense itself.'[52] At the same time, R. Petersen points out the distinction between violence (criminalized) and insult (non-crimi-nalized actions) in Greenlandic society. In his words, 'With regard to non-criminalized actions, the interest of both parties was often in efforts to prevent tension from developing into an uncontrolled conflict rather than in indemnifying the victim. In connection with criminalized actions, the reaction was most likely to be revenge.'[53]

The normative application of traditional Inuit systems of rules and beliefs fluctuated according to the situation. Graburn notes that at different times the members of Inuit society reacted in a different way to the same infraction. Inuit legal actions represented *situational* pluralism and also differed depending on the season of the year.[54] Inuit vision and application of law-ways were determined by specific Northern conditions. This implies a special spiritual connection with the wildlife and the land that is not apparent in modern Euro-Canadian law. Rouland notes that for each level in Inuit society there was a corresponding legal system: 'internal family disagreements were settled by the family leader; anything that could disturb the balance of the group as a whole belonged to the *umialik* [leader of the group].'[55] Inuit forms of regulation or the social order were based on self-control and methods of conflict resolution shaped in accordance with Inuit values and under-standing of right and wrong. For example, as Rasing notes, for violation of the norm of contributing to the survival of the group, a person could be mocked, gossiped about, ostracized, or castigated in a song, but 'vio-lations of this nature were not punishable under the Canadian law.'[56] Furthermore, emotionality and visual/musical perceptions of conflicts and moral norms, rather than contextual interpretation of legal canons, marked the traditional Inuit system. Postulates with juridical functions were embedded in mythological narratives, song duels, dancing, and music.[57] Generally, individuals avoided acting in contravention of such postulates not because of the threat of sanctions per se but because of their desire to be a part of the community. The Inuit language, which is full of metaphorical ways of describing situations and practices and lacks abstract legal terminology, also contributed to the development of normative visual culture in the traditional Inuit society.[58]

Allan Patenaude has described a range of responses to conflict resolution that existed within traditional Inuit societies. Informal methods included gossip, mockery, derision, ignoring, and threat of magical retribution in cases of insult, failing to share food, poor or lazy hunting, theft of property, offences related to women (e.g., failure to accept a spouse as a gift or failure of a wife to accept another man). Formal methods included song/drum duels, physical contests, banishment, and execution, which might apply in cases such as theft of a woman, witchcraft, insanity, and murder or retributive murder. Finally, there is individual duty – that is, action by an individual required in accordance with custom – which was evident in cases of infanticide, suicide, assisting suicide, and senilicide.[59] These methods of conflict resolution were not based on law-enforcement mechanisms in the form of an institutionalized authority.[60]

Song duels were of particular significance in the process of conflict resolution and restoration of peace in Greenland and Nunavut. As E.A. Hoebel observes, they were 'used to work off grudges and disputes of all orders, save murder.'

> The song duels are juridical instruments insofar as they do serve to settle disputes and restore normal relations between estranged members of the community, and insofar as one of the contestants receives a 'judgment' in his favour. But like the medieval wager of battle the judgement bears no relation to the rightness or wrongness of the original actions which gave rise to the dispute. There is no attempt to mete justice according to the rights and privileges defined by a substantive law. It is sufficient that the litigants (contestants) feel relieved – the complaint laid to rest – a psychological satisfaction attained; ... the juridical song contest is above all things a contest in which pleasurable delight is richly served, so richly that the dispute-settlement function is nearly forgotten.[61]

Such traditional dispute resolution acted as a sort of psychotherapy, whereby through recasting the conflict in the form of a song competition, and through dancing and singing, emotions and grievances were released and the confrontation was brought to the public and resolved openly and without judgment.[62] The idea was to give the victim and the victimizer a chance to air their frustration in such a way so as not to judge the offender. It is known that 'society stimulated the free expression of aggressive feelings. Song duels thus undoubtedly had a cathartic value for the individual opponents, and in this particular sense conflicts became "resolved."'[63] Evidently the main purpose of these duels was to restore peace rather than to exercise justice.[64] According to some scholars, formal song duels did not qualify 'as a kind of court with the audience acting as the judge ... since no judgement was passed nor any of the parties punished.'[65] Others argue that during song duels community members fulfilled the functions of a judge.[66] As Inge Kleivan further notes, 'by bringing inter-personal and inter-group antagonisms out into the open in this formalistic way, more overt forms of hostility were avoided ... and more importance was attached to their [song duels] function as punitive remedies for violation of the norms than to their role in preventing a breach in social relations.'[67]

In addition to their cathartic value, song duels had an ethical significance, and were compared by some to moral lectures.[68] At one time the phenomenon of song duels was one of the most important mechanisms of dispute resolution. Regrettably, with the imposition of Western culture, it has almost ceased to exist.

Breinholt-Larsen points out that traditional conflict management among the Greenlandic Inuit was based on personal restraint, including suppression of irritated feelings and hostile expressions. 'Most conflicts were dealt with in an indirect manner such as talking ill about a person behind his back, covert use of sorcery or antagonists simply moving away from each other until tempers cooled.'[69] Kleivan expresses a similar position. Examining the West Greenland Inuit, she notes that 'social order is maintained not only by external but also by internal controls. Through the socialization process the members of society acquire insight into which behaviour society does and does not value. This knowledge can act as a restriction, so that the wish to behave in a manner unacceptable to others either does not arise or is accompanied by so much mental discomfort that the idea is given up, even if the desire to violate the norms is still present.'[70]

The study of traditional Inuit law-ways and methods of social control shows that the Euro-Canadian legal culture is not universal. A system of social order and control based on Inuit practices and customs functioned as something resembling law for traditional Greenlandic and

Nunavut societies. There is another image of law, which may be determined by 'visual normativity' and morals conveyed by visual images of normative significance.[71] Perhaps, as Hanne Petersen notes, we need 'to consider whether the visual norms and normative visual cultures may be taking over some of the important functions carried out by the written normative culture – creating a minimum of common considerations, values and demands.'[72] According to this view, the traditional Inuit images of law-ways and beliefs could be regarded as law by Western jurisprudence.

Beginning with colonization, an alien social structure and legal culture were imposed on the Inuit. The adversarial nature of Western legal procedures sits in sharp contrast with the Inuit practices, which are oriented towards reconciliation and the restoration of peace. The clash of legal traditions can also be observed from the differing perspectives on punishment. The clash is a result not just of substantial differences between the modern administration of justice and traditional Inuit legal practices with respect to conflict resolution, but of a gap between two legal cultures, traditions, and approaches to justice.

The recognition of this gap raises the question of the cross-cultural transferability of Inuit natural justice and customs to the legal systems of Denmark and Canada. How is the Inuit *lex loci* reflected in the contemporary administration of justice in Greenland and Nunavut? If Inuit methods of social control and law-ways are alien to Western concepts of justice, how can imposed Qallunaat legal beliefs fairly and effectively regulate the Inuit?

These issues are a crucial aspect in the consideration of Greenland's and Nunavut's autonomy. For a long time, Western culture and institutions of governance have had very little respect for existing Inuit legal traditions. Traditional Inuit legal-ways as well as the complexity of *lex loci* and their effectiveness in dispute resolution challenge this exclusiveness. The existence of this prior system raises the question of whether parallel or independent Inuit judicial and law-enforcement institutions should be created or whether it is possible to go back to more traditional law-ways in dealing with certain aspects of modern justice systems in Greenlandic and Nunavut societies.

Until a few decades ago, the impact of Canadian law on the 'legal' acculturation of the Inuit of Baffin Island has been minimal, because of the fundamental differences in Inuit and Euro-Canadian legal concepts, the insignificant participation of the Inuit in the administration of justice, and their limited understanding of Canada's legal system.[73] For example, John S. Matthiasson found that in the 1960s the Tununermiut of Pond Inlet had a knowledge of Canadian laws limited to murder and game regulations, a cloudy understanding of the law-enforcement system, and almost no comprehension of the court system. He concluded that, despite more than forty years of contact with local police and exposure to Canadian law, the Inuit were influenced by these institutions to a minimal extent. The 'legal' acculturation progressed slowly as a result of continued reliance on the traditional Inuit legal system in dealing with property, territorial, and family matters.[74] In the 1970s Harald W. Finkler revealed an information gap among the Inuit that was impeding their understanding of the concepts and mechanisms inherent to Canadian law in addition to a lack of Inuit participation in the tasks of formal agencies of social control.[75]

Some may argue that Canada is a multicultural society, which absorbs various legal traditions – Western and non-Western – more easily than would the relatively homogeneous society of Denmark. Whatever the merits of that argument, it is apparent that the case of Greenland is different from that of Nunavut. The Danish civil law system is rather inquisitorial, in that it looks for the truth, whereas the Canadian common law system, which is dominant in Nunavut, is adversarial, with judges assessing the evidence. That said, the question of whether the contemporary Greenland and Nunavut systems of governance manifest any difference in making the legal system and administration of justice more amenable to Inuit traditional knowledge and ways of dealing with wrongdoers needs to be addressed. In other words, did the Inuit of these Arctic jurisdictions attain any powers for a greater degree of control over existing legal institutions or possibilities for the creation of an autonomous judiciary in the wake of the creation of Nunavut and the development of home rule in Greenland?

The Administration of Justice of Greenland and Nunavut

Inuit turn to the formal justice system much less than other people, preferring their own traditional methods of working out disputes within their social system ... It is important that an administrative framework for justice matters be developed with due regard to the cultural traditions and needs of the Nunavut people.

Nunavut Constitutional Forum

To understand the modern administration of justice in Greenland and

Nunavut, it is important to explore the nature of colonial legal systems and institutions from a historical standpoint. The legal evolution of Greenland and Nunavut did not parallel the development of law in other parts of Denmark and Canada. Therefore, the contemporary organization of the Greenlandic and Nunavut judiciary shows the unique nature of the administration of justice in these Arctic jurisdictions.

Starting with the assertion of Canadian sovereignty in the Arctic at the beginning of the twentieth century, the legitimacy of Inuit methods of social control was ignored.[76] Some of the traditional Inuit ways of conflict resolution, peace management, and rituals steadily eroded and almost ceased to exist. In Canada, the national legal system was imposed on the Inuit without accommodation for their cultural milieu.[77] This imposition was achieved largely by the activities of the North-West Mounted Police (NWMP, later the Royal North West Mounted Police and, since 1920, the Royal Canadian Mounted Policy [RCMP]), although the courts also played a role. The first murder trials of Inuit under Canadian law demonstrate how the legal system was imposed on them. In 1917 two Inuit men, Sinnisiak and Uluksuk, were charged with the murders of Fathers Rouviere and Le Roux. In the words of the prosecuting counsel,

> these remote savages, really cannibals, the Eskimo of the Arctic regions have got to be taught to recognize the authority of the British Crown, and that the authority of the Crown and of the Dominion of Canada, of which these countries are a part, extends to the furthermost limits of the frozen North. It is necessary that they should understand that they are *under the Law* ...; that they must regulate their lives and dealings with their fellow men, of whatever race, white men or Indians, according to, at least, the main outstanding principles of that law, which is part of the law of civilization ... They have got to be taught to respect the principles of Justice ... to resort to British justice ... The great importance of this trial lies in this: that for the first time in history these people, these Arctic people, pre-historic people, people who are as nearly as possibly living to-day in the Stone Age, will be brought in contact with and will be taught what is the white-man's justice.[78]

By contrast, in Greenland, prior to the administration of justice and law reforms in the early 1950s, 'the colonial dualistic law system made a distinction between Danish law and Greenlandic customary law.' Thus, one set of legal authorities administered Danish law and the other administered Greenlandic law.[79] In accordance with Greenlandic customary law, Greenlanders settled their own conflicts excluding serious offences. A specific Greenlandic conception of law later became fundamental in the development of the laws and administration of justice in Greenland.[80] Clashes and conflict between Greenlandic traditional lawways and the moral and legal systems of the colonizers led to the introduction of Danish legal patterns.[81] Throughout the eighteenth and nineteenth centuries, the Danes tended to consider more and more actions as criminal offences in accordance with their own cultural views. Nevertheless, the Danes were able to introduce their punitive measures only to a limited extent.[82] A hybrid kind of colonial law gradually evolved. One milestone was the creation in the second part of nineteenth century of 'Boards of Guardians' (or principal councils), which, in addition to other functions, kept order, administered law in civil and criminal matters, and acted as special Greenlandic courts.[83] As Jensen points out, 'Although the first legal regulations to be used by the principal councils laid down only a few rules on punishment for theft and other major violations, a Greenlandic practice in the administration of justice gradually developed through these courts. It has been stated that, as a starting point, these courts turned to the customary law of Greenland.'[84] The dualistic legal system was extended with the law on the administration of Greenland of 1925.[85] Conflicts between the Inuit and Danish cultures and the introduction of new technologies to Inuit daily life (e.g., motorboats) had prompted the emergence of new types of crime among the Inuit and increased criminal activity (e.g., drunk driving, damage to property).[86] The collision resulting from the overlapping of the Danish and Greenlandic legal systems, and the need for a common legislative scheme and administration of justice, led to the Juridical Expedition (Jurex), which was sent to Greenland in 1948, and the consequent reforms to the administration of the justice system and law in Greenland.[87]

Prior to the early 1870s the Hudson's Bay Company had almost total jurisdiction over law and administration in Canada's Eastern Arctic. In 1873 the dominion government appointed stipendiary magistrates. In addition, the commissioner and each superintendent of the newly established NWMP were entitled to function, by virtue of their office, as justices of the peace. Stipendiary magistrates presided over trials for the vast majority of offences, although the most serious cases (e.g., homicide) fell 'within the jurisdiction of one of the judges of a provincial Supreme Court, such as that of Alberta.'[88]

Major change to the judiciary of the NWT occurred in 1955, when a superior court of record (then called the Territorial Court but renamed the Supreme Court of the NWT in 1972) was created. This court was composed of one judge appointed by the governor in council. Mr Justice Jack H. Sissons was appointed as the first judge of the Territorial Court.[89] There was also a system of police magistrates and justices of the peace.[90] The work of the Territorial Court under Judge Sissons revealed numerous problems with the administration of the Canadian justice system with regard to the Inuit.[91] By attempting to bring justice to 'every man's door,' Sissons tried to blend Inuit concepts of right and justice into the Canadian system.[92] In his words, 'If the other culture lacks some concept allowance must be made for it ... Even with a full vocabulary of words it would not be possible to explain satisfactorily to all Eskimos the importance of some procedures in the white man's legal system.'[93] The necessity of adapting the Canadian justice system to Inuit legal practices and the particular conditions of life in the North was obvious.[94] Further, the judiciary of the NWT and later Nunavut attempted to bridge the gap between traditional Inuit and modern ways in the administration of justice.[95]

The late 1940s and early 1950s were a time for review and reform of the administration of justice and legal system in Greenland. The topic was considered in the 1950 report of the Royal Commission on Greenland (G-50), but the most important milestone in bridging the gap between Greenlandic customary law and Danish law was the work of the Jurex. A member of the Jurex, Agnete Weis Bentzon, notes that the purpose of the expedition 'was to clarify to what extent Danish law could be introduced unamended in Greenland as a common law for Danes and Greenlanders.'[96] The Jurex also aimed to clarify 'how far it was possible to introduce unity of law between Denmark and Greenland or at least between Danes and Greenlanders in Greenland.'[97] The legislative work was stimulated by the need to place Danes and Greenlanders on an equal footing.[98] In 1951 the Law Reform Committee was created. The committee was guided by the Jurex's findings 'to prepare legislation within all fields of civil law, in order to abolish the dualistic legal system in Greenland, and to unify Danish and Greenlandic law, as far as possible, but with due consideration of differences in material and cultural conditions between Denmark and Greenland.'[99] The work of the Jurex, the royal commission, and the Law Reform Committee led to the introduction of the Greenland Administration of Justice Act in 1951, followed by the adoption of the Greenland Criminal Code in 1954.[100]

These documents formed the basis for the modern justice system in Greenland. Because of possible changes to the administration of justice in Greenland connected with anticipated expansion of Greenland's jurisdiction in the framework of a new partnership arrangement on self-governance, and the recommendations of the Commission on Greenland's Judicial System (2004), including consideration of substantial revisions or amendments to existing legislation, or the enactment of new legislation dealing with Greenland's judicial and penal systems, only some features of the current Greenlandic judicial system warrant mentioning.[101]

The Greenland Administration of Justice Act of 1951 abolished the dualistic system of law in the island and made Greenlanders and Danes subject to the same rules. It separated the judiciary from the prosecution and allowed for the appeal of decisions by the Greenlandic courts.[102] As an abbreviated and simplified version of the Danish Administration of Justice Act, it incorporated an important feature – high priority was given to the lay judge institution.[103] Currently, there are eighteen judicial districts in Greenland with the Magistrate Courts (District Courts) of common jurisdiction (that is, courts of first instance).[104] Each court has two lay assessors without legal training and usually one lay judge (district judge), who does not have judicial training but who receives 'short specific training in connection with appointment and current advisory aid from the staff in the court of appeal of Greenland.'[105] Lay assessors for Magistrate Courts are elected by the local district council, whereas the lay judge is appointed by a judge from the High Court of Greenland for a renewable term of four years. Lay judges work part-time. In addition to the Magistrate Courts, 'Greenland's current administration of justice system comprises the appeal instances: the High Court of Greenland and the Danish courts, the High Court of Eastern Denmark and the Supreme Court.'[106] Decisions made by the Magistrate Courts can be appealed to the High Court of Greenland. Its presiding judge is a lawyer, who is assisted by two lay assessors. The High Court of Greenland judge is appointed by the monarch, and the lay assessors of the High Court are elected by the Landsting upon recommendation by the High Court judge.[107]

The current administration of justice in Greenland is based on the principle of proximity, as the lay judges and lay assessors are recruited from among the local population and speak Greenlandic.[108] This system is less expensive than hiring professional judges, and lay judges are more familiar with the cultural values and linguistic characteristics of their districts. Consequently, they are more adept at handling cases and make more intelligible decisions for Greenlanders. The Magistrate Courts try civil, criminal, matrimonial, and probate cases. If a case requires specific knowledge, the Magistrate Court or one of the parties may ask the Greenlandic High Court to try the case as a court of first instance.[109] Brøndsted notes that criminal cases are rarely referred to the High Court. 'The basic principle behind the Administration of Justice Act and the criminal code is that members of the local community, who are familiar with the accused and his background, are regarded as better qualified to act as judges than Danish jurists.'[110] The idea was that lay judges and lay assessors would consider the Greenlandic customary law.[111] 'This trait that the judges were lay people with close connections to the small, widespread Greenlandic communities was in itself a special feature of the culture ... The use of Greenlandic lay judges implied that the legislators to a great extent could leave it to the discretion of the judges to take the traditional way of life and ways of thinking into consideration as needed.'[112]

The Commission on Greenland's Judicial System (2004) proposed several changes to Greenland's court structure. The division of the judicial districts would be retained. Local District Courts (the Magistrate Courts) would have permanently employed and trained district judges, the number and location of which would be determined on the basis of case load, infrastructure, and the nature of district. To handle the most complex cases and to provide training and guidance to district judges, there would also be a lawyer-based court of first instance – the Court of Greenland – which would cover all of Greenland and would be headed by a professional judge. Thus, 'the district courts and the Court of Greenland will jointly handle court functions at first instance, while the High Court of Greenland will be second instance exclusively, and the Supreme Court of Denmark will be the third instance ...' The High Court of Eastern Denmark would no longer form part of Greenland's system for the administration of justice. Finally, to assist in the appointment of district judges, and, where necessary, to consider their dismissal, the commission recommended that a Council of Judges be created, composed of the High Court judge, the Court of Greenland judge, and a district judge.[113]

The administration of justice system in Nunavut differs from the Greenlandic system in several ways. Following the Nunavut Implementation Commission's recommendations on the 'unification' of the court system and consultations with the Inuit, and in light of some practical considerations, a single-level trial court was established in the territory to make the formal court system as simple and efficient as possible.[114] The Nunavut Court of Justice came into being on 1 April 1999. As a single-level trial court, it has powers of a superior court of record and the Territorial Court.[115] Its judges have the status of superior court judges and are appointed by the governor in council (i.e., the federal cabinet).[116] As yet, none of the judges have been Inuk or Inuktitut speakers. This problem has been partially resolved by the work of elders advising the judges, employment of mostly Inuit staff at the court, who are able to converse in Inuktitut with clients, and the role of justices of the peace – also called Nunalingni Iqqaqtuijit (community judges). Most of the justices of the peace are Inuit who have usually not received a legal education. Importantly, in February 2003 Alexina Kublu, an Inuk who is fluent in Inuktitut, was appointed as Nunavut's first full-time senior justice of the peace to the Nunavut Court of Justice.[117] Justices of the peace are appointed by the commissioner in executive council.[118] The participation of justices of the peace in restorative justice at the community level is extremely important. They act as a bridge between the judicial system and their local communities.[119]

The Nunavut Court of Justice is a circuit court, a 'fly-in' court that travels throughout the territory, whereas the Greenlandic magistrates are local courts.[120] Taking into account the expense of transportation in the Arctic, unpredictable climatic conditions, and the non-Inuit composition of the Nunavut Court of Justice, the Greenlandic system of magistrates' permanent residence in the communities seems to be a more appealing model for the administration of justice in circumpolar jurisdictions. Some authorities note that the model of delivery of justice services via a circuit court is foreign to the Inuit communities. For example, a group of researchers of community perceptions of the territorial court in 1995 found out that the lack of understanding of the role and activities of the court by Inuit residents was the major problem. As one Inuit elder expressed himself, 'To me, I find them useless. I am an Inuk and they are all Qallunaat. Yes, they deal with some people that have been charged with offences and they hold court. But those that go to jail never learn from their mistakes. They are sent away to jail, but it does not deter them from repeating offences once they are back.'[121] According to one social worker, 'This mumbo jumbo ceremony really has no meaning for people here. They fly away. They take a few people with them who magically reappear six months or a year later. It's like justice from another planet.'[122] Furthermore, the circuit court has a high rate of acquittals and is known for its delays.[123] In contrast, others point out that a circuit court system provides a bridge to traditional indigenous resolution practices and 'gives meaning to the representative and public involvement functions of the criminal jury.'[124]

Similar to Greenland's High Court, there is a Court of Appeal in Nunavut with the powers and rights that the NWT Court of Appeal had at the time Nunavut came into being.[125] The Nunavut Court of Appeal is composed of justices from other territories and provinces, and the court may sit in Nunavut or in any other territory or province,[126] whereas the High Court of Greenland sits in Greenland. However, at the fourth annual Northern Premiers' Forum, which took place in Iqaluit on 7 November 2006, it was suggested that a Northern Court of Appeal should be established, which would hear appeals on decisions made by the courts in Nunavut, Yukon, and the NWT. If created, this new institution is expected to be more reflective of Northern specifics and would establish 'a consistent body of northern jurisprudence.'[127]

Despite forthcoming law reforms of Greenland's judicial and penal systems, the current Greenland Criminal Code of 1954, which incorporated some unique features of Inuit traditional law-ways and customary law, deserves particular attention.[128] Codifying Greenlandic legal practice, the code installed a special system of sanctions that were 'determined by a global assessment of the offender's individual and social situation at the moment of conviction.'[129] The goal of the Greenland Criminal Code 'is not retribution (the word "punishment" is never used) but rehabilitation'; for the same reason, in this document 'the words "will be sentenced" are used instead of the words "will be punished."'[130] The code does not contain provisions concerning insanity.[131] It includes extensive possibilities for altering decisions made by retrying cases,[132] and 'reflects the community's condemnation of "criminal behaviour," regardless of the cause of crime.'[133] The drafter of the code, Verner Goldschmidt, underscored that this document 'has solely been based on systematic observation of *concrete legal reactions* and on information as to the *geographical and social background of the decisions made.* Thus the Code is an attempt at *expressing the pattern of behaviour of the legal authorities in legal terms.*'[134]

As it is based on Inuit legal tradition, which doesn't promote punishment but seeks to eliminate conflict and put forward a more restorative view of justice, the Greenland Criminal Code's sanctions are not measured by the gravity of the crime. Judges are given 'broad discretion to impose a wide variety of sanctions on the basis of the individual *offender's* personal background,' and can freely choose between a number of sanctions.[135] Created by the Greenland Criminal Code of 1954, the 'Arctic Peace Model,' which aims to restore social harmony, could work for small isolated communities, but it does not accommodate contemporary Greenland's realities.[136]

The Greenlandic system of law and justice has come under increasing scrutiny, and in general the advantages of codifying Inuit customary law have not been convincingly demonstrated.[137] The Greenland Criminal Code has been criticized for giving lenient sentences, as 'rapists and other sexual offenders are not given more severe sentences than, for instance, thieves.'[138] The Commission on Greenland's Judicial System (2004), which recommended revisions to the 1954 code, proposed to maintain its fundamental idea of rehabilitation as the basis of criminal sanctions. However, observing the development in case law and rapid changes in Greenland, the commission suggested reconsidering the application of the pure 'offender principle,' according to which 'only the individual offender's personal and social circumstances are considered, without regard for the type and gravity of the crime committed.' It also rejected the application of the pure 'offence principle,' which takes into account only the type and gravity of the criminal offence without consideration of the offender's personal and other circumstances. The commission proposes drawing on the advantages of both principles. Thus, it recommended that in choosing and meting out sanctions, the court has to consider 'the gravity of the offence, including the interest of society in discouraging acts of the type in question, and the offender's personal situation, including what is deemed necessary to keep the offender from committing further offences.'[139] The commission also proposed the application of a 'sanction ladder,'[140] based not just on the assessment of the severity of the criminal act but also on 'an overall assessment which may also include considerations such as age, motive and whether the offence is a first-time offence or a repeated crime.' Particular consideration would be given to flexible sanctions for mentally ill offenders, as an alternative to the ordinary sentences on the 'sanction ladder.'[141] In line with the provisions of the Danish Criminal Code, the commission also suggested introducing in Greenland's revised criminal code provisions that would regulate criminalization of acts such as child pornography, trafficking in human beings, computer fraud, and others that are currently not included in the code.[142]

Greenland's rapid development, the increasing complexity of legislation, the growing number of new types of crimes and cases before lay judges and lay assessors require specialized legal knowledge and further improvement of the district lay judges system. Lay judge Mille S. Pedersen notes from his experience that the largest problems are the recruitment of suitable lay judges, the high volume of juridical work falling within the normal working hours of their principal occupation, training and education, and remuneration for the work.[143] Consequently, the Commission on Greenland's Judicial System has recommended preserving the advantages of the proximity principle and recruiting local district judges and staff, but with a significant professional strengthening and increase in the legal expertise of the Magistrate Courts. The commission also suggested that magistrate judges complete a special district judge training program 'as a condition for permanent employment as a district judge.'[144]

The possibility of criminals being able to serve sentences in Greenland is hampered by several factors. These include a lack of maximum security penitentiaries and an urgent need for a high-security jail to reduce waiting lists for incarceration, poor training among Greenlandic staff working at detention centres and correctional facilities, and the need for qualified personnel to provide psychiatric treatment. Even though in 2006 'for the first time ever, a prisoner serving an indefinite sentence has been jailed in the Nuuk correctional facility,' there are still problems in connection with local incarceration.[145] Increased criticism by the community and victims calling for more protection and harsher sentencing, few facilities for alcohol and drug-abuse treatment, and financial difficulty in supporting the system add to the list of problems facing the administration of justice in Greenland.[146] Therefore, the Commission on Greenland's Judicial System has recommended reforms and a modernization of the entire administration of justice system, as well as the potential transfer of parts of it, including the creation of prison facilities and probation service, to the home rule authorities.

Problems connected with the administration of justice are not new for Nunavut. Among the problems it has faced partially as a result of the legacy of the NWT is the ineffectiveness of the circuit justice system to solve the issue of crime in the communities, given the scant knowledge of traditional Inuit wisdom by mostly Qallunaat juridical personnel. Other problems include language barriers, case delays, the adversarial approach of the Canadian criminal justice system, overcrowded correctional facilities as a result of the growing number of remand prisoners, and inappropriate leniency in sentencing (partially caused by the so-called double standard of justice).[147] Other critics have also noted that some regard the local correctional facility as an offenders' paradise. According to one research study, Nunavut residents referred to the Baffin Correctional Centre as 'the Baffin Hotel' or the 'Baffin Country Club.' Many offenders regard jail as the chance to get out the community. 'They look forward to it ... They see it as a reward.'[148]

To conclude, compared to their Canadian counterparts, who historically have imposed their own legal system upon the Inuit, Danish legislators have attempted to preserve some of the unique features of Greenlandic customary law. The question that arises is whether the creation of public governance in Nunavut in 1999 or the introduction of home rule in Greenland in 1979 made a difference in the Inuit political or legal capacity to maintain their traditional customs in the modern administration of justice or the legal systems existing in these Arctic jurisdictions.

Developments in the Justice Systems in Greenland and Nunavut

A consideration of the possibility of further integrating or reviving traditional Inuit law-ways in the contemporary justice systems in Greenland and Nunavut raises the question of the importance and validity of *lex loci* in bringing justice to the Inuit. The existing legal systems in Greenland and Nunavut are products of Western legal thinking. Further, according to some authorities, after obtaining home rule status, Greenlanders had to manage the conflict between remaining traditional customary law practices and modern legislation.[149] In both entities one can still observe the phenomenon of 'mimetic' legislation – that is, the duplication or 'imitation' of Canadian and Danish laws, which are not rooted in Inuit cultural values and are framed in Western legal language.[150] Understanding of this legislation by local practioners who do not have special legal training is hampered by a number of difficulties, which in Greenland's case include problems with translation of Danish legal concepts, or with following 'imported' laws that are frequently amended. This also alienates the local population from enforcement of such legislation.[151] At the same time, in the opinion of H. Petersen, contemporary Greenlandic legal culture is still strongly affected by Inuit tradition. Despite the growing influence of a rights culture, the Greenlandic system is still oriented towards situational consensus.[152] In Canada generally and in Nunavut in particular, some elements of Inuit customary law were incorporated into common law by judicial practice within the past decades,[153] and attempts were made to integrate customary law within the overall justice system in Nunavut.[154] Importantly, in Nunavut, all laws passed by the territorial Legislature must be translated in Inuktitut and most of them contain provisions for consideration of *Inuit Qaujima-jatuqangit* or even attempt to employ IQ as a 'legal principle.' At the same time, Canadian legal culture is still foreign to some Inuit. For example, recently there have been precedents where the accused did not understand what was happening in the court and pleaded guilty without knowing the meaning of the word 'complainant.'[155]

Despite these developments, the question remains as to whether the introduction of an Inuit judiciary in Nunavut and Greenlandic courts is feasible. The study of non-legal predicaments of any possible reform in that regard is not the focus of this chapter, nor is an assessment of legal impediments to the recognition and establishment of Greenlandic and Inuit courts or other changes to the justice system. My presumption is that Greenlanders and the Inuit of Nunavut would be able to negotiate with central governments to create a more or less independent Inuit judiciary or some parallel justice system if there were support from all the residents. This could be done on the grounds of extending the scope of autonomy within current Greenland and Nunavut legal arrangements and in the framework of the Inuit peoples' right to self-determination. Thus, Greenlanders can negotiate with Danish authorities for extended self-government, including Greenland's jurisdiction in judicial affairs. The Danish legal expert Frederik Harhoff sees no definitive reason why Greenland should be barred from establishing its own courts to settle questions under Greenlandic law.[156] As he notes, 'according to the Greenland view, the judiciary cannot be excluded from the areas as-sumed under Home Rule; any autonomous legal system has the right to establish a judicial structure for the solution of legal conflicts within the system itself. The Greenland authorities therefore believe that they are entitled to establish a separate Greenlandic judiciary with independent courts.'[157] Though a Greenlandic judiciary is legally feasible, in practice, 'the existing Danish courts have proved to be loyal to the Home Rule legislation and there has been no incentive to institute a parallel and costly separate system of courts.'[158]

The Commission on Greenland's Judicial System (2004) found that the Danish constitution does not prevent a transfer of all elements of the judicial system to Greenland but requires that 'the competence granted to the Home Rule Government must be exercised within the framework of the Constitution, including that the Supreme Court remains the "supreme court of the realm."'[159] Consequently, a connection between the Danish and Greenlandic judicial systems will remain, 'and the Supreme Court, as a court of last resort, will have to determine disputes, including control the administration and monitor observance of the limits of the legislative power.'[160] The transfer of legislative jurisdiction and administration of the judiciary to the home rule authorities is possible with the amendment of the Home Rule Act. However, the commission did not develop its proposals for reforming Greenland's judicial system with such transfer in mind, which might be highly burdensome for the home rule authorities.[161] The commission evaluated advantages and drawbacks of this transfer and considered it to be doubtful that 'the Home Rule Government will become able, within a foreseeable time, to build up the requisite administrative and professional capacity, especially legal capacity, to cope with both the issuing of rules for and actual administration of the fields of responsibility that a transfer involves.'[162]

There is no definitive answer as to whether the constitutional development of Nunavut provides for realization by the Inuit of their right to self-determination.[163] In the future the Inuit of Nunavut could negotiate the establishment of an independent justice system through the framework of self-determination. Further development of Nunavut's system of governance, and problems arising with the impact on the Inuit of a justice system based on the Canadian model, may at some point place this issue on the political agenda.[164] The Nunavut Act does not confer the authority to create an alternative Inuit system of courts or administration of justice. However, hypothetically, if residents of Nunavut wished so, there might be a legal possibility for this development based on Canada's constitutional law. For example, Patrick Macklem's analysis of the question of which level of government possesses the constitutional authority to create an Aboriginal justice system and the judicature provisions of the Constitution Act, 1867, concludes that there is no serious obstacle to 'the establishment of a separate or parallel system of justice for Aboriginal people.'[165] Moreover, section 35(1) of the Constitution Act, 1982, guarantees support for the recognition or creation of indigenous courts.[166] Macklem has also found that legislative initiatives aimed at vesting greater control over criminal justice in Aboriginal communities do not infringe upon constitutional guarantees enshrined in the Canadian Charter of Rights and Freedoms.[167] Macklem's arguments notwithstanding, the introduction of an Inuit justice system was not at the forefront of the debate when Nunavut was created in 1999.[168] This may be partially explained by the challenges the young government had

to face connected with the building of Nunavut and making it a homeland for all its citizens.

Today, the administration of justice in Nunavut is a subject of criticism. The complaints cover a variety of problems, including the serious
shortage of criminal defence lawyers, delays in the processing of civil
and criminal cases, lack of access to civil law among Nunavut residents
(and the low priority given to those cases in the court system), and mis-
guided attempts by non-Inuit in the justice system to show 'sensitivity' to
Inuit culture, which have resulted in cases of domestic violence being
condoned and a high number of repeat offenders. To protect Nunavummiut who are experiencing family abuse, the Family Abuse Intervention Act was passed by the Nunavut Legislature in 2006. However, a lot
of work remains to be done to deal with violence and escalating addic-
tion rates leading to criminal behaviour.[169] Nunavut elders say that the
Inuit are forced to use a court system they know nothing about and that
Inuit traditional law-ways should be integrated into the Canadian court
system, especially with respect to minor offences.[170] There is great concern about the way elders are treated in the justice system. As Piujuq
Enoogoo claims, elders are often invited to give their opinions before
sentencing at trials, but 'they are just being used ... The elders are lis-
tened to but they don't have any say.'[171] There is some desire among the
elders to see a system where they will share equal power with the judges.
Elder's representative Gamailie Kilukishak emphasizes that 'before the
white man came, Inuit treated people differently than today's culture ...
Elders can offer counsel and forgiveness.'[172]

In the words of former Crown prosecutor Pierre Rousseau, 'Nunavut's
dysfunctional justice system destroys lives, ignores Inuit culture and is a
major cause of inter-ethnic conflict.'[173] He further states that 'the use of
interpreters, local justices of the peace, diversion programs, provisions
for unilingual Inuktitut-speaking jurors, and elders' panels sitting with
judges are just "crumbs" thrown at aboriginal communities.'[174] One
solution, in Rousseau's opinion, is to restore the power that the Inuit
once had to resolve conflicts in their communities. To the list of concerns may be added letters from Nunavut residents who are 'furious
with [a] justice system' that does not sentence sex offenders to adequate
jail time.[175] Nunavut's rate of violent crime is the highest in Canada and
includes a high incidence of sexual and domestic assaults.[176] Clearly,
further change to the administration of justice in Nunavut is needed;
recognition of some form of Inuit judiciary, a return to more traditional
Inuit methods of social control and dispute resolution, and their further

introduction into the contemporary justice system are important reforms for consideration.

However, in the words of Frances Piugatuk, a court worker from Iqaluit, a separate justice system for the Inuit is never going to become a reality, 'because the crimes the Inuit people commit are the same as the crimes white people commit. The Inuit system is usually rehabilitation if possible. We have a system of justice in place and what we have to do is make the present system work to our advantage. Hopefully there will be Inuit lawyers in the future and maybe we can have a hand in making the system a little bit more flexible.'[177] Indeed, thanks to Akitsiraq Law School program – which was organized as a result of a partnership between the Akitsiraq Law School Society, the Faculty of Law at the University of Victoria, and the Nunavut Arctic College, and included some Canadian Aboriginal scholars – the shortage of Inuit lawyers has been alleviated. Inuktitut-speaking law graduates 'will naturally tend to look at customary and informal approaches to law.'[178] In the words of Akitsiraq Law School graduate Sandra Inutiq, we are 'going to challenge the "black letter approach" to law, where written legislation is valued in court, more than Inuit Qaujimajatuqangit (Inuit traditional knowledge).'[179] In a similar vein, Qajaq Robinson noted 'there will only be justice in Nunavut when Inuit traditional law is viewed as equal with Canadian written law.'[180]

Even though the legal system in Nunavut remains rooted in the Euro-Canadian justice system, there have been some initiatives for bridging the gap between Inuit values and the administration of justice. It is expected that eventually the role of justices of the peace and community-based justice committees will increase, and alternatives to the existing justice system that are based on Inuit traditions and values will be promoted. It is also hoped that over time the Inuit will take more responsibility for and control over justice issues in their communities.[181] Nunavut's residents themselves are taking steps to make the justice system more amenable to their needs. For example, the Kitikmeot Inuit Association has tried to banish repeat offenders from moving in and out of their communities and took their campaign to the federal government.[182] Victims of crime in Iqaluit are seeking justice from the elders. The collaboration of a group of elders and professional mediators in the Iqaluit Restorative Justice Society is one example of a popular alternative for handling lesser crimes, such as vandalism, petty theft, or minor assaults. Most of the cases the society mediates involve young offenders. In their work outside the official justice system, Inuktitut-speaking elders share their traditional knowledge with offenders about how the Inuit dealt with criminals in the past; they ask the perpetrators questions about the crime they have committed and give them advice. If the victim requests, the accused may also meet with a trained mediator, instead of the elder. These mediation sessions help the victim and the offender agree on some form of conflict resolution.[183] In 2005 the Restorative Justice Society launched a video across Nunavut explaining 'how elders would use age-old techniques to resolve crimes today.'[184] The hope is that, in the future, the justice system in Nunavut will develop towards more flexibility in dealing with dispute resolution outside the court system, and will involve more Inuit knowledge to accommodate cultural identity in the existing juridical structures.[185]

Greenlanders and the Inuit of Nunavut have some opportunities for employing their legal practices and incorporating Inuit legal culture into the administration of justice. It is not clear to what extent Inuit legal traditions and *lex loci* have survived the imposition of the Danish and Canadian legal systems. Because many Inuit law-ways are informal, it is debatable whether customary law is inconsistent with or complementary to Western legal traditions. Inuit legal culture is valuable itself, and there should be further dialogue between Inuit and non-Inuit legal traditions so that the legal systems in Greenland and Nunavut can embrace the best of both worlds. Although, according to some authorities, there are no legal obstacles to establishing an alternative Inuit judiciary in Nunavut and a more or less independent justice system in Greenland, in practice it is not clear how this can be done, given the erosion of traditional Inuit practices and the financial resources required. The cases of Greenland and Nunavut show that via self-governance, further evolution of Greenland home rule, and development of Nunavut's governance, bringing a community-based approach and increasing Inuit involvement in legal services and the judicial system should open more possibilities for the application of *lex loci*, and will enable the Inuit to be tried by their own peers. Recognition in the legal framework of autonomy of the possibility of Greenlandic or Nunavut administration of justice with strong Inuit involvement (as a part of the jurisdiction of the regions' governance) could make a difference in the delivery of justice to Northern residents.

5 Greenland and Nunavut in International Affairs

As Inuit, we have a responsibility to our people and our communities to secure greater international recognition of Inuit rights. At the same time, Inuit from all circumpolar countries must contribute to the integrity of the world environment and world peace, by advocating coherent policies and initiatives and the establishment of an international forum where all these concerns can be discussed and acted upon.

Mary Simon, president, Inuit Circumpolar Conference, 1987

The scope of the Home Rule Act, the Nunavut Land Claims Agreement (NLCA), and the Nunavut Act does not go so far as to permit Greenland or Nunavut jurisdiction over international relations or defence and security policy. Despite this, Nunavut and particularly Greenland want to be involved in the security activities of their national states when the issue at hand concerns their lands. They are also active in various forms of international cooperation and indigenous internationalism, although formally their legal personality in international or domestic law does not permit such activities.[1] In this chapter, I examine the legal capacity of Greenland and Nunavut in international affairs and security policy by looking at the main international forums in which these jurisdictions have a voice, regardless of the limitations imposed by their legal status.

There is no legal clarity on the competence and boundaries of subnational territories' participation in the international field.[2] Nonetheless, there is clear growth in the importance of international involvement by 'constitutional dependencies' such as Greenland and Nunavut. Since the first days of the home rule, Greenlandic authorities gradually took over elements of foreign affairs and pursued a strategy that allowed Greenland to 'become a genuine actor in its own sphere of foreign policy.'[3] The report from the Commission on Self-Governance (Greenland) highlighted the necessity of expanding Greenland's capacity to take a stand in foreign affairs and security policy issues in 'the areas of fishery, hunting, environment, tourism, transportation and business' in order to strengthen the country's economy.[4]

Unique cultural, geographical, environmental, linguistic, and economic conditions, as well as current trends towards globalization and the existing practice of Inuit internationalism have created a need to expand the legal vision of autonomy in some areas of the traditionally non-transferable domain of foreign affairs.[5] In this chapter, I argue that Greenland and Nunavut should have a legislated right to cooperate in international activities and the formulation of security policy as subnational territories, when the issue has direct or indirect significance for them. Recognition of this right would open up more opportunities to accommodate both local concerns and the development of these jurisdictions in the global and Arctic contexts. The transfer of this kind of jurisdiction, with specified limits on the autonomous regions' capacity in international forums, would not pose a threat to national sovereignty or statehood. The Danish and Canadian interests in the preservation of the legal status of Greenland or Nunavut are not based on international law. The protection for these interests is promoted by active Inuit participation in international organizations. Tacit approval by Danish or Canadian authorities for Greenland's or Nunavut's participation in international cooperation creates a precedent that justifies the limited international legal capacity of these Arctic jurisdictions. However, in the opinion of the Commission on Self-Governance, the practice that developed in the form of consultations built on goodwill will not be acceptable in Greenland's future self-governance agreement. Therefore, the Commission on Self-Governance called for a new arrangement recognizing Greenland's formal participation in this area. An important step in this direction was the introduction, after negotiations between the government of Greenland and the government of Denmark as equal parties, of the Act Concerning the Conclusion of Agreements under International Law by the Government of Greenland (the Authorization Act).[6] In practice some of the spheres in the field of foreign affairs are becoming legitimately transferable to Greenland. This may also become an option for Nunavut in the long run.

The Legal Status of Greenland and Nunavut as International Actors

There are striking similarities and differences in the legal status of Greenland and Nunavut with regard to international relations. Greenland and Nunavut have no special status in international law stemming from an international convention. Although in practice these jurisdictions could be subjects of the legal regime of 'Arctic' international law, constitutionally the territories are a part of Canada and Denmark.[7] Consequently, from a legal standpoint, the authorities of Nunavut and Greenland cannot undertake foreign affairs; their jurisdiction in the international domain is limited by rights and obligations derived from treaties or other international documents signed by Canada and Denmark; the Canadian and Danish authorities have exclusive priority in decision-making powers over foreign relations regarding the interests of their states; Greenland and Nunavut cannot be independent members of international organizations that are composed of sovereign states; these territories are not allowed to conclude unilateral agreements with foreign countries and cannot have their own diplomatic missions. All this means that Greenland and Nunavut do not have international legal capacity or an international legal personality and cannot be classified as subjects of international law.

This situation is changing to some extent, especially in Greenland's case. In order to advance foreign policy collaboration, in 2003 the governments of Denmark and Greenland signed in Itilleq (Greenland) a joint declaration on the involvement of Greenland's home rule government in foreign and security policy matters of significance for the island. This declaration supported Greenland's participation in international negotiations along with the Danish government for assertion of Greenlandic interests. It also noted that 'the government of Greenland must ... be consulted prior to the ratification of international agreements' whose implementation is incumbent on Greenland. Furthermore, apart from some areas (e.g., human rights) the declaration noted that 'it will normally be possible to accede to international agreements with effect solely for Denmark, so that Greenland can independently take a decision on the extent to which the agreement concerned should apply to Greenland.'[8]

Some areas of foreign affairs are in fact transferable to Greenland home rule when they do not limit the constitutional responsibilities and powers of the Danish government related to conclusion of agreements under international law. Since the introduction in 2005 of the Authorization Act, the Greenland home rule government is allowed to 'negotiate and conclude agreements under international law with foreign states and international organizations, including administrative agreements, which relate entirely to subject matters where legislative and administrative powers have been transferred to the Authorities of Greenland' (s. 1(1)). These arrangements, however, cannot apply 'to agreements under international law affecting defence and security policy, or agreements which are to apply to Denmark or which are negotiated within an international organization of which the Kingdom of Denmark is a member' (s. 1(4)). Further, these agreements 'shall be entered into on behalf of the Danish Realm by the Government of Greenland under the designation of the Kingdom of Denmark in respect of Greenland' (s. 2). It is presupposed that Greenland cooperates with Denmark and informs the Danish government about upcoming negotiations and before international agreements are entered into or terminated (s. 2(2)). The act also allows Greenlandic representatives to be appointed to the diplomatic missions of the Kingdom of Denmark to address issues related strictly to powers taken by Greenland home rule authorities (s. 3). Finally, according to section 4 of the act, 'where this is consistent with the constitutional status of Greenland' at the request of home rule authorities, the Danish government may grant or support Greenland's application to attain membership in its own name in international organizations that allow membership of entities other than states and associations of states.

Despite the fact that the home rule government was authorized to act on behalf of the Danish realm in international affairs related exclusively to legislative and administrative jurisdiction that was transferred to Greenland, the Authorization Act does not limit the constitutional powers and responsibility of the Danish government in the field of foreign affairs, including powers of the minister of foreign affairs and the Danish authorities in relation to Greenland (s. 1(5)). Also it does not replace the provisions of the Greenland Home Rule Act of 1978, which is still in force at the time of writing. The developments towards gradual expanding of Greenland's foreign policy involvement are taking place within increasing cooperation with Denmark and with special consideration of the Danish constitutional framework. According to section 19(1) of the Danish constitution, the king acts on behalf of the kingdom in international affairs, and the principle of national unity presumes that foreign affairs are part of the indivisible sovereignty of Denmark.

Correspondingly, the Commission on Home Rule has isolated foreign affairs as an absolute jurisdiction of the national authorities that cannot be delegated to the home rule authorities.[9] As a result, section 11 of the Home Rule Act vests jurisdiction in the central authorities of the realm regarding questions affecting the foreign relations of Denmark and obliges the home rule government to first discuss with Copenhagen any measures that would be of substantial importance to the foreign relations of the kingdom. Moreover, section 10(1–2) of the act stipulates that Greenlandic authorities shall be subject to obligations arising out of treaties and other international rules that are binding on Denmark, and that 'The powers delegated to international authorities under section 20 of the Constitution shall at all times prevail over the powers of the home rule authorities.'

The home rule system is meant to work in the interests of the Danish nation as a whole. Even if some spheres of foreign relations are transferred to the home rule government, Greenlandic and Danish authorities must cooperate if an issue falls under an international treaty or other obligation. Section 13 of the Home Rule Act obliges the central authorities to consult with the home rule government before concluding treaties that require the assent of the Folketing and that specifically affect Greenland's interests. Likewise, Denmark is not entitled to enter into an agreement of specific interest to Greenland without prior consultation with the home rule authorities.[10] When matters of particular interest to Greenland are at stake, Copenhagen may, at the request of the home rule government, authorize it to negotiate directly with the collaboration of the foreign service, provided such negotiations 'are not considered incompatible with the unity of the realm.'[11]

The Authorization Act extended and modernized some provisions of section 16 of the Home Rule Act dealing with employment of Greenlandic representatives within the Danish diplomatic missions. According to these changes, Greenlandic authorities may request that representatives of the government of Greenland be appointed to Danish diplomatic missions 'to attend to subject matters where legislative and administrative powers have been entirely transferred to the Authorities of Greenland.'[12] Thus, the previous term 'officers' was replaced with 'representatives of the Government of Greenland,' and the scope of activities was expanded from 'special commercial interests' to the powers transferred to the home rule authorities.[13] Clearly, according to the provisions of the Home Rule Act, before the introduction of the Authorization Act, Greenland had some say in international relations that included specific Greenlandic interests. Sometimes these interests were the cornerstone of the Denmark–Greenland relationship. For example, before 2005 the home rule authorities were not allowed to conclude agreements with foreign countries, even on matters exclusive to Greenland jurisdiction. In practice, however, Greenlandic authorities have concluded such agreements with some neighbouring countries.[14] According to Harhoff, 'the Danish government has tacitly accepted these treaties as true international agreements, indicating that only the Home Rule government could be held responsible in the case of breaches.'[15] Nonetheless, it was understood that 'this limited international treaty-making power applies only to local Greenlandic matters under Home Rule jurisdiction that have no general implications for Danish foreign and external security.'[16]

These precedents showed that national authority in foreign affairs was not absolute and was, in fact, transferable to some extent. It was not surprising, then, that in 2003 the Commission on Self Governance concluded that the Home Rule Act was limited in meeting Greenland's need for a greater say in international affairs. It recommended that the act be revised to reflect today's reality, particularly with respect to the legally recognized duty of state authorities to negotiate with Greenland's government before undertaking any international initiatives of significance to the island.[17] Greenlandic authorities saw international agreements only at the stage of ratification and did not have much chance to influence the context of the agreement. The commission suggested changing this practice so that 'mandates in principle to enter into international negotiations' were presented not just to the Folketing but also to Greenland's government and the Landsting, which should be in the position 'to express their views concerning the negotiation mandate.'[18] Also, the commission raised the question regarding the participation of Greenlandic representatives in Danish delegations in cases where international negotiations for Denmark concern the European Union (EU). The commission noted that 'in international relations, Denmark is sometimes used to cover all the parts of the Realm and in some cases Denmark is understood only as an EU member country.' Because Greenland is not a part of the EU, the commission suggested that in those areas where Denmark acts on behalf of the realm, it should be assumed that 'the necessary negotiations have taken place with Greenland concerning those areas that are marked by a Greenlandic interest.' When Denmark acts only as an EU member state and may be obliged by common EU policies, Greenland should be allowed to maintain other interests, whereas the Danish legislation should be revised to deal with this potential conflict.[19]

To conclude, despite increasing Greenland's jurisdiction in some areas of foreign affairs, the Authorization Act did not amount to an actual transfer of powers from Denmark to Greenland to act independently in international affairs, as the Danish kingdom is one subject in international law. Greenland's government was authorized only to act on behalf of the Danish realm in international affairs that related solely to Greenland and did not affect or challenge the integrity of other parts of the realm. Thus, the legal scope of the act was extended to already existing Danish-Greenlandic practices in the area of foreign affairs.

The case of Nunavut is different. Compared with Greenland, the territory has insignificant legal capacity to perform internationally even in the matters related entirely to Nunavut's jurisdiction. The Nunavut Act does not deal with the issue of Nunavut's participation in international affairs. In Canada foreign affairs are primarily under the direction and control of the federal government. However, the legislative jurisdiction to implement international treaties is divided along federal and provincial lines. Even though Nunavut does not have the full status of a province, the NLCA recognizes that 'any legislation implementing an international or domestic interjurisdictional agreement shall be interpreted and administered to treat Inuit on at least as favourable a basis as any other aboriginal people in Canada' and that 'the Government of Canada shall include Inuit representation in discussions leading to the formulation of government positions in relation to an international agreement relating to Inuit wildlife harvesting rights in the Nunavut Settlement Area, which discussions shall extend beyond those discussions generally available to non-governmental organizations.'[20]

Further, section 12.11.2 of the NLCA specifies that the government of Canada and the government of Nunavut, assisted by the Nunavut Impact Review Board, shall do their best in negotiations with other jurisdictions to provide for cooperation 'in the review of project proposals which may have significant transboundary ecosystemic or socio-economic impacts.'[21] Beyond this point, however, provisions of the NLCA do not provide the government of Nunavut with a solid jurisdiction in international matters.

Despite the extension of Greenland's authority in the area of international affairs and Nunavut's limited capacity in that sphere, the question remains as to the necessity of a legal recognition of the right of subnational entities to exercise jurisdiction in some areas of foreign affairs. The transferability of some areas of foreign affairs to subnational units such as Greenland and Nunavut is the subject of constitutional and international law and can be considered in the framework of the right to self-determination. I argue that limited jurisdiction in this area can be transferred to Nunavut and Greenland within the scope of the right to internal self-determination (self-government), and that this is already the case for Greenland. At the same time, though neither public international law nor the constitutional law of Denmark or Canada entitles Greenland and Nunavut to perform as independent subjects of international law, these Arctic jurisdictions are involved in fostering international relationships in order to realize their cultural, social, environmental, and economic interests. Danish–Greenlandic cooperation in foreign affairs is workable as long as it does not affect the major principles of Danish foreign policy. The continued evolution of Greenland, the growing desire for greater self-government, the need for sustainable economic development, and the capability to respond to global challenges support the involvement of Greenlanders in foreign affairs, particularly concerning international environmental and trade policy initiatives.[22] Steadily increasing recognition of subnational territories such as Greenland and possibly Nunavut as legitimate participants in international relations contradicts traditional conceptions of national sovereignty and reduces the sovereign powers of the state. However, the developing practice of involving subnational units in international affairs shows that they are progressing in this direction in cooperation with their respective national governments.

Inuit involvement in international relations – for example, via the Inuit Circumpolar Council (ICC), which will be discussed below – bears some similarity to the simultaneous involvement of both the Canadian and Quebec governments in la Francophonie. Yet the Inuit aspiration does not grow out of any interest in separatism.[23] Indeed, the Commission on Self-Governance has underscored that even in the renewed self-governance model there would be areas where jurisdiction in foreign affairs cannot be transferred to Greenland. Thus, the legal parameters for Greenland's activity in foreign affairs should be based on cooperation and partnership between the Danish and self-governance offices.[24]

Forms of Greenland's and Nunavut's International Activity

To understand the breadth of areas where jurisdiction in foreign affairs can be transferred to Greenland and Nunavut, it is useful to look at existing forms of their involvement in international forums and evaluate their potential interests in that area. The variety of forms, certain of which are summarized below, indicates that involvement in certain areas of international affairs is of the utmost importance for subnational Arctic entities. Greenland is more actively involved in this field than Nunavut, and it successfully pioneered and enhanced transnational diplomacy even within the context of its limited autonomous status.

   Greenland and Nunavut have particular interests in international cooperation, and these interests define their priorities and forms of international activity. These forms can be classified in the following principal ways:

- Regionally:
  - Arctic cooperation (e.g., via the Arctic Council)
  - Nordic cooperation (e.g., via the Nordic Council and the Nordic Council of Ministers) (Greenland only)
  - European cooperation (e.g., via the European Union)[25] (Greenland only)
  - cross-border cooperation between Greenland and Nunavut and between Greenland and Canada (e.g., Canada/Greenland Joint Commission on the Conservation and Management of Narwhal and Beluga)[26]
  - 'internal' cooperation indirectly affecting international decisions[27]
  - the North Atlantic Cooperation (e.g., Greenland)[28]

- Globally:
  - via the World Trade Organization (WTO) (Greenland only), the UN[29] (e.g., the Permanent Forum on Indigenous Issues), UNESCO, the ILO

- Functionally:
  - interparliamentary cooperation (e.g., summits of parliamentarians of the Arctic region, Greenland's participation in the Nordic Council and the West Nordic Council;[30]
  - intergovernmental cooperation (e.g., Greenland's participation in the Nordic Council of Ministers)
  - supranational cooperation (e.g., the EU) (Greenland only)
  - non-governmental cooperation (e.g., the Inuit Circumpolar Council [ICC]), the International Arctic Science Committee (IASC)

– indigenous cooperation (e.g., the ICC, the Indigenous Peoples Secretariat, etc.)

• By subject matter:
  – environmental cooperation (e.g., through the Arctic Council)
  – fishery and hunting cooperation (e.g., the Northeast Atlantic Fish-
    eries Commission, the Northwest Atlantic Fisheries Organization
    and the North Atlantic Salmon Conservation Organization, the
    International Whaling Commission, the World Council of Whalers,
    the North Atlantic Marine Mammal Commission (Greenland only),
    the Canada/Greenland Joint Commission on the Conservation and
    Management of Narwhal and Beluga)
  – international trade cooperation (e.g., Greenland's Trade Council)
  – cultural, educational, linguistic cooperation (exchanges between
    Greenland and Canadian universities, activities of the University of
    the Arctic
  – cooperation in defence and security matters

In many areas, Greenland and Nunavut have similar interests in international involvement as a result of their climatic, geographic, economic,
and linguistic similarities and because they face common environmental
and global challenges. However, there are some fields of interest for
Greenland only – in particular the island's involvement in Nordic cooperation and its relationships with the EU.

Greenland and Nordic Cooperation

Geographically, Greenland belongs to the North American continent.
Legally, as part of Denmark (itself part of Norden or Scandinavia),[31]
Greenland is involved in the process of Nordic collaboration, whose
legal basis today is the Treaty of Cooperation among Denmark, Finland,
Iceland, Norway, and Sweden, which was signed in Helsinki on 23
March 1962 (the 'Helsinki Treaty').[32] Amendments to the treaty show
that there has been a renewal and expansion of Nordic cooperation 'in
the light of the greater participation by the Nordic countries in the process of European cooperation.'[33]

Today, major Greenlandic interests are expressed via participation in
the activities of the pillars of Nordic collaboration, such as the Nordic
Council and the Nordic Council of Ministers.[34] The roots of the Nordic

Council date back to its predecessors in 1907 and even earlier.[35] Since its founding in 1952 as a forum for interparliamentary collaboration, the council has promoted discussion among the parliaments and governments of Denmark, Iceland, Norway, and Sweden, and, later, Finland, on matters of Nordic cooperation.[36]

The status of autonomous territories (i.e., the Åland Islands, the Faroe Islands, and Greenland) in the structures of Nordic cooperation was consolidated and clarified in 1980 in the report of the Petri Committee, composed of the executive body of the Nordic Council and the ministers of justice of the Nordic countries.[37] As a result, in 1984 Greenland entered the Nordic Council after having obtained the status of permanent participant within the Danish delegation.[38] The council consists of eighty-seven elected members, representatives of Nordic governments and governmental representatives of the Åland Islands, the Faroe Islands, and Greenland. As is the case for other autonomous territories, the Landsting of Greenland elects two members to the Nordic Council, and the home rule government appoints representatives it wishes to send. The Greenlandic delegation, although formed separately, joins the national delegation of Denmark on the council.[39] Because Greenland has only two elected members, representatives of home rule government are allowed to participate and speak on matters affecting Greenland in different committees of the council on which they don't have elected members. However, these governmental representatives do not have voting rights.[40]

As regards jurisdiction, the Nordic Council is an informal cooperative structure with purely advisory and supervisory functions. It may adopt recommendations, make representations, or issue statements on its views to the national governments of the Nordic countries or to the Nordic Council of Ministers.[41] Thus, it is not an independent decision-making body: each Nordic parliament has to separately enact the council's recommendations.[42] The Nordic Council's mandate makes it an exclusively consultative organ of the Nordic parliaments.[43]

Another structure of Nordic cooperation in which Greenland participates is the Nordic Council of Ministers, which was formed in 1971 as a forum for intergovernmental cooperation to develop collaboration between various governments and the Nordic Council.[44] De jure, the prime ministers 'are responsible for overall coordination of matters of Nordic cooperation,' and in each country they are 'assisted by a member of the Government (the Minister for Cooperation) and an Under-

Secretary of State or government official (a member of the national Standing Committee on Nordic Cooperation).'[45] In practice, overall responsibility for the Nordic Council of Ministers is delegated to the ministers for Nordic cooperation and to the Nordic Committee for Cooperation. The Nordic Council of Ministers consists of 'several individual councils of ministers ... Most of the Nordic ministers for specific policy areas meet in council of ministers a couple of times a year.' Thus, the composition of the council may vary depending on what issues need to be addressed.[46] As is the case for other autonomous territories, the home rule government of Greenland is allowed to take part in the work of the Nordic Council of Ministers. Greenland has representatives at various councils of ministers, and it cooperates via a minister for Nordic cooperation.[47]

Greenland views its limited participation in these high international forums as a chance for furthering its integration with other Nordic regions, and for broadcasting its 'international' voice within the Nordic community. According to one authority, if Greenlanders expressed their will to do so, there is no constitutional obstacle to their full membership in the Nordic Council or the Nordic Council of Ministers. However, it is not clear whether such an argument corresponds with Denmark's position.[48] That position may soon become apparent: in 2006 Greenland expressed interest in having its own delegation in the Nordic Council. Greenland wants to take part in decision-making processes and participate more independently in the work of the Nordic Council and the Nordic Council of Ministers.[49]

Currently, Greenland's far-reaching associate status within the Nordic Council and the Nordic Council of Ministers provides Greenlanders with some degree of authority in the processes of Nordic cooperation. This collaboration is further enhanced by cooperation between the Nordic Council and the West Nordic Council, which in 2006 signed an agreement allowing Greenland, Iceland, and the Faroe Islands to exert greater influence on the Nordic Council's decisions and agenda.[50] Although, according to some commentators, formal Nordic cooperation is in crisis, challenged by the growth of the European Union's supranational institutions, of which most of the Nordic countries are members,[51] Greenland's current participation in the institutions of interstate Nordic collaboration is a positive example of the potential for transferring some areas in international relations to subnational entities.

Greenland and the European Union

We confirm our relations with Denmark – and with Europe – but we have also realized that our full membership of the European Community as a 'European Region' is inadequate and unworkable along with our self-determination established through our Home Rule. Our climate, norms, culture, ethnicity, social structure, economic and industrial pattern, infrastructure and basis of existence are so different from Europe that we can never equate with the European countries or regions. Our country does not fit into Europe, and we do not fit within the European community. This is not to indicate that any relation to Europe should be cut off. But a loose relation with Europe would in a much more realistic way reflect the differences – and the connections – between Greenland and Europe. In political terms, the step out of the Community is one step away from all that, which for centuries has made us believe that we cannot manage on our own.

Moses Olsen, Greenland's Home Rule minister for social affairs, 1983

The complexity of Greenland's relations with the European Union is conditioned by two important factors. First, Greenland as a part of Denmark, an EU member state, has to harmonize its non-European features and home rule interests with EU policies. Second, Greenland has no direct jurisdiction in the supranational institutions of the EU. Despite this, Greenland's 'loose relation with Europe' has developed into a 'political love affair' marked by mutual cooperation and benefit. Some of Greenland's political figures publicly support EU membership for the island, imagining the use of the EU machine as a counterweight to the United States and speculating on the benefits of the EU taking economic responsibility for the island.[52] How did this 'political love affair' become legally possible for a subnational territory that is not an EU member?

In 1972 Greenland, as an integral part of Denmark, had to join the European Economic Community (EEC), notwithstanding the mixed reaction of Greenlanders to the idea.[53] On 23 February 1982, 53 per cent of Greenland's population voted to rescind its membership, and the home rule government requested that Danish authorities begin negotiations with the EEC regarding Greenland's withdrawal.[54] On 22 February 1983 the Commission of the EEC issued a formal communication approving Greenland's withdrawal, and Greenland left the EEC on 1 February 1985.[55]

Greenland had reaped some economic benefits from participation in the EEC, but withdrawal became necessary for several reasons.[56] Because of Greenland's history as a colonized entity, it was reluctant to further compromise its autonomy by ceding it to the supranational authority of the EEC.[57] Culturally, socially, and geographically, Greenland does not fit into Europe, and Greenlanders thought of themselves as quite separate from the continent.[58] Greenland's membership in the EEC suppressed expectations for home rule development and imposed limitations on possibilities for self-determination.[59] Membership in the European superpower was seen as a potential threat to Greenlanders' ethnic identity.[60] In economic terms, as a fishery-based society, Greenlanders found it humiliating that their politicians would have to bargain with EEC representatives about the right of Greenlandic fishermen to fish off their own coastline.[61] Finally, there were considerable practical problems in exercising Greenland's membership.[62] Legally, Greenland's withdrawal created a negative precedent in EEC law, but reluctance regarding Greenland's 'secession' was overcome by the exceptional circumstances.[63] In 1985, after numerous legal and political considerations, Greenland obtained a new legal regime designation within the EEC as an overseas country and territory (OCT), with special arrangements regarding its unique circumstances.[64]

Greenland as an OCT within the EU

The legal status of Greenland within EU law is regulated by the regime of the Overseas Countries and Territories.[65] On 1 February 1985, in accordance with so-called Greenland Treaty, Greenland was added to the list of the OCTs associated with the EEC.[66] The general OCT legal formula was applied to Greenland as a basis for reassociation with the EEC in 1985, with certain provisions tailored to fit Greenland's particular circumstances,[67] and the Protocol on Special Arrangements for Greenland was annexed to the treaty that established the EEC. This protocol exempted Greenland from customs duties, equivalent charges, and quantitative restrictions on import into the community of fishery products originating in Greenland with the condition that the EEC obtain access to fish in Greenland's waters in conformity with the Fisheries Agreement.[68]

The initial goal of the OCT's association with the EEC is 'to promote the economic and social development of the countries and territories and to establish close economic relations between them and the Community as a whole.'[69] This association also includes non-discrimination in trade arrangements between the OCTs and member states.[70] In addition, Declaration No. 25 of the Maastricht Treaty regulates Greenland's position as an OCT. According to this, Denmark is entitled in exceptional circumstances to act separately from the EU in the interests of Greenland, without this affecting the interests of the EU.[71] The detailed relationships between the OCTs and the EU are governed by periodically updated decisions of the Council of the EU on the association of the overseas countries and territories with the European community. Currently the OCT decision of 2001 still applies to Greenland until 2011. It contains an exhaustive mechanism of association with the EU on the principles of cooperation, dialogue, and partnership.[72] This collaboration, which is of the utmost importance to Greenland, comprises a wide range of areas such as economic, trade, social, regional, and cultural cooperation as well as fisheries, agriculture, industry, mining, energy, transport, finance, and water.[73] Thanks to Greenland's OCT status, the residents of the island have access to numerous EU programs in the fields of education, entrepreneurship, culture, research, information technology, and communications.[74] Thus removal from one end of the EU Treaty system (participation as an integral part of Denmark) to the other (association with the EU as an OCT) has turned out to be more favourable for Greenland, which, without direct membership in the supranational EU institutions, is still able to manage its own interests. This Greenland–EU relationship may be partially explained by Greenland's proactive approach to the decision-making process. One of Greenland's interests includes the possibility of having a policy-making mechanism to influence the EU legislative process with its unique Arctic perspective.[75]

As Greenland's system of home rule evolves, so too does its participation in the EU. Currently, it qualifies for a higher status than that of simply an offshoot of Denmark but less than that of a member state. Does this require a new partnership with the EU, or does the OCT status work well? Experience has shown that the Greenland–EU relationship is effective within the framework of the OCT and would be workable even if Greenland changed its home rule status.[76] At the same time, the current Greenland–EU relationship has evolved to the point that the need for negotiation of an ad hoc EU–Greenland partnership agreement and review of all the conditions and entitlements of OCT status and the fisheries agreement became apparent. Proposals for a new arrangements with Greenland based on a comprehensive partnership for sustainable development were considered at various bodies of the EU in light of priorities connected with the enlargement of the EU and the fact that the fisheries agreement and successive protocols did not reflect the real fishing levels (the quantities of fish had been worth much less than the level of financial compensation provided by the EU).[77] The need for a new partnership was urged by broadening the areas of the EU–Greenland collaboration. Thus, in 2006 the Commission of the European Communities submitted a proposal that a new comprehensive partnership with Greenland should be rooted in adoption of a new Greenland OCT decision based on Article 187 of the EC Treaty, which will regulate cooperation not related to fisheries, and the conclusion of a new Fisheries Partnership Agreement negotiated in accordance with general rules and principles applying to such agreements. Consequently in 2006 a new partnership between Greenland and the EU was strengthened and affirmed in a Joint European Community–Denmark–Greenland declaration, the EU Council decision on the relations between the parties, and a new Fisheries Partnership Agreement. Greenland–EU collaboration was further extended in areas other than fisheries (e.g., energy, tourism, research, mineral resources, culture, food safety, education, and training). Moreover, the EU Council's decision on relations between the European Community and Greenland and Denmark opened the possibility for the adoption of a programming document for the sustainable development of Greenland with support from the EU budget in the period of 2007–13. Since 1985 Greenland received development aid from the EU via the Fisheries Agreement and the successive fishery protocols instead of getting financial assistance through the European Development Fund (EDF). However, this situation has changed in 2006 with adoption of a new Greenland OCT decision that applies rules analogous to those of other OCTs that benefit from a territorial allocation from the EDF.[78]

Greenland–EU Fishery Relations

Fishery interests are a cornerstone of Greenland–EEC/EU relations. In light of a new Greenland–EU comprehensive partnership, on 1 January 2007 the Fisheries Partnership Agreement replaced the previous Fisheries Agreement, which had been in force since 1985.[79] The new deal reflects more adequately the system of payments from the EU to Greenland and their correspondence to actual fishery possibilities in Greenland's waters. It includes broader priorities in developing cooperation in the fisheries sector (e.g., sustainable management of fish stocks, enhancing scientific research and training) and provides fishing arrangements with regard to several species in Greenlandic waters. In addition to the EU financial contribution, substantial payment is expected to be collected from shipowners' licence fees.[80]

It is revealing to explore the developments that gradually led to these changes in fishery policy. In 1985 the framework Agreement on Fisheries between the EEC, the government of Denmark, the home rule government,[81] and the Fisheries Protocol[82] came into force. Fishing forms a substantial part of Greenland's economy. The framework Agreement on Fisheries established the principles and rules for regulating the fishing activities in Greenland's waters by vessels that fly the flag of, and are registered in, a member state of the EEC.[83] In return for the potential catch realized under this agreement, the EEC agreed to pay Greenland financial compensation as fixed in the implementation protocol.[84] Since 1985, there have been several fishery protocols concluded by the EU and the governments of Denmark and Greenland. Protocols specified the EEC/EU quotas and the annual compensation to be paid to Greenland for access to fishing areas in its exclusive economic zone. The Fourth Protocol, which was in force from 1 January 2001 to 31 December 2006, was criticized by EU member states for, among other things, providing Greenland with generous financial compensation despite the fact that catch quotas for fishing in Greenlandic waters were not met.[85]

Fishery relations between Greenland and the EU are the subject of much EU legislation. Before the new Fisheries Partnership Agreement came into force in 2007, a number of changes have been made that intended to improve the relationship between the parties and took into account the special development needs of Greenland's economy, including the vital importance of the fishery, and broader cooperation between Greenland and Europe. Greenland and the EU share mutual interests in managing fishery policies that make a joint contribution to the Greenlandic and EU economies.

Greenland and the Northern Dimension of the EU Policies

Launched in 1999, the Northern Dimension is an EU policy initiative that focuses on trans-regional and cross-border collaboration to draw the attention of the EU's members to Northern Europe and to develop cooperation with northwestern Russia and Northern Europe.[86] It aims at addressing the regional development challenges of Northern Europe, such as harsh climatic conditions, long distances, widespread disparities in living standards within the region, environmental challenges including problems with nuclear waste and waste-water management, insufficient transport, and poor border crossing facilities.[87] Framed and implemented in a number of documents, the Northern Dimension initiative has become a well-established part of policy making within the EU and in the partner countries (i.e., Iceland, Norway, the Russian Federation).[88] It plays an important role in enhancing integration and collaboration within the Northern region. Greenland has a unique position as a bridge between the Arctic region and the EU. As such, in 1999 the Greenlandic government presented the idea of emphasizing the Arctic dimension of EU policies by introducing the 'Arctic Window' into the EU's Northern Dimension. Greenland considers the Arctic Window the political space within the Northern Dimension where the Arctic nations and the EU share mutual interests. This initiative should help build a circumpolar dialogue on Arctic policies and initiatives and enhance Arctic–Northern Europe cooperative structures.[89]

At the first EU Ministerial Conference on the Northern Dimension, the Arctic Window was seen as an additional reason for fostering close links between the EU and Arctic jurisdictions, with a particular focus on indigenous people in the Northern Dimension region.[90] In order to define the main priorities of this cooperation, the home rule government produced a report on the Arctic Window. This document identifies the following as key areas of Arctic–EU collaboration: trade and industry in the Arctic, the Arctic environment, cross-border pollution, natural living resources, human resources development, telecommunications, research, Arctic know-how, and regional and cross-border cooperation.[91] Greenland regards its participation in the European Union's Northern Dimension policy as a political privilege that allows for involvement in the EU and contributes to that organization's initiatives.[92]

The Greenlandic authorities want the EU to become a constructive partner in supporting Greenlandic and Arctic interests even on the legislative level.[93] This development is an important milestone in strengthening relations between Greenland and Europe. It is also crucial for safeguarding common interests within the Arctic, dealing with structural and development needs of Greenland, and addressing the cultural, social, and economic challenges facing the Inuit of Greenland.[94] Greenland's relatively active participation in Nordic collaboration and its developed relations with the supranational institutions and mechanisms of the EU have added unique elements to the island's forms of international cooperation.

Although there is no direct link between Nunavut and the EU initiatives, Canada has observer status in the Northern Dimension and reflects its Arctic interests by participating in the ministerial and the senior official meetings. But there is more to the cooperation and acknowledgment of shared interests between the EU and Canada vis-à-vis the Arctic. There are implications for Nunavummiut from the implementation of *The Northern Dimension of Canada's Foreign Policy*, which emphasized the importance of Canada–EU Northern cooperation, and its 2005 evaluation that outlined Canada's progress in EU–Circumpolar North collaboration, as well as joint Canada–EU statements on Northern cooperation, defence, and security.[95] According to the EU–Canada Partnership Agenda, both parties are committed to fostering their Northern Dimension policies through coordinated actions in the field of environmental, health, and social issues; strengthening links in education via the University of the Arctic; enhancing cooperation in economic development, legal instruments, transportation, and communications; and deepening collaboration on cultural matters to ensure the multilateral promotion of recognition of cultural diversity.[96] These Canada–EU initiatives on the Northern Dimension are significant for Nunavut and suggest its greater participation in the implementation of Canada's foreign policy as it applies to the Arctic.

Nunavut and Greenland, as Arctic regions, share many similar challenges and problems, some of which can be solved by Arctic cooperation. As former premier of Greenland Jonathan Motzfeldt emphasized:

> We look to high-level forums such as the Arctic Council, the European Union, the Nordic Council of Ministers and others to support our efforts in protecting and developing the Arctic. We believe that our lessons learned may be of use to others. There are many similarities in the problems facing the Arctic part of Russia, in the Arctic parts of the EU, Greenland or Canada. Greenland therefore strongly supports northern and arctic bridge building. We have many mutual problems and challenges calling for the same type of solutions or rather, solutions based on cooperation.[97]

Thus, the next section focuses on Greenland's and Nunavut's representation in the Arctic collaboration.

Greenland and Nunavut in the Arctic Cooperation

Although international cooperation in the Arctic dates back to the nineteenth century, during the past few decades there has been enormous growth in the development of international initiatives centred on recognizing the Arctic as a distinct region.[98] The region is seen as an arena for the promotion and protection of numerous interests, which vary from environmental concerns to issues of Arctic governance and indigenous peoples' rights.[99] The Arctic has become an important area of international cooperation for both institutional and informal actions.[100] The establishment of the Arctic Council in 1996 by the eight Arctic states (Canada, Denmark, Finland, Iceland, Norway, the Russian Federation, Sweden, and the United States) is one example of an informal arrangement.[101] Having emerged as a result of efforts of various stakeholders, and based on a Canadian initiative, the Arctic Council was created as a high-level forum for promoting cooperation, coordination, and interaction among Arctic governments, indigenous communities, and other Northern residents on common Arctic issues.[102] In particular, these include issues of environmental protection and sustainable development in the Arctic; the dissemination of information; encouraging education and promoting interest in Arctic-related matters; and coordinating and overseeing activities established under specific Arctic programs.[103] At the end of its meetings, the Arctic Council issues 'soft-law' declarations and recommendations for further action.[104] Conducted under the auspices of the Arctic Council, the *Arctic Human Development Report* and the *Arctic Climate Impact Assessment Report* are examples of the council's initiatives.[105] Established as a 'high-level forum,' the Arctic Council lacks a legal personality and cannot be classified as an international organization under international law. This affects the mode of the council's operation. Its work is based on consensus.[106] Further, at the time of writing, it does not have a permanent administrative structure or resources of its own.[107]

Although it has been criticized for its limited organizational capacity, lack of authority to make binding decisions, severe shortage of financial and other resources, and increasing overlap in its activities with other international actors in the Arctic region, the Arctic Council plays an important role as a voice of the Arctic.[108] The Inuit of Greenland and Nunavut exercise their mandate in the Arctic Council via the Inuit Circumpolar Council (ICC), which holds the status of permanent participant. The ICC partakes in activities and consultations with the Arctic indigenous representatives within the Arctic Council.[109] The ICC can participate in all meetings and activities of the Arctic Council, and 'may be represented by a head of delegation and such other representatives as each Arctic State and Permanent Participant deems necessary.'[110] Ministerial meetings of the council are held in consultation with the permanent participants. In addition, the ICC can make proposals to the Arctic Council regarding cooperative activities.[111] The Indigenous Peoples Secretariat (IPS) functions within the Arctic Council to provide technical support to facilitate the work of the permanent participants.[112] Though the ICC does not have the status of a member state in the Arctic Council, its jurisdiction is similar.[113] The Arctic Council, through creating the category of permanent participant, considers the aspirations, needs, and opinions of Arctic indigenous residents in its activity. This involvement should bring about a new role for the participation of subnational entities in Arctic international cooperation. Although the perception of the Arctic Council as an intergovernmental structure of national member states does not allow much room for Nunavut's or Greenland's involvement via the ICC, the role of the latter should not be underestimated.[114] Active Inuit participation and support for the council's projects indicate strong potential for further indigenous peoples' collaborative initiatives in the Circumpolar North. Furthermore, according to some authorities, the work of the Arctic Council on the soft-law approach provides indigenous peoples with a better standing in intergovernmental cooperation and opens up more of an opportunity for international representation.[115]

The Inuit are involved in the activities of intrastate, intergovernmental, interparliamentary, and supranational forms of international cooperation via the Nordic Council, the Nordic Council of Ministers, the EU, the Arctic Council, and other forums.[116] This involvement is challenged and limited by the dominance of national states' doctrines and the limited legal capacity of subnational entities in international law. Greenland's and Nunavut's participation in the institutional complex of the Arctic is not based on a legally binding regime, and instead relies upon informal mechanisms. There are no adequate international or domestic regulatory provisions legalizing the international activity of Greenland and Nunavut. However, despite fragmentation and relatively weak institutional organization in the Arctic, non-state actors such as the Inuit Circumpolar Council are able to influence and express their interests within intergovernmental settings, thus enhancing the Inuit's voice in international forums. The level to which international cooperation between indigenous peoples can be promoted on a non-governmental level is closely connected with the modern phenomenon of 'indigenous internationalism,' 'Inuitism,' or 'Pan-Inuit' collaboration, to which I now turn.[117]

Indigenous Internationalism and the Inuit of Greenland and Nunavut

Indigenous internationalism is the cooperation of indigenous peoples with each other across or beyond national borders to share ideas, information, and inspiration; to concert moral and political influence on national governments and international bodies; and to establish better international standards for themselves and other indigenous peoples in matters of shared or universal interest.

Peter Jull

Inuit cooperation across Alaska, Canada, Greenland, and Chukotka and with other indigenous peoples has developed in a variety of forms. The Inuit of Nunavut and Greenland are geographic neighbours whose homelands and culture share similar natural features and characteristics. Their desire to foster and maintain extensive cultural, personal, and social relations led them to sign[118] the Memorandum of Understanding on Cooperation in 2000.[119]

Cooperation in several areas was given high priority. These areas included human resources, staff training, and professional development; sustainable management of the polar bear population; mutual growth in trade via private business initiatives and deeper collaboration among business schools, councils, networking organizations, tourist councils, trade unions, and interest organizations[120] common to both constituencies; sustainable fisheries management in their common waters; exchange of expertise in energy conservation and waste disposal; and collaboration between Statistics Greenland and Nunavut on data exchange and related studies.[121] The cooperation between Nunavut and Greenland has been attested to by the signing of other documents of mutual interest, visits by the premiers and other government officials, conferences and workshops, and cultural, trade, and educational ex-changes.[122]

Transborder or multilateral Inuit cooperation, as a form of indigenous internationalism, is distinguished by Inuit participation in indigenous peoples' organizations, governmental and parliamentary organizations, and non-governmental organizations (NGOs).[123] Today the Inuit Circumpolar Council provides a major international collective voice for more than 155,000 Inuit from Canada, Alaska, Greenland, and the Chukotka Peninsula. Having emerged in 1976 as an outcome of the indigenous internationalism movement, it obtained official status in June 1977 at the first ICC General Assembly.[124] The ICC came into being as a formal organization three years later, when the fifty-four delegates to the second ICC general assembly voted unanimously to adopt its charter.[125] According to article 3 of this document:

> the purposes of the Conference are: a) to strengthen unity among the Inuit of the Circumpolar region; b) to promote Inuit rights and interests on the international level; c) to ensure Inuit participation in political, economic, and social institutions ... [they] deem relevant; d) to promote greater self-sufficiency among the Inuit in the Circumpolar region; e) to ensure the endurance and growth of Inuit culture and societies for both present and future generations; f) to promote long-term management and protection of arctic and sub-arctic wildlife, environment and biological productivity; and g) to promote wise management and use of non-renewable resources in the Circumpolar region, incorporating such resources in the present and future development of Inuit economies, taking into account other Inuit interests.[126]

The ICC has become a leading organization in the Arctic in promoting international collaboration among the Inuit and other indigenous peoples of the world.[127] The scope of its activities, its achievements in advancing indigenous peoples' rights and interests, and its advocacy of policies safeguarding issues of importance to the Circumpolar region are impressive.[128] They cover Inuit rights on the national and international level, security, environmental, social, economic, cultural, educational, and scientific issues, communications, international development and trade, sustainable development, and human rights.[129] The ICC's strong stand on fighting climate change is breaking new ground in the environmental rights of indigenous peoples. Of particular significance in this regard is the ICC's petition to the Inter-American Commission on Human Rights against the United States for its failure to protect the environment and for violation of the human rights of people living beyond its borders, undertaken in response to human-induced climate change that threatens the survival of the Inuit and infringes on their environmental and other human rights.[130]

In 1983 the ICC was granted consultative status category 2 of a nongovernmental organization within the Economic and Social Council (ECOSOC) of the United Nations.[131] Despite its limited advisory status and lack of voting rights, the ICC has obtained a solid mandate for promoting Inuit/indigenous rights within the UN.[132] For example, it contributed to the establishment in 2000 of the UN Permanent Forum on Indigenous Issues, and it took part in the development of the UN Draft Declaration on the Rights of Indigenous Peoples, which was adopted by the UN Human Rights Council in 2006.[133]

The ICC's NGO status within the UN has advantages and disadvantages.[134] For now, the ICC plays an increasingly influential role in international public policy through its participation in numerous international organizations and forums. Because of its non-governmental nature, it is more effective than government bodies in lobbying national governments. Embracing the Inuit of four countries and based on Inuit culture, the ICC is a uniquely trans-Arctic NGO.[135] It was able to enhance a new diplomacy in the Circumpolar North by being 'a small organization whose voice is strong globally.'[136] Indigenous internationalism and the ICC's influential role prove that 'Inuit have a legitimate, extensive and varied role to fulfill in international matters.'[137] The work of the ICC shows that Inuit of Canada, Greenland, Alaska, and Chukotka are succeeding in their international activities and are often ahead of national governments in their vision of indigenous needs and the challenges of the Arctic rim.

The extensive international involvement of the Inuit of Greenland and Nunavut in intrastate, transnational, global, and indigenous politics is a manifestation of a new era in international relations development, and shows that these subnational entities are gradually becoming de facto subjects of international law. The evolution of Greenland's home rule system and a gradual increase in Nunavut's jurisdictional capabilities in the process of devolution of powers from Ottawa to the territory will further speed up the demand for the participation of these entities in international forums. This demand has also been prompted by the need for stronger representation of these entities in international bodies as a countermeasure against possible neglect and non-consideration by the mother states in fulfilling their international obligations.[138] These activities do not challenge the sovereignty of the former colonizers. However, they do require a new approach in national doctrines and international and domestic legal regimes regarding the legal personality and role of subnational regions in international affairs. The forms of Greenland's and Nunavut's involvement in international relations show that national jurisdiction in external affairs is transferable to subnational entities to some degree. This transferability can be legally regulated to safeguard Greenland's and Nunavut's interests in those areas of international relations that do not conflict with the management of Danish and Canadian foreign affairs. Currently, Nunavut has less of an interest in active participation in international policies because it is preoccupied with building its new government. Greenland has more specific priorities in this regard. Due to the structural, financial, and legal limitations on the current institutions of Nordic and Arctic cooperation, and constraints on the development of indigenous internationalism, these areas are less realistic arenas for Greenland or Nunavut to legitimate their international policy. Thus, international activities in trade and environmental policy issues will most likely become a priority for Greenland and Nunavut.[139]

Given their lack of jurisdictional power in decision-making processes and the fact that most of their participation in international forums is with only an advisory mandate, Greenland and Nunavut have a limited role to play in the institutional complex of the Arctic. Despite their active participation in Arctic collaboration, their potential for global impact is extremely small. At the same time, the impact of global issues (e.g., climate change, pollution, security, international trade) on the development of Greenland's and Nunavut's governance systems means that their authorities need to develop strategies and legal mechanisms to deal with the external challenges they face. Bogi Eliasen has argued, on the basis of empirical data, that the international and global community is open to flexible solutions to deal with non-sovereign polities, and a majority of international organizations would allow some form of full or associate membership to entities such as Greenland.[140]

According to some authorities, the legal possibility for recognition of indigenous internationalism can be rooted in the external aspects of the right to self-determination that do not entail secession. The representation and participation of the Inuit of Greenland and Nunavut in activities that transcend state boundaries can be regarded as an external dimension of this right.[141] However, it can be argued that this international activity and participatory rights of the Inuit of Greenland and Nunavut in international forums constitute a part of their internal right to self-determination and evolving right to autonomy, as this jurisdiction is crucial for addressing local matters and strengthening self-government. Some of the provisions of the Authorization Act (Greenland), discussed earlier in this chapter, recognize this right.

Greenland, Nunavut, and Defence and Security Policy

We do not wish our traditional territories to be treated as a strategic military and combat zone between Eastern and Western alliances. For thousands of years, Inuit have used and continue to use the lands, waters and sea ice in circumpolar regions. As aboriginal people, we are the Arctic's legitimate spokespersons.

Since our northern lands and communities transcend the boundaries of the four countries, we are in a unique position to promote peace, security and arms control objectives among states of the Arctic Rim.

Mary Simon

Because of strategic military interests, Inuit lands are vulnerable to militarization, missile defence plans, and other security/defence doctrines of their respective states and outside countries. Traditionally, jurisdiction in defence and security policy is the domain of national states. Significant changes in the approaches to security, caused by the end of the Cold War, technological developments, and the emergence of politically evolving Arctic entities, call into question the absolute non-transferability of security jurisdiction to subnational territories where the legitimate interests of those units are concerned.[142] In terms of the legal scope of autonomy and the competence of the Greenlandic and Nunavut governments, the following questions emerge: Is the fate of the Inuit homelands in the hands of Southern alliances and politicians, or of the Northern communities and governments themselves? Should citizens of the subnational entities of Greenland and Nunavut have some legal capacity in national defence and security policies when these policies concern or affect their homelands? Should security matters become a legitimate part of the home rule or Nunavut jurisdictions, or can they be regulated by informal methods, such as consultation, shared advisory councils, or meetings? These questions are linked to the issue of the extent to which there should be special consideration for the Northern indigenous peoples in the framework of the public governance systems.

Home rule in Greenland is developing greater competence in the area of external affairs policy, and the Nunavut system will eventually develop more extensive involvement in this area as well. Possible jurisdiction in security matters is a part of this evolution. In light of the principal elements of Greenland's and Nunavut's evolving interest in security policy, their governments should have greater opportunities for participating in the security agenda of their national states as it relates to the Arctic region. Moreover, this activity of the Nunavut and Greenland authorities should be legally regulated. The potential strategic-political importance of Greenland and Nunavut entitles their authorities to greater cooperation with national agencies on security matters. There is no challenge to Canadian or Danish sovereignty caused by Nunavut's or Greenland's representation in the security decision-making process regarding their lands. In light of new international political realities, the legal understanding of autonomy of Greenland and Nunavut has to be reassessed with respect to their jurisdiction in security issues, because curently the effectiveness and viability of their governance are challenged by the insufficient powers of local authorities to act on security matters. Thus, in its findings, the Greenland Commission on Self-Governance has emphasized that security policy should become a legitimate part of Greenland's jurisdiction, that Greenlandic authorities should participate in formulating defence and security agendas that concern Greenland, and these authorities should be able to contribute a Greenlandic perspective to the international security policy debate in matters of the common security of the realm as a share of mutual responsibility for Denmark's security.[143] An important step in this direction was the 2003 joint Danish–Greenlandic declaration on the involvement of Greenland authorities in foreign and security matters of significance to Greenland. This partnership-cooperation approach was further enhanced in 2004 with the modernization of the 1951 Defence Agreement, the upgrade of the Thule air base, and the signing of several important declarations. However, the Authorization Act of 2005, which enabled Greenland to conclude international agreements in certain areas on behalf of the Danish kingdom, does not apply to agreements affecting defence and security matters.

Greenland's and Nunavut's Interests in Defence and Security Policy

I am not going to analyse Greenland's and Nunavut's security policies within the broad frameworks used by some scholars within the last decades.[144] Instead, I mean to concentrate on defence issues that affect the development and livelihood of the citizens of Greenland and Nunavut. I will attempt, on the basis of existing facts, to show why it is of vital importance that these regions maintain some jurisdiction in defence policies regarding their lands. In so doing, a brief overview of the military significance of these territories is appropriate.

Being major parts of the Canadian North and the Arctic territory of

Denmark, Nunavut and Greenland have been strategically important because 'the Arctic has gradually been transformed from a *military vacuum* prior to World War II, to a *military flank* in the 1950–70 period, and a *military front* in the 1980s.'[145] Though 'Canadians have never been fully wedded to the primacy of a military understanding of security affairs,'[146] the Canadian military has played a definitive role in establishing Canadian sovereignty over the Arctic frontier by developing Northern infrastructure and by assigning military responsibility to the Canadian forces in the North.[147] Observers differ on the seriousness of attempts by the military to consult with or engage indigenous people in this assertion of sovereignty. However, it is clear that, since the negotiation of the NLCA, Inuit provide essential information before defence activities occur.[148]

Greenland and the NWT/Nunavut had to face similar challenges connected with the militarization of their regions. Besides, both entities share similar interests for involvement in security developments in the Arctic when it concerns their lands. Both Greenland and Nunavut are part of NATO member states, and Greenland and the NWT/Nunavut have been regarded through the lens of the alliance's security interests. Indeed, Denmark's main contribution to the security of NATO was through Greenland.[149] Thus, Greenland has far-reaching interests in the alliance's security policies. In the future it may seek to obtain first-hand information from NATO and the possible accreditation of the home rule's representative to its headquarters.[150] Modest Danish and Canadian defence abilities led to the extensive 'military discovery' of Greenland by the United States, and provided a long-term American presence in the Canadian Arctic, causing Canada's quasi-dependence on the military potential of its southern neighbour. Greenland and, to a lesser extent, the NWT/Nunavut have become integrated into American defence plans. Although this forced marriage has been regarded as a threat to Inuit sovereignty over their lands and has posed challenges to Canadian sovereignty in the North, it also had the positive effect of mobilizing Canadian civil activity on behalf of the Inuit.[151]

Generally, military activity in Greenland is alien to Inuit tradition. In the words of Greenlander Henrik Lund, then the mayor of Qaqortoq, war and the means of mass destruction are historically alien to Greenlanders, who are pacifists and cannot accept attitudes leading to the eradication of life that are a possible threat to the people.[152] This position is supported by Willy Østreng, who also emphasizes that Inuit tradition, the core value of which is civility, influences and shapes Greenlandic security policy. At the same time, Greenland and Nunavut, having experienced the consequences of the Second World War and the Cold War, should have developed some 'immunity' against militarization. Greenland's experience shows that there can be an external military threat to the island, and thus the government of Greenland must be involved in security policies.[153] The development of Nunavut, the increasing powers of Greenlandic authorities, and both territories' growing security concerns mean that national defence policies can no longer ignore the opinions of Greenlanders or the Nunavummiut.[154]

The Inuit Circumpolar Conference (now Council) has elaborated a wide range of measures to advance security and peace objectives in the Circumpolar North.[155] Representatives of the Inuit have developed a concept of sustainable security as an alternative to militarization.[156] These measures correspond to Greenland's and Nunavut's interests in security policies, which can be summarized as the right of Greenland's and Nunavut's authorities to be informed about all questions relating to the security policies regarding their homelands, waters (including offshore), ice, and air space; the protection of game and other limited resources from any sort of military activity; security for the population from any military actions on Inuit territories; the right of Nunavut's and Greenland's authorities to be included in the decision-making processes and formulation of national defence policies that directly or indirectly concern these Arctic entities; and the possibility of changes in legislation to enable Greenland and Nunavut to influence Denmark's and Canada's security policies, when relevant.[157]

The Greenland Commission on Self-Governance suggested evaluating Greenland's security through the prism of the geographical position of the island, including military aspects and soft security policy.[158] One can argue that the efficiency of the Greenlandic and Nunavut systems of governance is not conditioned by their possible jurisdiction in defence matters. Besides, economic and environmental security issues are of vital importance for Greenland and Nunavut.[159] In the meantime, there are direct connections between defence matters and questions of a safe environment and economic viability. Further economic development of Greenland and Nunavut is linked to defence/security policies. There is an interdependence of local economies on any fluctuation in the Arctic environment, which can have an impact on employment opportunities for Northern residents, game profits, hunting, fishing, climate change, and the prices on renewable and non-renewable resources. The scope of Nunavut's and Greenland's jurisdiction in matters related to the security of the territories is thus important.

Are there any grounds for legitimating the voices of Nunavut and Greenland in security and defence issues related to their lands? A historical perspective on the role of Inuit homelands in the defence strategies of superpowers and their national states shows that there is. The strategic importance of Greenland and Nunavut has fluctuated since the end of the Second World War, owing to the changes in the doctrines of the superpowers, technological developments, military capabilities, and competing East–West alliances. With the occupation of Denmark by the Germans in 1940, Greenland's strategic location took on international importance and acquired particular military significance to the United States.[160] Greenland's security was threatened by Germany's invasion of the Danish kingdom. Consequently, 'in May 1940 the Greenlandic authorities requested American protection and a US consulate was opened in Godthaab. By July 1940 the US Coastguard ship *Campbell* had moved to Ivigtut where some of its crew guarded the cryolite mines, a source of aluminium for the United States. After the Germans had extended their war-zone to the east coast of Greenland in March 1941, President Roosevelt allocated $5 million for the construction of air bases in Greenland.'[161] On 9 April 1941, the Danish government signed an agreement with the American government, allowing the latter 'almost unlimited rights to establish bases and military installations in Greenland.'[162] This led to the establishment of thirteen American army and four naval bases on the island.[163]

After the Second World War, the Cold War strengthened American military interests in Greenland. In 1946 the United States made an official offer to Denmark to purchase the island for $US100 million with the purpose of establishing military bases that could be used in the event of attack.[164] It is not clear whether the offer was turned down by the Danish government or simply ignored. With Danish membership in NATO in 1949, the U.S. request for long-term rights to existing military facilities in Greenland and the possibility of building new ones was satisfied.[165] This, in turn led to the signing of a new U.S.–Danish defence agreement in 1951.[166] As part of the implementation of the North Atlantic Treaty, the agreement set up a joint Danish–U.S. defence of Greenland under the national flags of both countries. It provided the American armed forces, including ships and aircraft, with free access to strategic facilities on the island.[167] Greenland's long-term concerns with and negotiations towards revising the agreement of 1951 and the upgrading of the only remaining military installation in the northwest of Greenland (the Thule base) form the crux of Greenlandic–Danish–American security policy interests today.[168]

Since its construction in 1951–2, the Thule air base has been the centrepiece of the American presence in Greenland.[169] During the Cold War, Thule's significance was increased by the installation and modernization of the early warning radar system with its large coverage capacity in the event of a nuclear attack.[170] The base has been crucial in the American missile-defence program.[171] In 2000 an American delegation visited Greenland and consulted with Greenlandic authorities regarding the upgrade of the Thule radar as part of the U.S. anti-missile defence shield scheme. As Henriette Rasmussen notes, 'The US visit, derided by one newsweekly as the American "Charmoffensiv," was one of only several high level diplomatic visits to Greenland (including the French foreign minister and the Russian ambassador to Denmark) that highlighted the strategic importance of the Thule radar should the US proceed with a national missile defense.'[172]

The importance of the Thule base to the United States is also evident in comments President George W. Bush made in his letter to the premier of Greenland in 2001: 'We will undoubtedly face a number of challenges in the years ahead. Like you, I am eager to work together on issues of mutual concern, like the base at Thule.'[173] Thule's significance can further be seen in numerous overtures made by the Bush administration to the Danish government, seeking permission to upgrade the base as part of the U.S. missile defence plans.[174] In 2002 the U.S. government asked Denmark to open negotiations on the future use of the base. Greenlandic representatives met with the U.S. secretary of state and the Danish minister of foreign affairs in Washington.[175] Greenlanders suggested that they would negotiate on any further upgrade of the Thule radar facility only if the renewal of the outdated agreement of 1951 could be negotiated in full partnership with the home rule government.[176] In 2004 an agreement on the upgrade of the base was reached. On 6 August 2004 an agreement to modernize the 1951 Defence Agreement, a declaration on environmental cooperation in Greenland, and a declaration on economic and technical cooperation were signed in Greenland by representatives of the American, Danish, and Greenlandic authorities.[177] The joint committee met in Nuuk on 5–6 October 2004 to establish further cooperation and concrete results in the framework of the signed agreements. A new partnership between the United States, Greenland, and Denmark was further enhanced in the subsequent meetings of the joint committee in Washington (2005) and Copenhagen (2006).[178] These instances show that Greenland is taking an active step towards greater independence in security and foreign affairs.

The Thule issue is extremely sensitive to Greenlanders for a number of reasons.[179] In May 1953, twenty-seven Inughuit families were relocated, or 'strategically banished,' from the community of Uummannaq (Dundas) mainly to the community of Qaannaq in order to provide additional space for the Thule air base.[180] This relocation was done without the consent of the local population, and the rights of Inuit were violated through appropriation of their hunting lands and the negligence of the Danish state in failing to compensate them for their economic losses. Lars Nordskov Nielsen, the former Danish ombudsman, concluded that the Danish–American agreement of 1951 was presented to the Folketing with inadequate information. The establishment of the base in 1951 took place without reasonably informing the local population or hearing their views on the matter. After the base was built, the authorities did not evaluate its economic consequences for the local population, nor did they offer them compensation.[181] In 1996 the Inughuit formed an association, Hingitaq 53, which launched a lawsuit against the Danish government. As Aqqaluk Lynge noted, 'They simply asked for their land back and to be justly compensated for the decades of lost hunting, whaling and gathering. They asked for justice for having been taken from a region that was not only rich in living resources, but one to which they were intimately linked. They had a deep understanding of the Uummannaq environment, developed over thousands of years, which included knowledge of its ocean currents, animal migration patterns, whale movements, and other environmental features required for survival.'[182]

On 20 August 1999 the High Court of Eastern Denmark rendered its decision:

> The relocation was decided upon and carried out in such a manner and under such conditions which meant a serious interference with the peoples who were moved from the settlement ... The High Court finds that in the stated circumstances, the interference must be considered an unlawful violation of the peoples of Uummannaq ... The loss to the Thule Tribe caused by lost and diminished hunting rights in connection with the establishment of the base and the relocation of the peoples can thus fairly be fixed at 500,000 Danish Kroner.[183]

While the court upheld the Inuit's claim for financial compensation for the losses suffered by the Thule people, it did not allow the hunters to return to their old settlements or regain their lost territories.[184] Yet, according to A. Lynge, the Inughuit must be allowed to return to Uummannaq. 'Otherwise, they will perish as a people.'[185] The population of Uummannaq appealed to the Supreme Court in October 1999. Furthermore, with regards to this relocation a representation was made in November of that year by the national confederation of trade unions of Greenland – Sulinermik Inuussutissarsiuteqartut Kattuffiat (organization of people who live by wage-earning) – to the International Labour Organization concerning Denmark's non-observance of the Indigenous and Tribal Peoples Convention, 1989 (No. 169).[186]

The Supreme Court of Denmark's ruling on 28 November 2003 did not acknowledge the Inughuit's right to return.[187] The court found that 'the population in the Thule district shares the same conditions as the rest of the Greenlandic people and does not differ from it in any other relevant respects.'[188] The Inughuit's land claim was not recognized, as 'the land traditionally occupied by the Inuit people has been identified and consists of the entire territory of Greenland.'[189] Furthermore, the court ruled that the Thule base had been established legally.[190] Finally, the Thule tribe's claim for compensation remained unchanged at DKK 500,000.[191] In May 2004 the members of Hingitaq 53 took their case to the European Court of Human Rights, seeking the right to return to their hunting and fishing grounds.[192] It should be noted that in February 2003 an agreement had been signed between the U.S., Danish, and Greenlandic governments allowing for the Inughuit's right of return to the Uummannaq peninsula.[193] However, this step was protested by several Inuit organizations because the Inughuit did not participate in the negotiations for the agreement and only a small portion of the hunting land was designated for their return.[194]

The Thule issue is crucial for Greenlanders because of the environmental impact of military installations on Inuit hunting. Radioactive pollution has already resulted from an incident on 21 January 1968, 'when an American B-52 Stratofortress carrying four hydrogen bombs crashed on the ice in Bylot Sound near the Thule base.'[195] Greenlandic and Danish workers did the cleanup after the crash without any protective equipment. They even made tea using snow contaminated from the crash.[196] Danish and American authorities agreed 'that between 500g and 1.8 kg of plutonium – enough for a whole bomb' – was missing.[197] Although official Danish policy did not allow nuclear weapons on the territory of Denmark, the Thule air base was used by U.S. aircraft for stationing and transporting nuclear weapons, with the informal consent of the Danish government.[198]

The state of Danish–American relations and the Danish manipulation of the 'Thule card' to please U.S. military interests prompted Greenland's authorities to seek participation in security issues without the intervention of Denmark.[199] Greenlanders were concerned that in the event of war, their territory would have been destroyed in a nuclear attack. The 'Thule issue' and U.S. strategic interests in Greenland show how vulnerable Greenland's position is and how weak the home rule system can be in challenging the superpower's policies. Despite Greenland's strategic military importance, the adoption of an international convention on the demilitarization of Greenland could be a solution.[200] However, this would be hard to achieve because of Danish membership in NATO and American interests in upgrading Thule. The Americans put pressure on Denmark and Greenland to finalize an agreement to upgrade Thule. Greenland wanted compensation for the upgrade. The United States categorically rejected this demand, and the agreement was revised without any financial compensation.[201] Some Greenlandic authorities have admitted that they had no choice but to support the modernization of the 1951 Defence Agreement by allowing the radar upgrade at Thule. As Mikaela Engell, then Greenland's deputy minister of foreign affairs points out, 'If Greenland had opposed the Thule upgrade, then the U.S. might have closed down the base entirely and headed off to Canada ... and we would lose any interest for the Americans.'[202]

Like Greenland, the Canadian Arctic (including what has come to be known as the territory of Nunavut) became a centre of military activity after the Second World War.[203] In 1947 Prime Minister Mackenzie King announced Canada's cooperation with the United States on Northern defence and Arctic research.[204] This meant that, 'for the remainder of the 1940's and throughout the 1950's, Canada's Arctic Islands would witness a flurry of military and civilian activity: joint exercises, the establishment of meteorological stations, and ultimately the creation of the Distant Early Warning (DEW) Line, and the North American Air Defence (NORAD) Command.'[205]

Not unlike the situation in Greenland, Canada's Arctic involvement in defence was a product of U.S. strategic concerns and the military's 'discovery' of the North. As Kenneth Eyre concludes, 'the United States used the Canadian North to carry the war to the enemy ... The United States, its troops, its money, its construction firms and its employees dominated the North. All of what the United States did – or caused to be done – occurred beyond the sight of ordinary Canadians; much of what they did occurred beyond the sight of even the Canadian government, despite not insignificant attempts to regulate and monitor these activities.'[206]

These activities were similar to what Denmark had faced with the presence of the U.S. military bases in Greenland. There were also similar military initiatives, such as the construction of the Distant Early Warning (DEW) Line, which stretched into northern Alaska, Canada's High Arctic, and eastern Greenland.[207] The DEW agreement, signed between the United States and Canada in 1955, in many ways paralleled the Danish–U.S. agreement of 1951. However, the DEW agreement contained some regulations regarding the Inuit. It addressed the issues of Inuit contact with outsiders, removal of Inuit settlements, protection of hunting grounds and burial places, employment possibilities, and the disposal of waste, supplies, and materials used by the military facilities.[208] Thus, if there were a need for extra military in-stallations, the United States would be entitled to remove Inuit settlements or burial grounds with the consent of the Department of Northern Affairs and National Resources.[209] There could even be a 'Canadian Thule.'[210] Furthermore, some parallels with the Thule tribe's relocation in Greenland can be drawn with the Canadian Inuit relocation of 1953, when the Inuit from Northern Quebec were relocated to the High Eastern Arctic to assert Canadian sovereignty, which was being challenged by American military activity.[211]

U.S. military presence, airfields, maps, roads, and construction played a crucial role in the opening up and development of the Canadian North for the projects of non-Northerners and had a significant impact on the economic development of Greenland.[212] However, Greenlanders continue to have a negative image of possible militarization of their lands, although many have resigned themselves to eventual cooperation with the United States.[213] Furthermore, environmental issues caused by military actions in the Arctic – contamination caused by inadequate local disposal of waste, decaying equipment with heavy metals, spilled petroleum, leaking transformer oil containing PCBs, and air pollution – put the question of cleaning up the DEW Line on the political and legal agenda.[214] Fortunately in Nunavut, there have not been any crashes of airplanes carrying hydrogen bombs, but the remediation of the fifteen DEW sites located in the territory is crucial for its residents.[215] Currently, unlike Greenland, Nunavut does not consider involvement in security issues as its priority. However, this may be a challenge for the government of Nunavut in the future.

Another foreign policy issue with vital implications for the residents of both Greenland and Nunavut is the continuing dispute between Canada and Denmark over Hans Island, located halfway between Greenland and Ellesmere Island. Because of the sovereignty dispute over the island, a 1973 agreement drew the continental shelf line excluding the island.[216] The Danes declared sovereignty over the island, and the Danish flag has flown there at least in 1984, 1988, 2002, and 2004, attempting to demonstrate that Canada could not prove its sovereignty by means of effective occupation. The Canadian government disagrees with this claim and started to conduct military patrols to demonstrate its ability to enforce sovereignty.[217] Although the dispute is only about the island itself, concerns have been raised over Canada's capability to maintain sovereignty in its Arctic. There is also speculation that the Danes are being so persistent with the ownership issue because there are valuable natural resources at stake. The Danes claim that Greenlandic Inuit were using the island for centuries and that it was first discovered in 1853 by an expedition with the famous Greenlander Hans Hendrik of Fiskenæsset.[218] In September 2005 Denmark and Canada agreed to develop a protocol for managing Hans Island, revealing that both countries will continue to pursue their claim and have agreed to disagree about the island's ownership.[219] Although the dispute continues, in February 2006 the Department of Indian and Northern Affairs Canada (INAC) granted Mr John Robins a five-year prospector's permit with an exclusive right to explore the island.[220] However, in September 2006 the Canadian government seemed to take a different approach, when the Ministry of Foreign Affairs refused a permit to conduct research activities on the island to a scientist with a licence from the Nunavut government and advised the scientist to cooperate with Danish partners.[221] Some Inuit in Nunavut state that Canada can claim Hans Island on the basis of historic use by Canadian Inuit of lands on the Queen Elizabeth Islands, which include Hans Island. At the same time, Greenlanders consider Tartupaluk – their name for Hans Island – as their territory, as it was historically used by hunters from Qaanaaq, and dispute over its sovereignty means that Greenlandic hunting grounds are at stake.[222] The dispute may be settled through the United Nations.[223]

Ottawa's various statements regarding missile defence and the agreement to link the U.S. missile defence system with the North American Aerospace Defence (NORAD) Command has caused concerns among the Nunavummiut, the Nunavut Tunngavik Incorporated (NTI), and other Canadians.[224] At the time of writing, it would seem that Nunavut may not play host to U.S. missile shoot-down sites, and Canada's Arctic bases are not going to be alternatives to Thule.[225] Nonetheless, the

Northern premiers have asked for a say in any missile defence developments and involvement in any security or defence negotiations leading
to Canada's involvement in the U.S. ballistic missile defence system.[226]

However, the premier of Nunavut, Paul Okalik, has stressed that Canada's participation in the missile defence debate is a national issue.
'Nunavut only wants "a positive role" in any projects such as the BMD
that take place in or affect Nunavut.'[227] Such a role would support a
'true partnership.'[228] To this point, at least, Nunavut is not asking for
jurisdiction in security matters regarding missile defence, as it considers
this best left to the federal government. However, the 'Inuit have a role
to play in northern projects that require an understanding of the Arctic
when it comes to such fields as engineering, climatology and environmental assessment.'[229] As the premier further noted, the Nunavut Land
Claims Agreement and the government of Nunavut serve as some guarantee that future development projects will take into account both positive and negative impacts on the Inuit.

Over the last few years, the Canadian armed forces have conducted
several operations and exercises in the High Arctic and Northwest Passage to assert Canada's sovereignty.[230] In addition to logistical problems
and limited capabilities of Canadian military exercises 'to ward off
future threats to the country's sovereignty in the region,' these activities
in the territory of Nunavut raised questions of the Inuit Rangers' participation and role in such undertakings.[231] According to some sources,
the Inuit play an invaluable role in Ranger patrols, but their participation is still insufficient.[232] The role played by the Rangers in helping the
Canadian military and in maintaining Canada's sovereignty in the Arctic
cannot be underestimated. Nunavut has a Ranger patrol in each community. The Canadian Forces Northern Area (CFNA) rely on Rangers.
Their reports on suspicious activities throughout the Arctic (e.g., a sub-
marine appearance near a community) supplement periodic aerial and
satellite surveys.[233] In Greenland, similar to the Canadian case, the
assertion of sovereignty is taking place with the assistance of Greenland's commando force (GLK), which also 'undertakes responsibility
for the Sirius Patrol, Station Nord, the Air Group Vest,' and the defence
patrols.[234] Over the years, several young Greenlanders have voluntarily
joined the GLK and the Sirius Patrol. The Commission on Self-Governance suggested expanding this practice by making Greenlandic men
and women a part of the Danish defence on the island to assist in the
coast guard, the navy, fishery inspection ships, and the dog sleds of the
Sirius Patrol.[235]

As an alternative to military operations in the North, it is possible to develop what Franklyn Griffiths calls 'the practice of civility' in the Arctic.[236] Some Nunavut authorities have also emphasized that a better way for Canada to exercise its claim over the Arctic is to work with Northern citizens in making their homeland a better place to live.[237] The Home Rule Act, the NLCA, and the Nunavut Act do not include defence policy issues as a subject for gradual transferral to the Greenland or Nunavut authorities. However, the liability and responsibility of these Arctic governments for sustainable development, economic prosperity, safe environment, preservation of Inuit culture, and de facto involvement in security matters, particularly by home rule authorities, encourage citizens of Greenland and Nunavut to insist on a share of jurisdiction in this field without threat to the national defence/security policies of Canada or Denmark.

New Security Challenges Facing the Inuit of Greenland and Nunavut

With the development of the Nunavut system of public governance, and the evolution of home rule in Greenland, the Inuit face new challenges related to security matters in their homelands. Where do these challenges come from? The end of the Cold War brought the Inuit greater opportunities for participation in the security policies of their national states. At the same time, it reduced the potential geo-political importance of the Circumpolar North. However, current U.S. missile defence plans and Russians activities in the Arctic show that it is of the utmost importance for Northern citizens to be informed of any future military activities in their territories and to be ready for whatever security challenges lie ahead.

The scope of Greenland's and Nunavut's security interests will evolve with any new strategic-military significance of the Arctic lands connected with the war on terror. This is already the reason for a U.S. upgrade of the Thule radar system. Security interests may also be advanced because of the changing political configuration in the local governments. For example, the December 2002 elections in Greenland brought to power radically minded politicians who were pushing for Greenland's say on defence matters related to the island. Finally, Greenland's or Nunavut's involvement in security matters may increase because of global challenges to the 'sovereignty' and viability of home rule and the Nunavut system in the areas of their jurisdiction. These challenges are real and result from possible Inuit interest in offshore waters, global warming and climate change, the increased feasibility of transport in the Northwest Passage (referred to by the Canadian military as 'internal waters'), and the environmental impact on traditional Inuit livelihood, dietary habits, hunting and fishing, and so on.[238]

Does the possible involvement of representatives of Greenland and Nunavut in national security decision making regarding Inuit home-lands represent a serious challenge to Canadian and Danish sovereignty in the Arctic? Arguably, it does not. However, challenges connected with the assertion of Canada's and Denmark's Arctic sovereignty are relevant to Greenlanders and the Nunavummiut.

Some authorities have noted that 'climate change in the Arctic is a serious threat to Canadian Arctic sovereignty and security.'[239] Though Griffiths has argued that 'Canada's Arctic sovereignty is not on thinning ice,' others question this position.[240] The possible melting of ice in the Northwest Passage and the consequent opening of Arctic waters to sea transportation will eventually pose a number of challenges to the Nunavut and Greenland governments. As Griffiths suggests, the policies regarding the Northwest Passage and Arctic navigation have to be re-considered from the perspective of Northern residents and their needs, including engagement of 'the people and government of Nunavut in the name of Arctic stewardship.'[241] The opening of the Northwest Pas-sage as a 'Panama canal North,' global warming, and the resultant changes will affect Inuit traditional hunting and cultural survival, and, in addition to security concerns, result in substantial economic and environmental problems for the Nunavut and Greenlandic authori-ties.[242] These may include illegal fishing, trapping, hunting, and naviga-tion of the waters by foreign vessels; increased traffic of cruise ships, oil tankers, and possibly U.S. warships; air and water pollution; change in traditional diet, habits, and hunting patterns; security challenges to Inuit homelands resulting from increased military construction and activities; accommodating new economic development; increased trade and commercial navigation in the waters between Nunavut and Green-land; an influx of newcomers to the regions; infrastructure issues; increased extraction of current or potential non-renewable/renewable resources, including exploration and mineral resource development by non-Native and foreign investors;[243] employment opportunities; and enacting legislation in conformity with these challenges. In fact, some of those challenges (e.g., the looming presence of vessel traffic), were clearly recognized by a number of people involved in the creation of Nunavut and gave them additional incentive to reach the Nunavut deal.[244]

When the Nunavut and Greenlandic governments begin to face these issues, they will need to develop a better partnership with national authorities and to have a say in security matters. The existing home rule system has had a dynamic impact on Greenland's involvement in security matters. Thus, in 2006 the Danish and Greenlandic governments agreed to develop a coherent strategy to deal with and secure their interests in the Arctic, including discussions of concerns connected with the Northwest Passage. Nunavut's authorities have also become involved in national discussions on security matters. At the same time, Inuit representatives are calling upon the federal government for development based on a long-term plan to assert sovereignty in the Arctic with strong Inuit engagement. Nunavut is seeking an equal partnership and responsibility within Canada concerning the status of Canada's Arctic waters. As a result of the devolution process, the territory is willing to assume jurisdiction over Canadian internal waters within its boundaries. According to Nunavut's premier, this process could help Canada's Arctic sovereignty claim and benefit the territory's development.[245] The Nunavut Land Claims Agreement reserves some Inuit rights in decision making concerning the use, management, and conservation of land, water, and resources. However, it fails to provide sufficient mechanisms to deal with the above-noted challenges. Needless to say, the Inuit of Nunavut and Greenlanders need to be more involved in issues determining Canada's and Denmark's Arctic policies and security developments when Nunavut's and Greenland's interests are concerned.

In Griffiths's opinion, it is important to build a stronger capacity for collective choice in the Canadian Arctic. This can be done by creating a consultative committee on the future of the Arctic Archipelago. This body could establish enduring coalitions on the basis of a new partnership between the government of Nunavut and the federal government to support priorities and sustained occupancy of the High Arctic. The Inuit of Nunavut would gain greater representation in the Arctic workforce. Their familiarity with the area and sensitivity to the local conditions would ensure the development of the most effective policy.[246] According to Griffiths, the Inuit should take the lead in protecting Canada's Arctic sovereignty and 'no longer be confined to a historical role in the federal government's endeavour to make a sovereignty claim in law.' Further, 'It is hypocritical (indeed shameful) to rely on Inuit when making a claim for exclusive jurisdiction but to exclude them from the exercise of that jurisdiction.'[247] It is important to recognize that Inuit participation in security policies will not be a challenge to the sovereignty of Canada or Denmark as further partnership between the Nunavut and federal governments, and the Greenland and Danish governments, develops. Danish–Greenlandic cooperation on the Thule issue and other initiatives taken by the Danish/Greenlandic authorities regarding security matters show that, compared to Nunavut, Greenland is in a better position in this respect as a result of its direct engagement with the United States.

The Inuit of Greenland and Nunavut should become the de jure spokespeople for their homelands. The Greenland and Nunavut governments should have some legal jurisdiction over security policies related to their homelands. The concept of Arctic governance is a dynamic and evolving issue whose flexible development will not be fulfilled until it provides local authorities with a proper mechanism for participating in decisions on national defence agendas concerning the Circumpolar North. Greenland's and Nunavut's jurisdiction in foreign relations, including security, is becoming more transferable in practice. To ensure more responsibility and liability on the part of the Arctic governments, there should be some flexibility in the scope of their competence when it concerns indigenous peoples' interests and the specifics of Northern geography. Some may argue that it is not essential that Greenland and Nunavut should carry a legal capacity in the above-mentioned matters of non-transferable jurisdiction, as there are other, more informal, options for conflict resolution and involvement in matters of security, defence, and foreign affairs. It is true that many such issues can be resolved by means of joint committees, consultations, advisory boards, or conferences. Canadian indigenous peoples have made significant advances through informal bodies, including the renegotiation of the national constitution, which would be unthinkable in the Danish case.[248] However, Greenland's experience with working groups, seminars, and the Parliamentary Committee on Foreign and Security Policy shows that informal methods are not sufficient. Alongside informal methods, which might work well in practice in Canada, the Greenland Commission on Self-Governance has underscored the importance of changes to existing legislation that would allow Greenlanders to influence the security policy of Denmark.

The international activity of Greenland and Nunavut has created a new dimension in Circumpolar, transborder, and transnational cooperation, and has shifted state-dominated initiatives in external affairs and security towards the involvement of subnational governments. This phenomenon is partially connected with the dynamics and development of home rule and Nunavut public governance systems towards greater autonomy and self-determination. The changing nature of the relationships between subnational entities like Greenland and Nunavut vis-à-vis their mother states, and their increasing role in the processes of Arctic cooperation and global challenges, demonstrate the importance of their voice and raise the possibility of expanding their competence in areas of non-transferable jurisdiction.

Conclusion

The concept of autonomy is complex. It is surrounded by ambiguity in law and political science scholarship.[1] Although it is housed within the concept of self-determination, one can best understand its content and scope in the context of a particular situation. An empirical analysis of Greenland's and Nunavut's governance systems shows that autonomy is not a static phenomenon. It is a dynamic concept constantly developing and evolving towards more recognition at the de jure level.

On the one hand, within the framework of territorial public governance and home rule structures, the Inuit of Nunavut and Greenland are able to secure their interests without de jure indigenous self-governance. Existing forms of public government are effective in meeting indigenous peoples' needs without the enactment of special forms of indigenous autonomy. As in Greenland, the Inuit majority in Nunavut transforms formal territorial autonomy into de facto indigenous governance. This shows that territorial autonomy alone can protect the rights of indigenous peoples and mitigates the need for a special type of Inuit self-governance. On the other hand, these subnational jurisdictions are constitutional hybrids with some competence comparable to the subjects of federations. The fact that Nunavut is embedded in a federal system, whereas Greenland is a part of the unitary structure of the Kingdom of Denmark that is shifting towards some federative elements, does not make a significant difference for the implementation of autonomy. Despite the profound differences between Danish and Canadian legal and political settings, both Greenland and Nunavut evolved alongside political territorial autonomy in the form of public governance, but in practice they aim to protect the Inuit needs and aspirations for greater self-governance and regaining control of their lands and lives.

In the framework of internal self-determination, the concept of autonomy is consistent with Greenlanders' and Nunavummiut effective political participation in the institutions of democratic governance (legislative and executive bodies and other structures); is inclusive of cultural, linguistic, and ethnic differences; and is oriented towards achieving economic sustainability and taking greater responsibility, and assuming liability, for managing their own affairs. At the same time, the human development factor is of the utmost importance for understanding governance systems in Greenland and Nunavut. Autonomy starts with the will and ability of residents of these regions to be a part of existing and emerging institutions in their homelands and to make them more amenable to citizens' concerns and needs. Accordingly, I have focused on the bottom-up approach, revealing how empirical or de facto comprehension of the right to autonomy is evolving towards greater recognition on a de jure level and is advancing our legal understanding of autonomy. This development is already happening in regard to areas of non-transferable jurisdiction that can be partially transferred to subnational entities in the process of devolution of powers from the centre.

Regardless of the political importance of the Greenland and Nunavut cases, their models of governance may not be applicable to all Arctic areas where indigenous peoples are the majority. Internal self-government may not be a panacea or the best solution for realizing Arctic and other indigenous peoples' right to self-determination. Forms of autonomy in the North vary and should be understood in the context of each particular situation. The Arctic promise means that there is room for a unique vision of governance in the North, inclusive of indigenous knowledge and values, Southern experience, and flexible legal imagination on the scope of autonomy.

The lack of a precise legal definition and unanimous understanding of the concept of autonomy makes it more attractive to those who are involved in the process of governance building and more flexible in response to their aspirations to self-governance. Yet, the experiences of the Inuit of Greenland and Nunavut in practice show that there are many challenges in terms of culture clashes, conceptual differences, and bridging the gap between the Inuit and non-Inuit perceptions on autonomy, especially within the legal framework of existing constitutional arrangements. For example, despite being a modern treaty, the Nunavut Land Claims Agreement (NLCA) reveals problems with authenticity and comprehension in Inuktitut, difficulty of its implementation by various stakeholders as a result of the lack of a unanimous interpretation by different government of Nunavut departments, and vague formulas. Furthermore, the NLCA has failed to meet the expectations of the Inuit in regard to guarantees for women's rights or consideration of socio-economic rights. Based on a 1970s vision of indigenous rights and territorial development, it raises concerns regarding Inuit ownership rights and is not adequate in meeting contemporary challenges caused by globalization and the necessity of sustainable economic development.

The actual development of home rule transcended the scope of the Greenland Home Rule Act. Indeed, Greenland's system functions in such a way as to advance the significant changes that have occurred in the region's relationships with Denmark, the Arctic, and the global community. The growing desire for an extended autonomy is justified by changes in national and international realities, the demand for global visibility, greater independence in taking care of its own affairs,[2] and, most importantly, by a self-sufficient economy that could substantially reduce financial dependency on transfers from Copenhagen.

In the Canadian context of interpretation of the right of indigenous peoples to autonomy, it can be argued that because the Inuit were self-governing prior to colonization, their right to autonomy, being inherent, continues to exist notwithstanding any governance structures created by Canada afterwards. If the Inuit of Nunavut had so chosen, they could have created a system of indigenous autonomy with all the necessary components based on their traditional beliefs and values. Prior to colonization, the informal character of Inuit social organization was based on the extended family structure. The Inuit of Greenland and Nunavut were transformed by dominant states from a people without a formal 'government' to a people with one. Despite this, the Inuit in both regions were able to move rapidly from their traditional forms of self-regulation to institutions and practices that are not indigenous. They have undergone a quick transformation and adaptation to the alien governmental systems of their former colonizers and attempted to introduce some elements of their traditional societal practices and customs into the modern administration of governance. This is of particular significance in Nunavut, where the incorporating of *Inuit Qaujimajatuqangit* (IQ, Inuit societal values, knowledge, wisdom of elders) into governance machinery and the lives of Nunavummiut is a focal point of the government of Nunavut's policy and priority set out in the government's plan *Pinasuaqtavut* (2004–9), 'Our Commitment to Building Nunavut's Future.' Despite considerable efforts to make IQ the 'living policy' in Nunavut, the introduction of

IQ principles in government is a work in progress, marked by ambiguity and by financial, epistemological, and other challenges. At the same time, Inuit values and traditional livelihood are changing over time and interconnect with the perceptions of the dominant and other societies. Therefore, adapting Inuit customs to legislation or institutions of governance will always be a challenge.

In both regions we witness the unique relationship between national and Greenland and Nunavut authorities. However, despite remarkable achievements towards greater political and legal autonomy of these subnational entities, Greenland and Nunavut continue to display 'voluntary' colonialism because of paternalistic practices and policies of Danish and Canadian towards the Inuit, some features of colonial legacy in Greenland's and Nunavut's legal arrangements, and Inuit dependency on the dominant societies. The Inuit need time to regain control of their lands and their lives. Despite some limitations, existing legal arrangements provide a starting point for the expression of the Inuit right to internal self-determination, and show that constitutional entrenchment of autonomy, though important, is not required for its effectiveness. Modern systems of governance are evolving towards greater Inuit involvement in the management of their affairs. The success of autonomy will depend on its progress in practice.

From a legal standpoint, the Greenland Home Rule Act, the NLCA, and the Nunavut Act do not recognize Inuit self-governance per se. Yet, because of the dynamic development of Nunavut, there might be a shift towards more political autonomy of the territory, just as Greenland moves towards an extended self-governance. This autonomy does not stem only from the fact that Inuit are a majority of the population in both regions – the effectiveness of Inuit self-governance and its institutions stems largely from thoughtful and active Inuit participation in politics. Internal developments and political institutions of autonomy in Greenland and Nunavut are viewed not just through the prism of the normative dimensions of the Greenland Home Rule Act, the NLCA, and the Nunavut Act but also through the policies of Greenlandic parties and the Nunavut Inuit organizations that are the driving force behind the normative and functional validity of autonomy.

The effectiveness of Nunavut's public governance and Greenland's home rule substantially depends on the breadth of powers delegated to the governing authorities. The legal framework of home rule and the government of Nunavut's jurisdiction are pulled in two directions – by Inuit aspirations and their expectations for effective governance, and by the realities and pragmatic expectations for future economic sustainability in the severely isolated North. Currently, neither Greenland nor Nunavut can function without substantial financial assistance from the central authorities. They do not have an economic basis for self-sufficiency. That causes the problem of reconciling the idea of autonomy, which means self-reliance, with the necessity of assuring significant funding from the national governments. It further challenges the viability of self-governance in the Arctic, and makes the concept of autonomy rather 'artificial.' In this respect, the capacity of subnational entities like Greenland and Nunavut to take over some additional responsibilities is questionable.

The legal authority of Nunavut and Greenland is limited by Canadian and Danish legal paradigms that are not always able to meet the specific interests of the Inuit population. In practice, the Nunavummiut and Greenlanders can shape their own policies but can make changes towards expanding their jurisdictions to only a minor extent. Their ability to shape their own policies is driven by the development of political consciousness and public initiative among residents of Greenland and Nunavut and by economic and socio-cultural factors. Despite jurisdictional limitations of Greenlandic home rule and the government of Nunavut, the evolution of these governance systems suggests increased local involvement and a greater responsibility for matters not envisaged by their jurisdictional frames. Therefore, the study of Greenland's and Nunavut's competence reveals the tendency of regional authorities to obtain more responsibilities in areas not covered by their current legal arrangements, as the set of delegated powers does not address all the challenges faced by the Inuit. The Inuit of Greenland and Nunavut have used the methods and 'language' of their former colonizers to overcome their subjugation. They have demonstrated how they value their own cultures by their aspirations for self-determination and autonomy. Arctic indigenous peoples have an image of governance and its institutions that differs from that of their former colonizers. There is a need for more flexibility and a rethinking of the boundaries of Danish-European and Anglo-Canadian legal imaginations that would adapt to Inuit realities and better serve their aspirations self-governance. At the same time, in the Canadian context, federal principles and practice facilitate the Inuit's coping with the 'white man's' outlook and ease transitions.[3]

There are important differences between Greenlanders and the Inuit of Nunavut in their relationship with their respective parent states. The process of nation building in Greenland has resulted in rapid changes in home rule and its political settings. The current governance structure does not fully meet the needs of Greenlanders in responding to the challenges of modernization, globalization, and a gradual transformation of home rule towards an extended version of self-governance. Home rule has evolved since its introduction in 1979, and Greenlanders are now taking a new look at their own future. It remains to be seen what kind of partnership will develop within a new agreement on self-governance. The Commission on Self-Governance (2003) examined several models (complete independence, personal union, free association, federation, extended self-governance, home rule, integration) that are relevant for defining a new relationship between Greenland and Denmark. But the future of Greenland depends on choices that can be made by Greenlanders who have publicly acknowledged their long-term goal of independence or at least a new 'partnership' agreement with Denmark on Greenland's self-governance, including possible autonomous jurisdiction in non-transferable fields such as foreign affairs, the justice system, and defence/security policy.

Nunavut is on a different political trajectory than Greenland. Even though it was established with active Inuit involvement and accommodated Inuit interests to a significant extent, it is unclear yet whether Nunavut is going to develop towards any form of self-governance for all residents of Nunavut or towards Inuit autonomy, or if it will eventually become a province of Canada. For Greenlanders, the Greenland Home Rule Act is a political compromise with the Danes. Similarly, the Inuit of Nunavut had to compromise with the federal government and the Canadian public in political and practical terms: the NLCA was separated from the quest for self-government, and the concept of public territorial governance was accepted by the Inuit as more palatable to the Canadian system. The creation of a new territory and the transfer of substantial responsibility to the public government postponed ideas for Inuit self-government. The Inuit of Nunavut show a strong affiliation to their parent country and pride in being Canadian. They look at the Nunavut arrangement, which is supported by the NLCA, as a victory for the Inuit and an opportunity to realize major developments. The right to a separate Inuit self-government agreement is reserved for the future in case of changed demographic or political situations unfavourable to the Inuit. The citizens of Nunavut consider their future constitutional development as occurring within Canada, aided by the increasing influence of Inuit traditional values and knowledge in the institutions of public government.

The constitutional recognition in Canada of Aboriginal and treaty rights distinguishes the Inuit of Nunavut's claims and the road to self-determination. Thus, in Nunavut, despite the existence of the system of public government for all Nunavummiut, special consideration is given to the values and rights of the Inuit beneficiaries of the NLCA, who represent a majority of the territory's population. Greenlanders have never considered Aboriginal rights as a focal point in their struggle for autonomy. Furthermore, in Greenland demands for rights put in ethnic terms have been interpreted into rights for the territorially defined population of the island.

At the same time, in both jurisdictions, the Inuit are facing the challenges of adjusting to the non-Inuit values of other societies in the administrative institutions of government. The Inuit's recognition of their participatory rights in the structures of Western democracy leaves very little room for any indigenous autonomy. However, unlike Greenland, Nunavut has more possibilities for participating in the institutions of the Canadian federal system. That involvement would expand the territory's political autonomy in practice. Moreover, the existence in Nunavut of the Nunavut Tunngavik Incorporated (NTI) – a powerful land claims organization with 100 per cent Inuit membership – creates a sort of second level of corporate governance along with Nunavut's public government. This phenomenon does not exist in Greenland.

The fields of non-transferable jurisdiction will gradually obtain more importance in Nunavut with Ottawa's devolution of powers and with the region's increasing participation in intergovernmental and international relations. Due to unique Northern geography and substantial involvement of Greenlanders and Nunavummiut in their governments' affairs, the legal understanding of the concept of autonomy is gradually changing, with consideration for the capability of Northern residents to take over responsibility in some areas of traditionally non-transferable jurisdiction.

No matter what constitutional path Greenland and Nunavut may follow in the future, there is no need for a special model of indigenous autonomy in the North. Yet the legal scope of autonomy in the Arctic has to be reconsidered. Although there are always informal methods of conflict resolution and consultation, the role of law is still valuable when it comes to defining the boundaries of Greenland's and Nunavut's jurisdiction in international, defence/security, and judicial matters.

I have attempted to show in this book that even the confusing legal concept of autonomy can be rendered more determinate by means of comparative research and the application of original information from those who actually try to build it in practice. This journey has revealed that the current legal arrangements of Greenland and Nunavut carry some potential for being influenced by indigenous values and perspectives on governance. Given Inuit majorities and increasing indigenous involvement in the administration of the institutions of Nunavut's public governance and Greenland's home rule, these Arctic jurisdictions constitute unique legal arrangements. Being by their legal nature models of territorial political autonomy, Greenland and Nunavut are evolving towards greater autonomy within Denmark and Canada. The case of Greenland is of particular significance for Nunavut. It tells us how it is possible, by means of diplomacy, increasingly to take over some elements of foreign policy and become a genuine actor in international affairs to promote local interests. It is remarkable how, despite the isolation, harsh Arctic environment, and economic dependency on external sources, Greenland has substantial promise for a great and self-sustainable future. Since 1979 its home rule system has developed into a highly democratic form of governance with a growing need for extended self-governance based on mutual respect and equal partnership with Denmark. Importantly, Greenlanders keep their options open as regards the exercise of their right to self-determination.

Nunavut may not be following the path of Greenland within the next few decades. Nunavut's future depends on economic self-sufficiency, environmental and societal sustainability, a better partnership with the federal government, and to some extent on further developing Arctic and global collaboration. As in Greenland, the participation of every citizen in making Nunavut a success story is crucial. The first eight years of the existence of Nunavut have shown that its system of public governance is constantly evolving. There were some important initiatives and developments in the dialogue with Ottawa, which show that the future of Nunavut rests in stronger partnership and mutual cooperation with the federal government and other parts of Canada.[4] Thus, the de facto evolution and development of Greenland's and Nunavut's governance reveal that there is room for flexibility in the legal image of governance in the North to keep the Arctic promise alive.

Notes

Introduction

1 This is evident from most of my interviews with Inuit representatives in Nunavut and Greenland, and is stressed by the Inuit Circumpolar Council. However, there might be objections to this statement.

2 Statistics Greenland (2001:43).

3 Harhoff (1986:31–2) gives a good explanation of the difference between autonomy in constitutional legal terms and local autonomy. This book does not aim to look at local Aboriginal self-government arrangements in the North or elsewhere. Local autonomy is similar to municipal government, whereas autonomy in constitutional legal terms is usually delegated to a distinct region or territory, which, in terms of the administrative territorial division of a state, constitutes a separate level of powers between the central or federal bodies and the local municipal authorities.

4 See *Report from the Commission on Self-Governance* (2003:19).

5 Dahl (2005a:31–2).

6 M.U. Jensen (2004:28).

7 Dahl (2005a:32).

8 Key Figures about Greenland, www.statgreen.gl/english/key.html.

9 'Nuuk Soon the Largest Municipality ... in the World,' *Nunatsiaq News*, 15 December 2006.

10 For Greenland, see Baunbæk (2005:3–4). For Nunavut, see 'Nunavut's Population Still Growing,' *Nunatsiaq News*, 31 March 2006.

11 See Larsen (2004) and note 6 in chapter 4 below.

12 Even though Nunavut had come into being after its strategic significance collapsed and Greenland's geopolitical significance has eroded, there are some

arguments to support the notion that these regions are important in a geo-political sense. See the discussion below in chapter 5.

13 There is a general tendency in Nordic countries to consider indigenous rights as little as possible. For more information see Alfreðsson (1999:529) and Hannikainen (1996:1).

14 D. Smith (1993:41); Nuttall (1994:14).

15 For a traditional approach to the notion of autonomy, see, for example, Lindley (1969), Dinstein (1981), Hannum (1993, 1996), Lapidoth (1997), Hannikainen and Horn (1997), Suksi (1998), Petersen and Poppel (1999), Welhengama (2000), Cook and Lindau (2000), Aikio and Scheinin (2000), Skaale (2004), and Skurbaty (2005).

16 Husa (2000:353).

17 Ibid., 354.

18 Merryman (1998:773).

19 See Grinde and Johansen (1991) for an exploration of indigenous influ-ences in American constitutional history.

20 See the *American Journal of Comparative Law* 46 (1998). The issue is devoted to the problems of comparative law and methodology.

21 Curran (2002:11). I have also found the basic principles of comparative method in Reitz (1998:617–38) to be useful. These principles contributed to my decision to choose two different legal jurisdictions for comparison and to underscore their most important similarities and differences.

22 Ewald (1998:702).

23 Ibid., 702–3.

24 Ibid., 704–5.

25 See, for example, *Polar Peoples* (1994) and Ashlee (1984). For recent develop-ments in Greenland, see H. Petersen (2006).

26 Gallagher-Mackay (2000:5–6).

27 Poelzer (1996:14).

Chapter 1. The Inuit of Greenland and Nunavut: From Subjugation to Self-Government?

1 Hicks and White (2000:45), Purich (1992:24), Moss (1995:60).

2 Caulfield (2000:170).

3 Duffy (1988:196).

4 Rigby, MacDonald, and Otak (2000:97).

5 Creery (1993:6).

6 Jenness (1964, 1967), Sørensen (1995:85–105), Duffy (1988).

7 In her study Ashlee (1984:22, ii) also designates the following phases: the

foreign policy phase, the paternal phase, and the industrial integration phase. The foreign policy phase is characterized by the barter of European explorers and whalers with the Inuit. This occurred in Greenland from 1550 CE to 1721. In the NWT foreign activity began more than a hundred years after it ended in Greenland. This phase lasted until 1903 with the creation of permanent posts by the North-West Mounted Police. The paternal phase is characterized by the extension of state administrations to regulate and govern the Inuit. In Canada this phase was marked by ad hoc administration of the Inuit by police, traders, and missionaries. The industrial integration phase, which occurs in both entities after the Second World War, is marked by the reorganization of the colonial relationship and integration of the Inuit with Denmark and Canada.

8 Ibid., 22.
9 See McNeil (1982:6–12). See also Order of Her Majesty in Council Admitting Rupert's Land and the North-Western Territory into the Union, June 23, 1870, in Ollivier (1962:157–61). About the 1880 Order of Her Majesty in Council admitting all British Possessions and Territories in North America and islands adjacent thereto into the Union, see McNeil (1982:44).
10 Regarding the Norse legacy, early settlers, and stages of Greenland's colonial history, see Fitzhugh and Ward (2000:281–349), Vahl et al. (1929), and Schuurman (1976:19–20).
11 Ashlee (1984:40).
12 Sørensen (1995:88) notes that there were few permanent Danish settlers in Greenland. Individuals stayed there for varying periods of time. According to Jenness (1964:8–9), in Canada most of the settlements were created at the end of the nineteenth century to establish the dominion's sovereignty in the area.
13 Ashlee (1984:43).
14 This point is debatable. In a personal communication, Peter H. Russell notes that Canada did not make treaties with some Aboriginal peoples who had the same status as those with whom treaties were made. Besides, neither Great Britain nor Canada acknowledged the full sovereignty of the Native people with whom they made treaties. In the case of Nunavut the lack of treaties with the Inuit can probably be explained by the remoteness of the region and the particular nature of the colonization process in Canada's Eastern Arctic.
15 In 1814 the Norwegian-Danish Crown union collapsed. Norway was ceded to Sweden, but Greenland remained under the Danish Crown according to Art. 4 of the Treaty of Kiel. However, because of long-term historical relationships (Greenland was under the Norwegian Crown from 1261 to 1380, when it

came under the joint Crown of Norway and Denmark) and the particularities of Greenland's colonization, the Norwegians claimed rights over Eastern
Greenland. See *Legal Status of Eastern Greenland* (1933:27–38).

16 On 10 July 1931 the Norwegian government declared that it had proceeded
to occupy certain territories of Eastern Greenland. On 5 April 1933 the Permanent Court of International Justice ruled that the declaration of occupation and any steps taken in this respect violated the existing legal situation
and were accordingly unlawful and invalid. *Legal Status of Eastern Greenland*
(1933:75). The claim was judged in favour of Denmark. On this dispute and
the legal particularities of Norway's claim, see Berlin (1932), Skeie (1933),
Hyde (1933:732–8), Preuss (1932:469–87).

17 Purich (1992:31–4). To confirm sovereignty through effective occupation,
the dominion would have to show a continuing interest in the North –
through creation of permanent settlements, for example.

18 Ashlee (1984:218). Other countries – the United States and Norway, for
example – claimed interests in the Canadian Arctic, and Canada had to
assert its sovereignty. See G. Smith (1952), chs 4 and 14.

19 Jenness (1967:30).

20 Justice Hall of the Supreme Court of Canada characterized the proclamation
as 'an executive order having the force of an act of Parliament and as the
Indian Bill of Rights. "Its force as a statute," he comments, "is analogous to
the status of *Magna Carta* which has always been considered to be the law
throughout the Empire."' Quoted in Royal Commission on Aboriginal Peoples (1993b:16).

21 McNeil (1982:3). McNeil notes that the Supreme Court of Canada in *Sigear-
eak El-53 v. The Queen,* [1966] S.C.R. 645, decided that the Royal Proclamation of 1763 did not apply to Rupert's Land. This decision was followed by
Mahoney, J., of the Federal Court in *Hamlet of Baker Lake v. Minister of Indian
Affairs,* [1980] 1 F.C. 518. McNeil (1982:3).

22 McNeil (1982:3) refers to Brian Slattery, *The Land Rights of Indigenous Cana-
dian Peoples* (Saskatoon: University of Saskatchewan Native Law Centre,
1979), 204–12, 221–7, 233–46, 258–60, 295–302, 309–10; Kenneth M. Narvey,
'The Royal Proclamation of 7 October, 1763, the Common Law, and Native
Rights to Land within the Territory Granted to the Hudson's Bay Company,'
(1973–4) 38 *Saskatchewan Law Review* 123; Narvey, 'The Supreme Court, the
Federal Court of Canada, and the Royal Proclamation of 1763 in Rupert's
Land,' (1980) 2 *Canadian Native Law Reporter* 109.

23 See the Address to Her Majesty the Queen from the Senate and House of
Commons of the Dominion of Canada to the Queen's Most Excellent Majesty, 16–17 December 1867, and the Memorandum, Details of Agreement

between the Delegates of the Government of the Dominion, and the Directors of the Hudson's Bay Company, 22 March 1869, both in Ollivier (1962:162, 165). The quote is from the Royal Address. See also the Indian Act, 1876, in Venne (1981). It is debatable whether Inuit were regarded as Indians in 1876.

24 *Reference re: British North America Act, 1867 (U.K.), s. 91,* [1939] S.C.R. 104.

25 Dahl (1986a:101–3).

26 Ashlee (1984:51–3).

27 Jenness (1967:30); emphasis in original. Jenness states that this philosophy was influenced by the concept of Rousseau's Noble Savage, 30–1.

28 Ibid., 32.

29 Ashlee (1984:219).

30 Duffy (1988:1–18), Ashlee (1984:72–100), Jenness (1964:7–17).

31 The year 1882–3 was declared to be the First International Polar Year. As a result, the Germans created a research station in Cumberland Sound on Baffin Island, the Americans at Fort Conger/Ellesmere Island, and the British at Fort Rae. Canada did not establish such a station. In 1898 Otto Sverdrup claimed the islands that are named after him in the Arctic archipelago for the King of Norway. From 1903 to 1906 the Norwegian Roald Amundsen navigated the Northwest Passage. Furthermore, there was substantial evidence that in the early 1900s Inuit from Greenland hunted on Canada's Baffin and Ellesmere Islands. Purich (1992:31–2). See also Zaslow (1981:61–78), Schledermann (2003:101–9).

32 Jenness (1964:10).

33 R. Petersen (1995:119). Alfreðsson (1982a:307–8) also notes that the Danes have been 'mild' colonizers. From the Western viewpoint, Danish contributions brought improvements to Greenland. By contrast, the Greenlander Finn Lynge 'has described these activities as constituting "not suppression, but suffocation"' (307). See also Alfreðsson (1982b).

34 R. Petersen (1995:119).

35 The Moravian missionary Samuel Kleinschmidt created a grammar and standard orthography for Greenlandic. Nuttall (1994:14). On social stratification see Ashlee (1984:57–9).

36 In 1906 a commission was named to investigate conditions in Greenland. As a result of that investigation, a law was passed in 1908, which led to structural changes in Greenland's administration. The law of 1925 established a permanent Greenland Commission for the annual examination of the social conditions in Greenland. See Høegh (1973:374–5).

37 On the Board of Guardians and municipal councils, see Schuurman (1976:34–5). On the provincial councils, see Ashlee (1984:66–7), Sørensen

(1995:92). A single elected provincial council for all of Western Greenland was created in 1950. Schuurman (1976:41).

38 Dahl (1986a:20–1). See also Schuurman (1976:36).

39 Ashlee (1984:68)

40 Sørensen (1995:92).

41 Ibid. Dahl (1986a:20) emphasizes that, compared to the Inuit in Canada and Alaska, Greenlandic children have traditionally attended school and learned to write and read Greenlandic.

42 Ibid., 104.

43 Jenness (1964), chs 2–6. Police imposed Canada's law and sovereignty, missionaries were concerned about the welfare and religious education of indigenous peoples, and traders were interested in the profits to be made from Inuit goods. The Inuit became dependent on the fur trade and European goods. Native leaders were replaced by outside representatives of the fur trade at the trading posts; hunting began to decline. Ashlee (1984), ch. 4. In 1905, with the creation of the provinces of Alberta and Saskatchewan from the NWT, an Ottawa-based commissioner was appointed as a controller of the Royal North West Mounted Police (RNWMP). Together with the NWT Council they were all senior federal bureaucrats until 1947. Purich (1992:37).

44 For example, the Northwest Game Act of 1917 dealt with regulation of fur trapping, and the Musk-Ox and Reindeer Commission of 1919 suggested the development of reindeer herds for the Inuit. The experiment to produce reindeer meat as an Inuit enterprise failed, as did the government's attempt to develop a standard orthography in the North. Ashlee (1984:84–95).

45 Purich (1992:38–40). For a detailed account see chapter 4 below and Grant (2002).

46 However, there was a mutual dependency between the colonizers and the Inuit. As Sørensen (1995:88) notes, 'only the Greenlanders could exploit the country's living resources, and only the Danes could provide the Greenlanders with the European goods on which they had gradually become dependent.'

47 Sørensen (1995:97–9). See also chapter 5 below.

48 Ashlee (1984:158–9). See also chapter 5 below.

49 See Robertson (2000:112–14), ch. 6, 'Canada Discovers the North, 1953–1957.' This department is now called Indian and Northern Affairs Canada (INAC).

50 Jull (2001b:4).

51 Sørensen (1995:97), Ashlee (1984:102).

52 Schuurman (1976:41). See also Ashlee (1984:102–3).

53 Jenness (1968:26, 27).

54 Wareham (1993:8).

55 Ashlee (1984:162), Jull (2001b:4).

56 Ashlee (1984:162–3).

57 See Alfreðsson (1982b:103–4).

58 Alfreðsson (1982a:301).

59 Constitution of the Kingdom of Denmark Act, 5 June 1953, in Henry and Miller (2003).

60 See Alfreðsson (1982a:303). See also Alfreðsson (2003:453–9, 2004:93–4).

61 Dahl (1986b:316–317).

62 Alfredsson (1982a:303).

63 Jull (2001b:4).

64 Brody (2000:92).

65 Hicks and White (2000:49 and 100n.43) note that, technically, since 1954 there were no barriers to Inuit voting territorially but that at the time it could not be realized because constituencies were established in the eastern and central Arctic only in 1966.

66 Comment by an anonymous reader.

67 Nuttall (1994:7).

68 The G-60 policy gave the Greenlandic elite a chance to seek wage parity with Danish workers in similar occupations (Ashlee [1984:109]). However, the problem of wage disparity and the shortage of equal opportunities with Danes remained a political issue in Greenland for decades. See Sørensen (1995:101).

69 Nuttall (1994:8).

70 In 1925 eighty-five Inuit families were transported from Ammassalik/Tasiilaq to found Scoresbysund/Ittoqqortoormiit so that Norwegians could not claim Northeast Greenland. See Petersen, Petrussen and Petersen. (1991:179–190). About the 1953 relocation of the Inuit of Greenland, see chapter 5 below. There are several publications on the nature of the 1953–5 Canadian Inuit relocation to the High Arctic and the 1934 relocation from Cape Dorset (southern Baffin Island) to Dundas Harbour on Devon Island in the High Arctic. The Inuit argue that they were relocated to assert Canada's sovereignty in the Arctic, Canada's last frontier. The government argues that it was motivated to launch its relocation plan by the shortage of game and with the humane intention of improving the economic situation in Inukjuak. The Inuit counter that they were not in danger and that the relocation was imposed on them without their informed consent. See Grant (1991), Dussault and Erasmus (1994), Tester and Kulchyski (1994), Marcus (1992, 1995).

71 Sørensen (1995:101).

72 Inspired by the Saami's struggle for their rights within the majority society, and by Alaska's Native Federation and the Inuit Tapirisat of Canada, Green-

landers, as a majority within their territory, wanted to reduce the Danish dominance and take the lead in administering their society themselves. Sørensen (1995:102).

73 The official title of the White Paper was the *Statement of the Government of Canada on Indian Policy* (Ottawa: Department of Indian and Northern Affairs, Queen's Printer, 1969). See Weaver (1980). The Alaskan oil discovery prompted multinational companies and governments to look at the Arctic riches. This boosted the political mobilization of the Inuit of Canada, whose concerns with possibly extensive resource exploration and exploitation in their homelands by the outsiders could be best addressed via activities of the Inuit organizations. See Amagoalik (1994:23). The *Calder* decision is *Calder v. A.G.B.C.*, [1973] S.C.R. 313. The James Bay and Northern Quebec Agreement was signed in 1975 by the governments of Canada and Quebec, and the Cree and Inuit of Northern Quebec. The Naskapi Indian Band negotiated the Northeastern Quebec Agreement, signed in 1978 and amending the James Bay agreement.

74 See Appendix: Nunavut – A Chronology, in Hicks and White (2000:94). Originally, there were two proposals by the ITC on Nunavut. The second formed the basis for the eventual NLCA. Ibid., 101n. 59.

75 For the text of legal documents and information regarding comprehensive land claims agreements settled with the Inuvialuit and other indigenous peoples in the NWT, which include Dene, Métis, Sahtu, Gwich'in, Tłįchǫ, see the website of the Department of Aboriginal Affairs and Intergovernmental Relations of the Government of the Northwest Territories (www.daair.gov.nt.ca).

76 Dahl (1988a:82).

77 See Agreement Between the Inuit of the Nunavut Settlement Area and Her Majesty the Queen in Right of Canada (Ottawa: Minister of Indian Affairs and Northern Development and the Tungavik, 1993); Nunavut Act, S.C. 1993, c. 28, as amended. For other preconditions and factors that led to the creation of Nunavut see Purich (1992:43–77), Creery (1993:14), Inuit Committee on National Issues (1987:29–35), Hicks and White (2000:50–7), Jull (2000:121–9).

78 The chronology is as follows: 1990 the Tungavik Federation of Nunavut (TFN) together with the federal and Northwest Territories governments signed a Nunavut Land Claims Agreement-in-Principle; May 1992, the majority of votes in the NWT approved the suggested boundary for division; October 1992, TFN and government representatives signed the Nunavut Political Accord; November 1992, the Inuit of Nunavut ratified the Nunavut Land Claims Agreement, with 69 per cent of eligible Inuit voters supporting the

settlement; 1993, the NLCA and the Nunavut Act were adopted by Parliament and received Royal Assent; 1994, the Nunavut Implementation Commission was created; 1995–6, the commission released its reports, *Footprints in New Snow* and *Footprints 2*; 1998, amendments to the Nunavut Act are adopted by Parliament; 1 April 1999, the Nunavut Territory is created; see Appendix: Nunavut – A Chronology, in Hicks and White (2000:94–6), see also Kusugak (2000:22–5).

79 Dahl (1986b:318).

80 Wilson (2002:30).

81 Dahl (1988a:74); emphasis in original.

82 Dahl (1988b:313).

83 Dahl (1988a:83).

84 Kusugak (2000:25).

85 Harhoff (1983:17). See also chapter 5 below.

86 The council's reaction was also motivated by the example of the Faroe Islands; the islands, a home rule territory of Denmark since 1948, were able to decide for themselves whether or not to follow Danish membership in the EEC.

87 The Home Rule Committee was created in 1973 with an all-Greenlandic membership. Its task was to study possible constitutional and structural changes that would provide Greenland with greater self-determination. Schuurman (1976:48–9). By contrast, Denmark and Greenland were equally represented on the Home Rule Commission (ibid., 49).

88 In a referendum in January 1979, Greenlanders approved the enactment by the Folketing of a bill on home rule (Henry and Miller [2003:53]). See also the Commission on Home Rule, Resumé of the Report, and the Greenland Home Rule Act No. 577 , 29 November 1978 (hereinafter Home Rule Act), published in Blaustein and Flanz (2003).

89 Kusugak (2000:27).

90 Jull (2000:119, 118).

91 Russell (1996:60). Some see this Inuit pragmatism as a continuation of the colonial relationship and as a reflection of the fear and corruption among the Inuit leaders who supported the government of Canada's policies on land claims. Thus Taiaiake Alfred (2005:122) notes that John Amagoalik 'stated bluntly that the Inuit were awarded a territorial government and land rights in Canada because "we are not Indians, who run around on blockades with guns causing trouble."' For Alfred, 'this [the statement by Amagoalik] was a supreme example of ignorance, spite, greed, and fear all rolled into one shameful display of kowtowing to the colonial master.'

92 Dahl (2005b:176).

93 Jull (2001b:11; 1998a).
94 Jull (2001b:11).
95 Ibid.
96 Brody (2000:28).

Chapter 2. The Constitutional Dimensions of the Governance of Nunavut and Greenland

1 During my interviews in Iqaluit in 2002, eleven of fourteen Inuit respondents expressed the view that Inuit were self-governing prior to European contact. Three noted that there was no form of actual government (self-government or otherwise) because they lived in a camp structure. Representatives of Pauktuutit – the Association of the Inuit Women of Canada – state that despite the lack of formal governmental institutions and written law, Inuit societies were self-governing and maintained a stable and peaceful existence. See Pauktuutit (2006a:9).
2 Report of interviews with Inuit leaders on self-government and treaty rights issues, quoted in Moss (1995:117).
3 Interviews with the Inuit respondents in Iqaluit and Nuuk.
4 During my interviews in Nunavut and Greenland, the respondents were asked whether they consider modern institutions of governance as imposed, unknown, or alien structures. Many said that they are alien to the Inuit culture, but that at the same time the Inuit are highly adaptive to everything new.
5 Canadian Arctic Resources Committee. Aboriginal Self-Government and Constitutional Reform. Ottawa, 1988, 118–123. Quoted in Moss (1995:81).
6 Established in 1971, the Inuit Tapirisat of Canada is a national voice for all Canadian Inuit.
7 Inuit Tapirisat of Canada (1994b:8).
8 On the views of the Inuit of the different Canadian regions, see Inuit Committee on National Issues (1987:19–40).
9 Interview with senior official of the ICC, Iqaluit, 16 October 2002.
10 J.B. Nielsen (2000:157).
11 About political demands for rights posed in ethnic terms see Gad (2005, chs 3 and 4).
12 See, for example, Lyck (1988:345).
13 See R. Petersen (1992:183–94). Sørensen (1995:89) notes, 'There were no racial prejudices in marriages, so many of which were mixed that at the end of the 19th century the authorities gave up distinguishing between Europeans, Greenlanders, and people of mixed origin in the censuses.'

14 A similar situation occurred with the Saami in Scandinavia, where there were difficulties in determining whom to consider Saami and based on what criteria. For an analysis of the delimitation of Greenlandic identity in present political debates, see Gad (2005).

15 Many of the leaders of the Canadian Inuit, such as Mary Simon, Sheila Watt-Cloutier, and Minnie Gray, are descendants of such intermarriages.

16 Pauktuutit (1991:35).

17 Inuit Tapirisat of Canada (1994b:43–4).

18 Rosemarie Kuptana, 'The Inherent Right to Self-Government: Its Nature and Source,' presentation to the Canadian Bar Association conference on Constitutional Entrenchment of Aboriginal Self-Government, 27 March 1992, quoted in Moss (1995:92).

19 Inuit Committee on National Issues (1987:5, 6, 14–15, 7, 6).

20 Moss (1995:112, 113). On fiduciary duty see Rotman (1996).

21 Jull (1991:54).

22 Territorial principle means that autonomy is given to the population of the whole area and is not based on ethnic criteria.

23 Craig and Freeland (1999:7).

24 H. Rasmussen (1995:48).

25 Johansen (1992:34).

26 Gulløv (1979:139).

27 Ibid.,141.

28 This account should be taken with consideration of the fact that the evolution of the home rule system continues. The new partnership agreement on self-governance is expected to expand Greenland's jurisdiction in a number of areas. See *Report from the Commission on Self-Governance* (2003).

29 Nunavut Act, S.C. 1993, c. 28, as amended. The Nunavut Political Accord, 1992.

30 See NLCA, art. 4 'Nunavut Political Development.'

31 About home rule status of the Faroe Islands and their constitutional development, see Rógvi (2004:13–48).

32 Comment by an anonymous reader. Cameron and White (1995:90) also note that the Inuit character, particularly patience and pragmatism, contributed to the acceptance of a form of public government that was considered to be effective in meeting Inuit political goals.

33 J. Amagoalik in Canadian Arctic Resources Council, *Aboriginal Self-Government and Constitutional Reform: Setbacks, Opportunities and Arctic Experiences* (Ottawa: Canadian Arctic Resources Council, 1987), 68, quoted in Gallagher-Mackay (2000:223).

34 Kusugak (2000:27).

35 Interview with a senior official of the Government of Nunavut, Department of Justice, Iqaluit, 15 October 2002.
36 Quoted in Nungaq (1999:28).
37 Trish Crawford, 'The Year of the Indian,' *Toronto Star*, 18 April 1993, B1; cited in Kersey (1994:429).
38 Anawak (1993:8).
39 Art. 2, part 7, s. 2.7.1 of the NLCA reads:

> In consideration of the rights and benefits provided to Inuit by the Agreement, Inuit hereby:
>
> a) cede, release and surrender to Her Majesty The Queen in Right of Canada, all their aboriginal claims, rights, title and interests, if any, in and to lands and waters anywhere within Canada and adjacent offshore areas within the sovereignty or jurisdiction of Canada; and
> b) agree, on their behalf, and on behalf of their heirs, descendants and successors not to assert any cause of action, action for a declaration, claim or demand of whatever kind or nature which they ever had, now have or may hereafter have against Her Majesty The Queen in Right of Canada or any province, the government of any territory or any person based on any aboriginal claims, rights, title or interests in and to lands and waters described in Sub-section (a).

> It should be noted, however, that neither this clause nor anything in the NLCA preclude the Inuit as Aboriginal people of Canada from enjoying all constitutional rights or government programs. See art. 2, part 7, s. 2.7.3 (a) and (b).

40 Interview with one of the key negotiators of the NLCA, Iqaluit, 2 October 2002.
41 Gulløv (1979:131).
42 The NLCA consists of 42 articles, filling about 400 pages. The Home Rule Act fits on 3 pages; the Nunavut Act contains 79 sections on 29 pages. On the one hand, this can be explained by the different relationship between the Inuit and the Danish and Canadian governments, differences in legal traditions, and legal modelling of Greenland's home rule on the Faroese Home Rule Act of 1948. On the other hand, it can be attributed to the longer negotiation process between the Canadian Inuit and the federal and territorial governments, the lessons learned from other Aboriginal groups' experiences, and improved Inuit understanding of their rights.
43 Kersey (1994:467) states that because the NLCA is too long and complex, disagreements over its interpretation and implementation are inevitable. Thomas Berger, the conciliator who was appointed to resolve the dispute

over a new implementation contract for the NLCA, also noted that 'it's fuzzy, nearly meaningless words contained in the land claim agreement that present the biggest problem in figuring out how much to spend on Nunavut's "Institutions of Public Government."' Cited in Jim Bell, 'Berger Chides Both Sides in Land Claims Dispute,' *Nunatsiaq News*, 21 October 2005.

44 On women's rights and a referendum on equal representation by gender in the Nunavut Legislative Assembly, see chapter 3 below.

45 To deal with this problem, in 2004 the NTI (a watchdog organization for the NLCA) published a simplified, 88–page version of the agreement called *Tukisittiarniqsaujumaviit? A Plain Language Guide to the Nunavut Land Claims Agreement. Tukisittiarniqsaujumaviit* means 'would you like to have a better understanding?'

46 *The Inuit of Nunavut as Represented by NTI v. the Queen*, para. 12. Claim by the NTI filed to the Nunavut Court of Justice, 5 December 2006. See also Bell, 'Berger Chides Both Sides' and note 121 in chapter 3 below. Importantly, the NTI oversees the implementation of the NLCA. See Nunavut Tunngavik Incorporated (1999). There are also annual reports on the implementation of the NLCA published by Indian and Northern Affairs Canada; see also Vertes, Connelly, and Knott (2000).

47 *Report from the Commission on Self-Governance* (2003).

48 Foighel (1980:5, 2005:232–4).

49 Foighel (1980:6).

50 The Greenland Home Rule Act, no. 577, 29 November 1978, ch. 1, s.1(1).

51 Foighel (1980:6).

52 Autonomous parts of Denmark include Greenland and the Faroe Islands.

53 Eliasen (2004b:170).

54 Harhoff (1994b:254).

55 Harhoff (1993:515). Harhoff also notes that Denmark cannot 'be classified as a "suzerain state," since Greenland and the Faroe Islands enjoy a higher status than mere vassals. A proper union or commonwealth would, however, require a more independent status for the two overseas territories' (1994b:254).

56 J.B. Nielsen (2000:157).

57 Breinholt-Larsen (1992:222).

58 Jull (1995:2).

59 The Nunavut Political Accord, s. 2.1, reads, that 'the legislation proposed to establish Nunavut (the "Nunavut Act") shall be similar to the present *Northwest Territories Act*.' Nunavut thus became the third territory within the Canadian federation. See also Nunavut Act.

60 Cited in Frideres and Gadacz (2001:281).
61 Isaac (1992:399–400).
62 It should be noted that the Faroe Islands also have substantial jurisdiction within Denmark, and their legal status is similar to Greenland's in some respects.
63 There were other reasons for such a delegation. Evidently, however, Denmark was looking for some relief from the responsibility for Greenland. As Harhoff (1994–5:71) notes, 'Denmark, to be sure, had a clear interest in reducing the financial burdens of its responsibilities in Greenland.'
64 Ibid., 60.
65 Lyck (1995:482).
66 Harhoff (1986:37); emphasis in original
67 Nowlan-Card (1996:58).
68 S. 28 of the Nunavut Act reads: '(1) A copy of every law made by the Legislature shall be transmitted to the Governor in Council within thirty days after its enactment. (2) The Governor in Council may disallow any law made by the Legislature or any provision of any such law at any time within one year after its enactment.'
69 In contrast to the Danish unicameral Folketing, the Canadian Parliament is bicameral. Therefore, one representative from Nunavut is elected to the House of Commons, another is appointed de facto by the prime minister to the Senate.
70 For discussion of whether the Danish Parliament can impose upon itself a permanent obligation not to withdraw or restrict in any way the Greenland's home rule arrangement, see Harhoff (1986:38).
71 Art. 2, part 2, s. 2.2.1 of the NLCA reads, 'the Agreement shall be a land claims agreement within the meaning of Section 35 of the Constitution Act, 1982.' See also the preamble. For analysis of the effect of section 25 of the Canadian Charter of Rights and Freedoms (Constitution Act, 1982, Part I, being Schedule B of the Canada Act, 1982 (U.K.), 1982, c. 11) on the Nunavut Agreement-in-Principle, see Isaac (1992:400–2).
72 Constitution Act, 1982, Part II, being Schedule B of the Canada Act, 1982 (U.K.), 1982, c. 11, s. 35 reads:

35(1) The existing aboriginal and treaty rights of the aboriginal peoples of Canada are hereby recognized and affirmed.
(2) In this Act, 'aboriginal peoples of Canada' includes the Indian, Inuit and Métis peoples of Canada.
(3) For greater certainty in subsection (1) 'treaty rights' includes rights that now exist by way of land claims agreements or may be so acquired.

(4) Notwithstanding any other provision of this Act, the aboriginal and treaty rights referred to in subsection (1) are guaranteed equally to male and female persons.

73 Isaac (1992:399).
74 Gallagher-Mackay (2000:217).
75 Gray (1994:315).
76 Regarding these options, see Kleist (2004:120–1).
77 Harhoff (1994b:250).
78 Ibid., 251.
79 Harhoff (1994–5:63 and 61–2). He outlines seven arguments for the permanent and irrevocable nature of the home rule jurisdiction. Harhoff (1994a:15) also notes that the Danish government intended at some point to rescind part of the home rule arrangement but refrained from doing so because such a move would have contravened international law.
80 J.B. Nielsen (2000:157).
81 Ward (1993:142).
82 Ibid., 143.
83 *Report from the Commission on Self-Governance* (2003).
84 Regarding the Inuit Qaujimajatuqangit (IQ) and incorporation of its principles into the Government of Nunavut, see chapter 3 below. (Inuit Qaujimajatuqangit means 'traditional Inuit knowledge').
85 Nowlan-Card (1996:31).
86 Interview with an Akitsiraq Law School program student, Iqaluit, 5 October 2002.
87 See art. 2, part 7 of the NLCA. The government of Canada has officially recognized that existing Aboriginal rights under section 35(1) of the Constitution Act include the right to inherent self-government. Canada, Department of Indian Affairs and Northern Development (1995:3). On the position of the Royal Commission of Aboriginal Peoples and the Supreme Court of Canada regarding this, see: Royal Commission on Aboriginal Peoples (1993b; 1996a:202), Russell (2005:170–89), Marecic (2000:286), and Macklem (2001:174).
88 Interview with a senior official with the Government of Nunavut, Office of the Premier, Iqaluit, 8 October 2002.
89 Aboriginal self-governance can take different forms, and the Royal Commission on Aboriginal peoples recognizes public government as a form of Aboriginal government, but it is not clear whether this form 'can be seen as a form of the inherent right of self-government' (Gallagher-Mackay [2000:223]).

90 Isaac (1992:398–9).
91 Gray (1994:303).
92 For example, Gray (1994:309) considers that the NLCA 'does not abandon
    the issue of self-government but rather reworks it to fit current models of
    government in Canada based on democratic representation.' In his words,
    'Instead of mono-ethnic self-government, public government transplants the
    Euro-Canadian system of popular representation into a jurisdiction where
    most of the citizenry are Inuit. The interests and rights of the majority are
    preserved by government.' Marecic (2000:293) does not share Gray's opti-
    mism and states that 'an incorporation of aboriginal governance into a pub-
    lic type of government may ultimately undermine *self*-government for the
    Inuit. Thus they may destroy what they have set out to preserve'; emphasis in
    original.
93 Marecic (2000:291–2).
94 Employing the theory of the overdeveloped postcolonial state, Dahl
    (1986b:321) refers to Greenlandic home rule as 'overdeveloped' relative to
    its social foundation inside Greenland. In other words, the home rule system
    was not based on adequate economic or social development. By its nature
    and the scope of its powers, it is deeply rooted in the Danish presence on the
    island for more than 250 years. Without an economic basis, it is not feasible
    to maintain the existing level of housing, wages, and social security benefits,
    and the high standard of living.
95 Aviâja Egede Lynge (2006).
96 Comment by an anonymous reader referring to Quebec Inuit leader Charlie
    Watt.
97 Alfreðsson (1982a:306) notes that 'introduction of limited autonomy called
    home rule can in no way be described as an exercise of the right of self-deter-
    mination.' Wutzke (1997–8:540) assumes that 'the Nunavut Act and the
    NLCA provide the "high water mark" for the aboriginal right of self-determi-
    nation in Canada.'
98 For example, Nowlan-Card (1996:60) makes this conclusion regarding
    Nunavut.

Chapter 3. Territorial Government versus Home Rule: The Structure of Nunavut's and Greenland's Institutions

1 The Nunavut Implementation Commission was created in 1994 with a mandate to advise the three parties to the Nunavut Political Accord 1992 – that is,
   the Tungavik Federation of Nunavut (succeeded by the NTI in 1993), the government of the Northwest Territories (GNWT), and the federal government –

on aspects of the creation of Nunavut. The Nunavut Political Accord (s. 6.1) specified that 'the Nunavut Act shall provide for a Nunavut Implementation Commission (NIC) in accordance with this Accord.' Comprising nine commissioners, appointed by the governor in council (i.e., the federal cabinet) (s. 6.3), the commission, in accordance with s. 6.6.1, provided its advice on: '(i) a timetable for the assumption of service delivery responsibilities from the GNWT, federal government or other authority, by the Government of Nunavut; (ii) the process for the first election of the Government of Nunavut and for the determination of electoral districts for Nunavut; (iii) the design of and funding for training plans; (iv) the process for the identification of a capital city of Nunavut; (v) the principles and criteria for an equitable division of assets and liabilities between the GNWT and the Government of Nunavut; (vi) capital infrastructure needs of Nunavut resulting from division and the creation of a new territory, and scheduling for construction; (vii) the appropriate administrative design for the first Government of Nunavut which may include personnel to administer the functions described in 7.1 with due regard for efficiencies and effectiveness ...' Consequently, the NIC has developed a number of reports, which were crucial for the establishment of Nunavut.

2 The Commission on Home Rule, Resumé of the Report, in Henry and Miller (2003:67–78). The original Danish report consists of four volumes (*Hjemmestyre i Grønland* [Copenhagen, 1978]). *Report from the Commission on Self-Governance* (2003:37–41 and 107–20).

3 The Greenland Home Rule Act, ch. 1, s. 1(2).

4 It is important to note that the chief executive officer for Nunavut is called commissioner of Nunavut. He appoints the members of an executive council (cabinet) on the recommendation of the Legislative Assembly of Nunavut (Nunavut Act, s. 11). In accordance with s. 12 of the act, the Nunavut Legislature consists of the commissioner and the legislative assembly. See also Legislative Assembly and Executive Council Act, S. Nu.2002, c. 5, as amended.

5 Breinholt-Larsen (1992:206) notes that until the mid-1970s Greenland did not have a party system despite a few attempts in 1950s and 1960s to create branches of Danish parties on the island. About Greenland elections, see Dahl (1986b:320–1).

6 Dahl (1985:176–7, 1986b:320) underscores that at the moment of introduction of home rule, the Siumut Party was organized nationwide and had an effective leadership based on goals formulated by the Greenlandic elite. Between 1975 and 1979 it was this elite that determined the party's politics.

7 Dahl (1986b:320).

8 Breinholt-Larsen (1992:206).

9 Statistics Greenland (2001:25). The Siumut Party was founded in July 1977.

10 Charles Bremner, 'Greenland Shows Its Support for Nation Status,' *Times* (London), 5 December 2002.
11 Atássut started as a political movement in 1976–7. The actual party was founded in April 1978. Statistics Greenland (2001:27).
12 Statistics Greenland (2001:27).
13 The Inuit Ataqatigiit Party, which became a formal party in 1978, started as a gathering of 500 young people from all over Greenland in 1976. Eventually this party was based on Marxist ideology and on independence. See Inuit Ataqatigiit Party platform, adopted 21 November 1978, in Dahl (1986a, appendix 3). See also Lyck (2000:99) and 'Coalition Collapse Sends Greenlanders Back to the Polls,' *Nunatsiaq News*, 23 September 2005.
14 Jack Hicks, 'Who's Who in Greenland Politics,' *Nunatsiaq News*, 9 December 2005.
15 'New Independence Movement in Greenland: Inussuk, Launched on May Day, Represents up to 30,000,' Siku Circumpolar News Service, 6 May 2006.
16 For analysis of the political culture in Nunavut, see Henderson (2004:133–54). As she notes, 'Political parties operate federally and thus contest the single constituency that Nunavut represents.' Many members of the territorial legislature are members of national political parties, mostly the Liberal Party (ibid., 136).
17 Ibid., 137.
18 Interviews with Nunavut residents suggest that there might be a party system in the future because of population growth.
19 Lyck (2000:102–10).
20 Dahl (1986a:144).
21 On the political system of the NWT prior to the division, and Inuit participation in it, see Hicks and White (2000:68–9).
22 Canada, Department of Northern Affairs and National Resources, Northern Administration Branch, Welfare Division, *Quajivaallirutissat* (Ottawa: Queen's Printer, 1964) at 38, quoted in Hicks and White (2000:68).
23 Dahl (1985:172–3) notes that during the Second World War, a Nazi group was established in Sisimiut. In 1946 an attempt was made to found a communist party in Qullissat. In the mid-1950s Greenland's Radical Citizens Party was established in Qaqortoq. In 1955 Greenland's Social Democratic Party was founded. 'An unsuccessful attempt in 1963 to establish a Greenlandic elite party (the Inuit party) on a purely ethnic foundation was followed by the formation of the Sukaq party in 1969, based on working class as well as ethnic appeal' (172). The Conservative Party of Greenland was established – and dissolved – in 1972. None of these parties succeeded, but they were all predecessors of the main political parties in Greenland today.
24 Legaré (1998:295–6 n.18). Nunavut, as a part of Canada, has generally inher-

ited the British Westminster system of parliamentary democracy, one notable characteristic of which is strict party discipline.

25 White (1991:503).

26 'The political system of Greenland is very similar to the Danish style of parliamentarian democracy.' Dahl (2005b:170).

27 F. Lynge (1989:68).

28 About 'the North Atlantic Group' – the body in the Folketing that aims to work towards independence for Greenland and the Faroe Islands – see www.dnag.dk.

29 'All Danish citizens may vote, provided they are aged 18, are not disqualified by insanity, and have been permanent residents in Greenland for at least six months prior to the election.' Statistics Greenland (2001:23).

30 The Greenland Home Rule Act, s. 2(1).

31 In 1995 the Siumut Party switched its coalition partner. In 1984–8 and 1991–5, the coalition was formed with the left-wing nationalist Inuit Ataqatigiit. In 1995 a coalition was formed with the liberal Atássut Party. This was a surprise for Greenlandic politicians because the Siumut Party had formed a minority government with liberals only for a short time, from 1988 to 1991 (Thomsen 1994–5:30).

32 Dahl (2006:34).

33 Ibid.

34 The new premier, Hans Enoksen, who speaks only Greenlandic, brought a new dimension to Greenlandic politics and replaced the longest-serving premier, Jonathan Motzfeldt.

35 The coalition agreement between Siumut and Inuit Ataqatigiit was announced on 8 December 2002. See Jan M. Olsen, 'New Social Democratic–Led Government Coalition in Greenland,' Associated Press, 9 December 2002.

36 'Greenland's New Home-Rule Government Coalition Has Practically Broken Up after Just a Month,' BBC Monitoring, 10 January 2003.

37 Lyberth's actions outraged Greenland's bishops and many of the senior politicians. He was fired, but this did nothing to restore Greenland's damaged reputation. See 'Greenland Civil Servant Who Used Spiritual Healer Fired by the Premier, Averting Political Crisis,' Associated Press, 13 January 2003; Andrew Osborn, '"Cleansed" Greenland Cabinet Falls,' *Guardian* (London), 11 January 2003.

38 Coalition agreement between Siumut and Atássut, 17 January 2003, www.nanoq.gl.

39 Info was provided by the Inuit Circumpolar Conference (since 2006 Council) (ICC) Greenland, 10 September 2003. See also M.U. Jensen (2004:28).

40 Coalition agreement between Siumut and IA, 13 September 2003, www.nanoq.gl.
41 'Greenlanders Demand Election,' *Nunatsiaq News*, 9 September 2005.
42 'Coalition Collapse Sends Greenlanders Back to the Polls,' *Nunatsiaq News*, 23 September 2005.
43 Jack Hicks, '"Northern Lights" Coalition a Return to Normal for Greenland Politics,' special to *Nunatsiaq News*, 9 December 2005. See also Jane George, 'Right-wingers May Be Crucial in Greenland Coalition,' *Nunatsiaq News*, 18 November 2005.
44 Dahl (2006:36–7).
45 According to Hicks, in the 1999 election voters were able to vote for one candidate out of 206 names on the ballot. The most popular candidates from each party were elected and '31 seats in the Landsting were divided up according to the percentage of vote obtained be each party' ('Greenland Parliament Shifts to the Left,' special to *Nunatsiaq News*, 18 February 1999). For details on the earlier system, see Thomsen (1998–9:26).
46 Thomsen (1998–9:26).
47 Greenland, in *Indigenous World* (1999–2000:29).
48 Thomsen (1998–9:27).
49 *Report from the Commission on Self-Governance* (2003:118–19).
50 See information about the Qikiqtani Inuit Association at www.qikiqtani.nu.ca, about the Kivalliq Inuit Association at www.kivalliq.org, and about the Kitikmeot Inuit Association at www.polarnet.ca/polarnet/kia.htm. See also NLCA, art. 39.
51 In 1993 the NTI was created as a private corporation representing Nunavut Inuit to ensure that promises made in the NLCA were carried out. It took over from the Tungavik Federation of Nunavut, the body that had negotiated the NLCA. The NTI has a ten-member board of directors that meets regularly in various Nunavut communities to debate issues and make decisions that affect the territory's Inuit. Four executive board members are directly elected by the Inuit of Nunavut. The remaining six board members are nominated by regional Inuit associations and include their presidents. The chair of Nunavut Trust also sits as an ex-officio member of the NTI board. See www.tunngavik.com; Legaré (2003:117–38).
52 Greg Younger-Lewis, 'Newly-minted NTI Prez Thaws Relations with GN,' *Nunatsiaq News*, 26 March 2004.
53 The importance of the NTI and the necessity for the government of Nunavut and the NTI to work closely together were emphasized in the Clyde River Protocol (27 October 1999), which governed working relations between the government of Nunavut and the NTI. Subsequent to the Clyde River Proto-

col, on 28 May 2004, the premier of Nunavut and the NTI president signed a new protocol – *Iqqanaijaqatigiit: Government of Nunavut and Nunavut Tunngavik Incorporated Working Together* (2004). Regarding this unique relationship see, for example, Joint Review of the Clyde River Protocol (2000:1–11); *Iqqanaijaqatigiit: 2004–2005 Annual Review of Priorities* (2005).

54 Nunavut Act, s. 17.

55 The 1997 Nunavut Electoral Boundaries Commission suggested different options for electoral districts. *Report of the Nunavut Electoral Boundaries Commission* (1997). At the January 1998 Nunavut Political Leaders Summit it was agreed to divide Nunavut into nineteen electoral districts. Hicks and White (2000:75).

56 See *Election of the First Legislative Assembly of Nunavut – 1999: A New Beginning* (Iqaluit: Published by the Chief Electoral Officer,1999), 37–65; *Election of the First Legislative Assembly of Nunavut – 1999: Official Voting Results* (Iqaluit: Published by the Chief Electoral Officer, 1999), 26–71. Regarding Nunavut's elections and constituency profiles, see www.cbc.ca/nunavutvotes2004/ridings/resultMain.html; 'Nunavut Votes: Constituency Profiles,' 17 February 2004, www.cbc.ca/nunavutvotes2004; 'Okalik Wins Second Term as Premier,' 5 March 2004, www.north.cbc.ca.

57 For some thoughts on 'consensus' government in Nunavut, see O'Brien (2003–4:6–10) and Henderson (2004:137–8). As White (1991:509) notes, with consensus government 'political decisions are arrived at not by strict majoritarian principles but through discussion, in which the views of all members are taken into account and accommodated.' See also the chapter 'Consensus Government in Nunavut and the Northwest Territories' in White (2005:58–63) and White (2006a:13–14 and 18–24).

58 Regarding the Legislative Assembly of the NWT in the context of British parliamentarianism, see White (1991, 1993a:322–39, 1993b:5–28), Cameron and White (1995), ch. 3. Regarding the nuances of the operation of the Nunavut Legislative Assembly and its unique features, see White (2006a:8–31).

59 S. 60 (1) of the Legislative Assembly and Executive Council Act, S. Nu. 2002, c. 5, reads:

(1) There shall be an Executive Council of Nunavut composed of
(a) a Premier chosen by the Legislative Assembly from among its members; and
(b) persons appointed by the Commissioner on the recommendation of the Legislative Assembly.

About the speaker, see s. 41(1).

60 The Greenland Home Rule Act, s. 3.

61 I am grateful to Ulrik Pram Gad for his comment. Notably, non-Inuit parliamentarians are well informed about specific conditions in Nunavut and Greenland and usually are fluent in Inuit languages. For example, following Greenland's 2005 election, of the thirty-one members of the Landsting, only one was an ethnic Dane and one was a Greenlander who does not speak Greenlandic. See Hicks, '"Northern Lights" Coalition.'

62 The first and the second elections for premier were conducted under the same rules. The premier of Nunavut was selected by the MLAs via secret ballot. Previously, the Nunavut Implementation Commission elaborated a detailed report called *Direct Election of the Nunavut Premier: Schemes for Legislative Enactment* (1998).

63 Re direct elections of the premier, see Legislative Assembly of Nunavut, *Nunavut Leadership Forum*, Official Report, Day 1, 6 June 2006, 27–9; Jim Bell, 'When They're Mad at the Premier' (editorial), *Nunatsiaq News*, 30 June 2006.

64 Quoted in Nunavut, Legislative Assembly (2000:6).

65 During the 1999 election, only one woman – Manitok Thompson – was elected. In the 2004 election two women were elected. They received the most important positions in the cabinet. Levinia Brown was made deputy premier, minister of health and social services, and minister responsible for the status of women. Leona Aglukkaq became the government house leader and minister of finance (Jane George, 'Okalik Shares Power with Assembly's Women,' *Nunatsiaq News*, 12 March 2004). In Greenland after the 1999 election, 20 per cent of the members of the Landsting were women; after the 2005 election, thirteen of thirty-one (or 42 per cent) were women (Hicks, '"Northern Lights" Coalition').

66 See Wilson (2002:43–66). For a bibliography on gender parity in the Nunavut legislature, see, Nunavut Implementation Commission (1996b:99–104). See also Dahl (1997:42–7); Gombay (2000:125–48); Young (1997:306–15); Hicks and White (2000:69–75). For NIC recommendations, see the Nunavut Implementation Commission 1995a; 1996a; 1996b:31–67; 1996c:56–7; 1995b:4–14.

67 The referendum was conducted on 26 May 1997. See Appendix: Nunavut – A Chronology in Hicks and White (2000:95).

68 H. Rasmussen (2004; 1998: 265, 269). For discussion of Greenlandic women's participation in other areas, see Dybbroe (1988:111–31).

69 Thomsen (1990:241–2) shows how Greenlandic women had to fight for their political rights, and how their contribution to the functioning of home rule has been unacknowledged. Women were discriminated against, and

their political involvement was hampered by the development of party politics, which undermined the unity among the outspoken minority of female activists.

70 Regarding Inuit women's participation in various Canadian political organizations, see Thomsen (1988:85). Pauktuutit is a national non-profit association representing all Inuit women in Canada. Its mandate is to foster a greater awareness of the needs of Inuit women to encourage their participation in community, regional, and national concerns in relation to social, cultural, and economic development. See the group's website at www.pauktuutit.ca.

71 The Nunavut Implementation Commission paid special attention to the size of the Nunavut parliament. See Nunavut Implementation Commission (1995a:17–18; 1996b:13–18). The 2006 Nunavut Electoral Boundaries Commission exercised its mandate within s. 21 of the Nunavut Elections Act, S. Nu. 2002, c. 17. The commission was chaired by Justice Beverly Browne. See Nunavut Electoral Boundaries Commission (2006: 24–5, 4–5).

72 The Landsting presidency consists of one chairperson and four deputy chairpersons elected by the parliament at the beginning of each parliamentary year. Before 1988 the same person acted as chair of the parliament and the head of the government. See 'The Home Rule/The Parliament' at www.nanoq.gl. Re the Nunavut speaker, see the Nunavut Act, s. 19, and Legislative Assembly and Executive Council Act, S.Nu. 2002, c. 5, as amended.

73 See 'The Home Rule/The Parliament' at www.nanoq.gl. and Legislative Assembly Statutes Amendment Act, S.Nu. 2005, c. 8, s. 2.

74 Comment by an anonymous reader. There were several arguments for accepting the concept of decentralization. The Nunavut Implementation Commission elaborated a number of principles and elements of the decentralized government. Regarding principles, see 1995a:23–4; 1996a:43–5. For elements, see 1995a:25–6; 1996a:46–7. See also Nunavut Consulting and Ekho Inuit Originals (1999:1–82). The latter contains responses and recommendations from the communities on the subject of decentralization. See also *Building Nunavut through Decentralization* (2002:1–32), which includes findings and recommendations on the effect of decentralization and challenges associated with such a model.

75 *Building Nunavut through Decentralization* (2002:9); emphasis in original.

76 Interviews with Nunavut residents in 2002 revealed that, while many view decentralization as a general phenomenon, it also coincides with the Inuit tradition of sharing things. The distribution of government services is shared among all Nunavut communities. As White (1991:506) states regarding the NWT, 'Natives generally prefer that power be decentralized and widely shared.'

77 Dahl (1986a:219–20).
78 Cited in *Building Nunavut through Decentralization* (2002:1).
79 'As an Inuk employee said, '*This is decentralization, but major decisions are still made in Iqaluit*' ibid. (2002:19; emphasis in original). See also Hicks and White (2005).
80 Jim Bell, 'GN Should Review Decentralization' (editorial) *Nunatsiaq News*, 26 August 2005. 'Decentralization "a Figment of Someone's Imagination"' (letter to the editor), *Nunatsiaq News*, 9 September 2005. The Auditor General of Canada, Sheila Fraser, concluded in her report to the Legislative Assembly of Nunavut (2005) that decentralization is a major factor in the government of Nunavut's significant financial problems. See Fraser (2005), chs 7–8.
81 Bartmann (1996:158).
82 Inuit and Western traditions are incompatible in several ways: decentralization versus centralization; collectivism versus individualism (the system of individual representation does not mesh with Inuit ideals of collective representation); consensus making versus majority rule.
83 Mark G. Stevenson prepared a paper for the RCAP entitled 'Traditional Inuit Decision-Making Structures and the Administration of Nunavut' (1993). Written from an anthropological perspective, it does not show particularly which Inuit ways have been working in the government of Nunavut.
84 The second government of Nunavut reaffirmed its commitment to the Bathurst Mandate and is focused on building an economy based on *Pinasuaqtavut (2004–2009)* principles and the incorporation of Inuit societal values through the application of IQ. See Government of Nunavut (1999b, 2004).
85 Government of Nunavut (2004:3–4).
86 Government of Nunavut, 'Inuit Qaujimajatuqangit Katimajiit Established,' news release, 8 September 2003.
87 Government of Nunavut, 'Second Inuit Qaujimajatuqangit Katimajiit Council Appointed,' news release, 7 September 2005.
88 The term 'living policy' is used by McCready (2003). For discussions of the IQ policy, see Wilman (2002:33–8); Government of Nunavut (1999a); Jaypetee Arnakak, 'Commentary: What Is Inuit Qaujimajatuqangit?' special to *Nunatsiaq News*, 25 August 2000; Arnakak (2001:17–19); Government of Nunavut (2002a); Levesque (2002); McCready (2003), Henderson (2005:1003–4).
89 Wildlife Act, S.Nu. 2003, c. 26, as amended. The act was passed by Nunavut's Legislature in December 2003 and came into force on 9 July 2005. Government of Nunavut, 'Nunavut Day Chosen for New Wildlife Act,' news release, 8 July 2005.
90 For instance, it is not apparent what IQ means for the justice system. See

Crnkovich, Addario, and Archibald (2000:22–4). About the efforts of the
Nunavut Wildlife Management Board to incorporate IQ into its activities
and challenges from incorporation of IQ into existing governance structures, see White (2006b:406–12). Re IQ in the Nunavut Legislative Assembly, see White (2006a:25–8, 15–18). He concludes that IQ has a limited
influence on the Nunavut Legislative Assembly (ibid., 28). Re IQ in the government of Nunavut bureaucracy, see Timpson (2006:517–30).

91 Nunavut, Legislative Assembly (2001:1). I am grateful to Bob Carson for
   telling me about this document.
92 The NLCA establishes the Nunavut Wildlife Management Board (art. 5,
   part 2, s. 5.2.1); the Nunavut Planning Commission (art 11, part 4, s. 11.4.1)
   to ensure effective land use and Inuit involvement in the planning process;
   and the Nunavut Impact Review Board (art. 12, part 2, s. 12.2.1) to protect
   and promote the existing and future well-being of the residents and communities of the Nunavut Settlement Area, and to protect the ecosystemic
   integrity of this area. For water management, see Nunavut Water Board
   (art. 13, part 2, s. 13.2.1); for promotion of Inuit participation in the development of social and cultural policies, see Nunavut Social Development
   Council (art. 32, part 3, s. 32.3.1).
93 See NLCA; 'Co-management and Judicial Review: Emerging Normativity
   and Old Institutional Relations,' in Gallagher-Mackay (2000:22–101);
   Rodon (1998:119–35). Gray (1994:327–33) distinguishes between self-man-
   agement and co-management. He finds that the Nunavut system resembles
   co-management, as Nunavut boards do not have final decision-making
   power and their 'decisions are ultimately subject to government approval'
   (331).
94 Gallagher-Mackay (2000:23) points out that advisory functions of these bodies constitute a hallmark of the system of co-management.
95 Anawak (1993:8).
96 Paul Quassa, 'Inuit Have a Good Deal Says Quassa,' *Nunatsiaq News*, 22
   December 1989, 1, quoted in Mitchell and Tobin (1999:21).
97 White (2002:94).
98 Gurston Dacks, 'Nunavut: Aboriginal Self-Determination through
   Public Government' (unpublished paper), 26, quoted in Nowlan-Card
   (1996:38–9).
99 Rodon (1998:130, 131).
100 Gallagher-Mackay (2000:71).
101 White (2006b:407), analysing the Nunavut Wildlife Management Board
    (NWMB), concludes, 'that while the NWMB has successfully integrated IQ
    and Western science into the empirical knowledge base upon which its

decisions rest, important elements of its structure and operation remain essentially rooted in the Western bureaucratic paradigm.' Similarly, Rodon (1998:129) notes that the structure created by the NLCA facilitates 'the integration of Inuit hunters into the bureaucratic apparatus of the Canadian State ... Indigenous knowledge is used only to supplement scientific data in the harvest study. The only part of the agreement where indigenous knowledge is explicitly recognized is in the Inuit Bowhead Knowledge Study (art. 5.5.2) ...'

102 The Greenland Home Rule Act, s. 17(1); the high commissioner replaced the office of the governor. The home rule authorities inform the high commissioner about new acts or regulations of the Landsting and other legislation of general application made by the home rule institutions (s. 17[3]). The high commissioner might be invited to participate in the Landsting's or the Landsstyre's debates, although he or she is not allowed to vote in them. See Statistics Greenland (2001:15). See also 'The High Commissioner of Greenland' and 'The History of the High Commissioner,' both available on the website of the Ministry of Foreign Affairs of Denmark www.stm.dk.

103 Nunavut Act, s. 6(1).

104 Ward (1993:69–70) suggests that the Greenland Home Rule Act resembles classical colonial legislation, as it does not include provisions that the Rigsombudsmand should be Inuk. However, she further notes that the tendency is that Greenlanders prefer a Danish-born high commissioner.

105 Before the creation of the Nunavut territory, there was an interim commissioner for Nunavut, Jack Anawak.

106 For details on Danish administration representation in Greenland, see Statistics Greenland (2001:14–15). Regarding police in Greenland, see Wacker and Hojbjerg (1992:163–70). See also Commission on Greenland's Judicial System (2004:98–107). I am grateful to Pierre Rousseau for providing me with this document. Regarding court systems, see chapter 4 below.

107 Thomsen (1994–5:30–1).

108 Any person can file a complaint with the ombudsman. The ombudsman's main task is to protect individuals from encroachment by the authorities; see J.B. Nielsen (2000:156). See also Thomsen (1994–5:30–1).

109 Also, from 1 January 1997, the ombudsman acts as supervisor for the Greenlandic Housing Company, as the latter can make decisions on behalf of the home rule government or any municipal authority; see Statistics Greenland (2001:8).

110 On deriving from the Danish institution, see 'The Home Rule: The Ombudsman' at www.nanoq.gl and www.ombudsmanden.dk. On the West-

ern tradition, see the Law on Ombudsman in Greenland, act no. 7 of 13
June 1994, which copies the Danish law.

111 For details, see Martens (1988:358–9).

112 Lytthans (1999:117).

113 For problems with the size of the public sector, see *Report from the Commission on Self-Governance* (2003:37–41, 59–62). On the work force, see ibid., 63, and J.K. Nielsen (2001:12).

114 The Commission on Self-Governance has emphasized the importance of increasing the educational level of the labour force, providing continuous education so that workers' skills are always up to date, and financing for training of the marginalized persons. *Report from the Commission on Self-Governance* (2003:42–3, 61–9).

115 Ibid., 39.

116 Jim Bell, 'Was Nunavut Worth It?' *Nunatsiaq News,* 8 July 2005.

117 There are numerous discussions in the *Nunatsiaq News* on that matter. See Janson Biggs, 'Nunavut's Trainee-led Government Is Facing Collapse,' *Nunatsiaq News,* 5 March 2004; 'Incompetent GN Management Needs Overhaul' (letter to the editor), *Nunatsiaq News,* 30 July 2004; Jim Bell, 'The GN: A Haven of Racism and Incompetence?' (editorial), *Nunatsiaq News,* 5 November 2004.

118 Gray (1994:326).

119 In 2005 the government of Nunavut announced that 46 per cent of its employees are Inuit (Jim Bell, 'Nunavut's DIAND Office Faces "Desperate" Staff Problems,' *Nunatsiaq News,* 13 May 2005).

120 'Inuit Still Less Than Half of GN Workforce,' *Nunatsiaq News,* 10 March 2006.

121 See *The Inuit of Nunavut as Represented by NTI v. The Queen,* para. 55; claim by the NTI of 5 December 2006. Before this $1 billion lawsuit was launched against the government of Canada, the NTI was asking Ottawa for $10 to $20 million a year over ten years to implement article 23. A partial deal to fund the institutions of public government was expected to be reached in 2006 (Jim Bell, 'IPG Funding Deal May Be Less Than Meets the Eye,' *Nunatsiaq News,* 7 April 2006). The conciliator for the implementation of the NLCA, the Honourable Thomas Berger, suggested in his final report that an extra $20 million a year will be required to deal with Nunavut's failed training system and recruitment of young Inuit with the government of Nunavut, and that much more funding is needed to create a bilingual (Inuktitut/English) program from kindergarten to Grade 12. See Berger (2006).

122 Lytthans (1999:122–3).

123 'Greenland' in *Indigenous World* (2000–1:27); for further considerations of
Greenlanders in Denmark, see Chemnitz (2005:54–9).
124 'Greenlandic Only, Suggests Siumut Party,' *Nunatsiaq News*, 3 March 2006.
125 Kleist (2004:116).
126 Lytthans (1999:122). See 'Greenlandic Managers,' *Sermitsiaq News*, 21 September 2006; 'Hire Greenlanders for Leading Positions,' *Sermitsiaq News*, 5
November 2006.
127 The francophone population of Nunavut encounters difficulties in receiving qualified services in French. There are also challenges with Inuktitut
funding for education and providing services in that language. See Sara
Minogue, 'GN Prepares to Fight for Federal Inuktitut Funding,' *Nunatsiaq
News*, 28 January 2005. For recommendations regarding language policy in
Nunavut, which are crucial for implementation of article 23, see Berger
(2006:23–59). Re the new Official Languages Act and the Inuit Language
Protection Act, see Nunavut Legislative Assembly, 3rd sess., 2nd Leg.,
Report of the Standing Committee Ajauqtiit on the Review of the 2004–5
Annual Report of the Languages Commissioner of Nunavut, June 2006; re
new government policies requiring senior officials to be fluent in Inuktitut,
and controversy surrounding this issue, see 'Learn Inuktitut or
"Iqqanaijaaqajjaagunniiqtutit," Mandarins Told,' CBC News, 7 June 2006;
Derek Neary, 'Bureaucratic Inuktitut,' Nunavut News/North, 10 July 2006;
John Curran and Derek Neary, 'Mixed Reaction to Inuktitut Policy,'
Nunavut News/North, 10 July 2006.

Chapter 4: The Jurisdiction of Greenland and Nunavut

1 *Report from the Commission on Self-Governance* (2003).
2 Jim Bell, 'Martin Commits to Nunavut Devolution by 2008,' *Nunatsiaq News*,
17 December 2004; 'Devolution Deal Easier to Reach in Nunavut Than
N.W.T.: Prentice,' CBC News Online, 4 December 2006, www.cbc.ca.
3 Developments in international law show that the right of indigenous peoples
to autonomy is a stronger case than for other minorities. For some considerations, see Anaya (2004), Skurbaty (2005), Loukacheva (2005:12–17).
4 The Commission on Self-Governance underscored that self-governance
should be based upon a self-sufficient economy, with considerable reduction
of the block transfer from Denmark to Greenland. *Report from the Commission
on Self-Governance* (2003:29).
5 *The Commission on Self-Governance – a Presentation* (2003), available at
www.dk.nanoq.gl.
6 On obstacles to sustainability, see, for example, Lyck (1997); R.O. Rasmussen

(2000:41; 2002); N. Larsen (2004); and *The Economic Competitiveness of Greenland: Financial Returns, Labor Productivity and International Gaps*, ICON Group International, May 2006. On Greenland's economic dependence, see Larsen (2002), who has investigated by means of statistical data and econometric analysis the possibilities of economic development and dependency in Greenland from 1955 to 1998.

7 Jane George, 'Greenland, Iceland Set to Become Hydrogen Fuel Leaders,' *Nunatsiaq News*, 18 November 2005; Jon Harding, 'Big Oil Targets Greenland: Fields of 500m Barrels: EnCana among 13 Firms Eyeing Bid for Offshore Rights,' *National Post*, 19 July 2006; 'Eldorado Opens Up off Greenland,' Siku Circumpolar News Service, 20 July 2006; R.O. Rasmussen (2006:40–7).

8 Jane George, 'Clean, Locally Produced Energy Fuels Greenlandic Election Campaign,' *Nunatsiaq News*, 18 November 2005.

9 Vail and Clinton (2001); Clinton and Vail (2005).

10 In 2005 Nunavut's economy declined by 0.5%; government of Nunavut expenditures on services and goods represented 89 per cent of GDP. Opportunities for economic expansion are seen in the development of the Jericho diamond mine and construction of the Doris North gold mine, investment in communications (e.g., satellite services), air transportation, cruise ships during the summer months, personal travel, restaurant, and accommodation services; Statistics Canada (2006:21); see also Myers (2000:25–40).

11 Regarding mining in Nunavut, see McPherson (2003). 'Arctic Port Location by Year's End: Defence Minister Tours Resolute, One of Seven Potential Sites for Deepwater Docking Facility,' *Edmonton Journal*, 15 July 2006.

12 Jim Bell, 'Economic Outlook: Nunavut Poised for Growth,' *Nunatsiaq News*, 18 November 2005.

13 Some of these steps are well described in *The Naujaat Challenge: Working Together. A Framework for Discussions about an Economic Development Strategy for Nunavut* [Government of Nunavut, (2002b:7, 11)]. There is also the *Nunavut Economic Development Strategy*, which lays the foundation for the development of the territory's economy [Government of Nunavut (2003)].

14 *The Naujaat Challenge* (2002b:8–10, 2).

15 For 2005–6, Nunavut's own revenue was $81.5 million, whereas the federal government provided $890.9 million. See 'Then and Now: How the GN's Budget Has Swollen since April 1, 1999,' *Nunatsiaq News*, 4 March 2005.

16 See 'Debate Rages, but Nunavut Has Human Rights Act,' CBC News Online, 5 November 2003, www.cbc.ca; Patricia D'Souza, 'Human Rights Bill Passes by Narrow Margin,' *Nunatsiaq News*, 7 November 2003; Human Rights Act, S. Nu. 2003, c. 12.

17 *Lex loci* means local law. This term is widely employed by Lester (1979:65) in his study of Inuit land rights. Analysing the practice of Inuit place naming, he notes that *lex loci* existed in the Inuit communities through a system of land occupancy and use despite imposition of sovereignty by colonizers.

18 E.A. Hoebel (1940–1:663–83) uses the term 'law-ways.' In this study, I generally use 'law-ways' as the equivalent term of 'legal ways.'

19 R. Petersen (1996:279–82).

20 Nungak (1993:86–104); Ittinuar (1985:47–53); Inuaraq (1995:255–61); Oosten et al. (1999:1–237); R. Petersen (2000:9–12); Pauktuutit (1995, 2006a:9–14); *Suvaguuq* (1993); Canada, Department of Justice, (1997); Inuit Tapirisat of Canada (1994a).

21 W. Anderson (1974–5:73–81); Van Den Steenhoven (1956a:531–8, 1966:90–4); E.A. Hoebel (1967:255–62, 1968:67–99); Lester (1981); Patenaude (1985); K. Rasmussen (1929); Yabsley (1984); Richstone (1983:568–97); Rasing (1984, 1989); Finkler (1985a:141–52, 1985b:321–5, 1990:113–19); Rouland (1978:120–31, 1979b); Pospisil (1964:395–431); Sonne (1982:21–50); Carswell (1984:303–8); Matthiasson (1992); Tomaszewski (1995); Rousseau (1995:263–75).

22 In the Canadian context there have been attempts to bridge the gap between indigenous and non-indigenous visions of the legal system. See, for instance, Royal Commission on Aboriginal Peoples (1993a, 1996b). However, the Inuit views on the justice system deserve special attention.

23 Rasing (1994:38).

24 E.A. Hoebel (1968 [1954]:68), Van Den Steenhoven (1959:62). Van Den Steenhoven (1962:112) in his research found only two cases of a legal norm. In his words, 'sorcerers and dangerous insane persons are liable to be executed as public enemies.'

25 In his work, Rouland (1979a:11) shows the specific nature of legal sanction in Inuit populations, and the legal processes of coercion.

26 Cited by Patenaude (1989:32).

27 Fossett (2001:5).

28 Hallendy (1994:2).

29 Inuaraq (1995:256, 261).

30 Nungak (1993:86).

31 Van Den Steenhoven (1956b:25). There might be objections to this statement today; see Brice-Bennett (1997).

32 Graburn (1969:46).

33 These proposed features are not exhaustive and leave room for further analysis. The basic approaches to the theory of law were used to identify features

that can be further categorized into groups (e.g., spiritual norms, proce-
dural, institutional, written or unwritten, mandatory and non-mandatory
norms, etc.).

34 R. Petersen (1996:279). Rasing (1993:100) also states that the Iglulingmiut
rules were unwritten but 'existed in people's minds, particularly in those of
the elders and leaders.' See also Birket-Smith (1929:261).

35 Cited in Oosten et al. (1999:14).

36 Birket-Smith (1929:260–1).

37 For a detailed account on the interpretation of *inua*, see Oosten (2000). On
isuma, see Rasing (1994:69).

38 Birket-Smith (1959 [1936]:162–3).

39 E.A. Hoebel (1940–1:668).

40 Ibid.

41 Ibid., 669.

42 Rouland (1979a:14).

43 E.A. Hoebel (1940–1:665–7).

44 Birket-Smith (1929:261).

45 Van Den Steenhoven (1962:123).

46 E.A. Hoebel (1968 [1954]:74).

47 See, for example, the Inuit's interpretation of Robert S. Janes's murder,
which took place in Pond Inlet in 1920, in Matthiasson (1967:46).

48 Rouland (1979a:18).

49 The term 'legal action' is used in E.A. Hoebel's interpretation: Hoebel (1968
[1954]:73).

50 Van Den Steenhoven (1962:123) notes that although the Inuit of Keewatin
District did not know justice as an independent concept they employed a
common and strong sense of fairness in their daily interactions. Rasing
(1994:144) shows that justice through punishment was never an aspect of
Iglulingmiut social control. See also Rouland (1979a:14).

51 Birket-Smith (1959 [1936]:149).

52 Schechter (1983:82).

53 R. Petersen (1996:282–3).

54 Graburn (1969:58).

55 Rouland (1979a:20).

56 Rasing (1994:147).

57 See Holtved (1974–5:15–24); H. Petersen (1998:75–87).

58 H. Petersen observes that 'Greenlandic lacks the European type of abstract
terminology, which has to be re-created, inevitably in a circumscribed form,
when "translated" from Danish to Greenlandic' (ibid., 78). This is also true
for Inuit languages in Nunavut.

59 Patenaude (1989:41). For the Inuit explanation of their traditional methods of social control, see Pauktuutit (2006a:10–13).
60 Rouland (1979a:29) states, however, that gossip was a sort of institution. Spreading information and putting pressure on the person in question prepared the community to make a judgment.
61 E.A. Hoebel (1940–1:678, 681–2).
62 According to Eckert and Newmark (1980:198), thanks to song duels the outcome of the conflict was kept out of the everyday context, and life was relatively free of overt confrontation.
63 Balikci (1970:188–9).
64 Rouland (1979a:8) notes that song duels aimed 'to restore the internal balances within the group.'
65 Jensen (1992:122).
66 Rouland (1979a:59) notes that community acted as a judge and participant. See also Kleivan (1971:9) and H. Petersen (1998:77).
67 Kleivan (1971:9, 13).
68 Ibid., 11.
69 Breinholt-Larsen (1996:50).
70 Kleivan (1971:10–11).
71 H. Petersen (2000:177).
72 Ibid.
73 Atsainak (1993:36).
74 Matthiasson (1967:119).
75 Finkler (1975: abstract).
76 C.T. Griffiths et al. (1995b:135–6).
77 Pauktuutit (2006a:13) and Finkler (1975:20).
78 C.C. McCaul's opening address was privately printed after the trial; a copy exists in the Alberta Provincial Archives. The quote here is taken from Moyels (1979:38–9); emphasis in the original. See also Grant (2002).
79 The division between Danes and Greenlanders was based upon how they attained their livelihood, and not on their place of birth in Denmark or Greenland. Greenlandic customary law 'was in force for people living by traditional Greenlandic "free occupation" i.e. hunting and fishing,' whereas Danes, as Greenlanders who worked in various state agencies, were under Danish law; Bentzon (1986:201). See also Goldschmidt (1956:218), Brøndsted (1973:554).
80 H.G. Jensen (1992:123).
81 As Goldschmidt (1956:220) notes, the missionaries were appalled by practices of senilicide, infanticide, and polygamy, which were accepted in traditional Inuit societies.
82 Ibid.

83 H.G. Jensen (1992:124–5), Kleivan (1971:33).

84 H.G. Jensen (1992:125).

85 Ibid., 125–6.

86 Goldschmidt (1956: 224).

87 Ibid. The Jurex consisted of three Danish jurists: Dr. Verner Goldschmidt, Per Lindegaard, and Agnete Weis Bentzon. See Bentzon (1996:97). After eighteen months of investigation in 1948–9, the expedition submitted to the Ministry of Greenland a six-volume report. On the reforms, see Bentzon (1986:202–4).

88 Finkler (1975:32–3), the quote is at 33. On stipendiary magistrates, see also Price (1986).

89 The Territorial Court of the NWT (1955–72) was the first circuit court in the Eastern Arctic, which, thanks to guidelines established by Judge Sissons, attempted to provide justice to everyone. Sissons (1968:76). There were numerous changes to the court structure of the NWT. Until 1978 the Territorial Court of the NWT was known as the Magistrate's Court. See the Territorial Court Act, R.S.N.W.T. 1988, c. T-2, s. 2(1), as amended.

90 Finkler (1975:33–4).

91 On the Territorial Court, see Rowe (1990). Sissons (1968) points out that 'there were many cases in the eastern part of the Territories where charges were laid and never came to trial because there was no court to try them. In other cases the police did not lay charges because they could see no prospect of getting them tried' (79). He further notes that the Inuit had no concept of the meaning of being guilty and 'sometimes "plead guilty" to something because they wish to please you by doing so'" (123).

92 See Sissons (1968:123).

93 Ibid., 123, 125.

94 Sissons tried to accommodate two legal systems and recognized customary practices in his judgments. As he writes, 'I soon became very reluctant to accept a plea of "guilty" from an Eskimo' (ibid., 123). 'When the significance of some procedure was beyond the experience of an Eskimo I relaxed the rules ... On other occasions I enlarged the rules of the territorial court to encompass the Eskimo custom of seeking corroboration from the crowd while giving evidence' (125). Judge Sissons's successor, justice W.G. Morrow, adhered to the belief that some special treatment or adjustment was required for the Inuit. See W.H. Morrow (1995).

95 See Finkler (1975:49). According to an official of the Nunavut Court of Justice, the court tries to follow the principles laid by Judge Sissons and his successor Judge Morrow as much as possible. Interview with a senior official of the Nunavut Court of Justice, Iqaluit, 2 October 2002.

96 Bentzon (1996:100).
97 Bentzon (1986:202).
98 Bentzon (1966:122).
99 Bentzon (1986:205).
100 Act no. 271, 14 June 1951; for more information on the 1951 reform of the administration of justice, see Bentzon and Brøndsted (1983:607–10). See also H.G. Jensen (1992:128–34) and Greenland Criminal Code (1954).
101 *Report from the Commission on Self-Governance* (2003). To review the judicial system in Greenland in 1994, the Danish government and the home rule authorities set up the Commission on Greenland's Judicial System, which made its recommendations in 2004. Commission on Greenland's Judicial System (2004).
102 Brøndsted (1973:555–6).
103 Brøndsted (1996:120–1).
104 Commission on Greenland's Judicial System (2004:24).
105 Bentzon (1986:207). 'Nuuk, however, has two district judges, and the district judges of Aasiaat [*Egedesminde*] and Paamiut [*Frederikshåb*] are also district judges of Kangaatsiaq and Ivittuut respectively' (Commission on Greenland's Judicial System [2004:23]).
106 For details, see Commission on Greenland's Judicial System (2004:22–3).
107 Ibid., 24.
108 Ibid., 21–2.
109 Brøndsted (1996:121), Commission on Greenland's Judicial System (2004:22).
110 Brøndsted (1996:121–2).
111 Bentzon (1996:106).
112 Bentzon (1999:130).
113 Commission on Greenland's Judicial System (2004:15 and 26–7). The Supreme Court of Denmark would be the court of third instance 'upon leave from the Board of Appeal in Denmark.' The current system has the same rule.
114 In *Footprints 2* the Nunavut Implementation Commission considered the merger of the Supreme Court and territorial court of Nunavut as an important step towards unifying the court system and opening up the possibility for the community-based justice of the peace network to take on an enhanced role. Recommendation #11–23. Nunavut Implementation Commission (1996a:266–8). Sanders (2007) notes that the reasons underlying the recommendation for the single-level trial court were largely practical, and had to do with efficiency, simplicity, and the reduction of levels of administration: this was not an indigenous justice initiative.

115 See An Act to amend the Nunavut Act with respect to the Nunavut Court of Justice and to amend other Acts in consequence, S.C. 1999, c. 3, assented to 11 March 1999. The territorial legal authority for the Nunavut Court of Justice is the Nunavut Judicial System Implementation Act, S.N.W.T. 1998, c. 34. It enacts a new Judicature Act, S.N.W.T. 1998, c. 34, s. 1 and Justices of the Peace Act, S.N.W.T. 1998, c. 34, s. 2, both of which were consequently amended by the Nunavut Legislature.

116 The Judicature Act, s. 4(1), as amended.

117 The office of the senior justice of the peace for Nunavut was established in 2002. See Kublu and Sharkey (2003:8). 'The Justice of the Peace Court is an integral part of the Nunavut Court of Justice. Nunavut communities have lay Justices of the Peace (JP) who regularly sit on bail hearings and do some of the summary conviction criminal work (sentencing and/or trials). All JPs are Inuit or long-term northerners.' Sharkey (2000:4).

118 Justices of the Peace Act, s. 2, outlines the requirements for persons eligible for justices of the peace appointments.

119 Sharkey (2000:4).

120 There has been a lot of criticism of the circuit court system, including complaints that the key justice personnel are usually unfamiliar with the Inuit communities. There are concerns that this system does not reflect the communal procedures or account to the communities. Stevens (1993:385).

121 Quoted in C.T. Griffiths et al. (1995a:114).

122 Ibid.

123 Vertes (2002:40–6).

124 Ibid., 46.

125 Nunavut Act, s. 31(1), as amended; Judicature Act, s. 15(3).

126 Judicature Act, s. 17(1) and s.18(1).

127 'The North's Place in Canada's Future,' Statement by Northern premiers from the fourth annual Northern Premiers' Forum, Iqaluit, 7 November 2006, www.gov.nu.ca.

128 As Goldschmidt (1963) notes, for preparation of the code 'In 1948/49, about 2000 law cases were compiled and verbal information received from 53 of the 62 municipal councils and from the magistrates in the judicial districts of West Greenland' (113). 'Both the political council and the local authorities, interviewed in 1948/49, expressed strongly their wishes for preserving and codifying Greenland law' (115).

129 Goldschmidt (1956:232).

130 Schechter (1983:80) and Goldschmidt (1956:237).

131 Goldschmidt (1956:235).

132 Ibid., 240. Schechter (1983:80) points out that unlike most criminal sys-

tems, the code provides no protection against double jeopardy: 'Cases could be reviewed again and again, and sentences shortened, lengthened ... or re-designed to promote the Code's goal – that the offender not repeat the undesirable antisocial behaviour.'

133 Goldschmidt (1956:254).

134 Ibid., 250; emphasis in original.

135 Schechter (1983:80); emphasis in original. In Nunavut judges prescribe sentences in conformity with the maximum and minimum boundaries of the Canadian Criminal Code, section 718(2)(e), which reads: 'all available sanctions other than imprisonment that are reasonable in the circumstances should be considered for all offenders, with particular attention to the circumstances of aboriginal offenders.' Martin's Annual Criminal Code of Canada (2004:CC1281).

136 The term 'Arctic Peace Model' is Verner Goldschmidt's. See Schechter (1983:82), H.G. Jensen (1996:141).

137 For scrutiny of the system, see C.T. Griffiths (1996:10–11). Regarding possibilities for codification of Inuit customary law in Nunavut, see Haysom and Richstone (1987:103).

138 H.G. Jensen (1996:144).

139 Commission on Greenland's Judicial System (2004:75, 77).

140 This sanction ladder includes (from the mildest to most severe form of punishment) caution, fine, suspended prison sentence, supervision, community service; prison and supervision, prison, and safe custody. Ibid., 77–82.

141 Ibid., 78, 83.

142 Ibid., 68–74.

143 M.S. Pedersen (1999:138).

144 Commission on Greenland's Judicial System (2004:27).

145 Cited in 'Danish Parliament's Ombudsman Criticizes Greenlandic Prisons,' *Sermitsiaq News*, 28 September 2006; 'Greenland Needs a Jail,' *Nunatsiaq News*, 21 July 2006. 'Aasiaat and Qaqortoq have two small institutions with room for ten delinquents.' Nuuk has a larger one for fifty-four. Statistics Greenland (2001:219); see also Brochmann (2001).

146 'Summary of the Commission's Proposal on the Future of the System of Correctional Institutions and Probation in Greenland' (2001).

147 'Iqaluit city council members condemned Nunavut's court system for imposing too many lenient sentences on people convicted of serious violent crimes and for failing to protect the community.' Jim Bell, 'Iqaluit Councillors Slam Court System,' *Nunatsiaq News*, 1 July 2005; Jane George, 'Nunavut Cells Overflowing as Remands Grow,' *Nunatsiaq News*, 3 Novem-

ber 2006. On the 'double standard,' see 'The Territorial Court,' ch. 6 in
C.T. Griffiths et al. (1995a:101–56).

148 Justice of the peace, quoted in C.T. Griffiths et al. (1995a:164).

149 Rousseau (1994:169); Schechter (1983:81). On some considerations of
customary law in Greenland and its conflict with modern legislation, see
Ørebech et al. (2006:chs 2 and 10).

150 H. Petersen (1999:101); Spakowski (2001:14); Bayly (1985:285).

151 H. Petersen (1999:101–2).

152 H. Petersen (2001:70).

153 In Canada until a few decades ago there was relatively little jurisprudence
on Inuit customary law. Morse (1988:108) notes that in Canada the clear
weight of courts' decisions dealing with Inuit customary law is focused on
the validity of Inuit customs 'concerning marriage, divorce, and adoption,
as well as their impact upon inheritance, spousal immunity in evidence, and
related matters.' See, for instance, the decision of Justice Browne in *SKK v.
JS*, unreported decision of the Nunavut Court of Justice, File No. 01000053
CV, 4 June 2002.

154 Haysom and Richstone (1987:91–106). *Justice that Brings Peace* (1997). In
1998 at the conference Towards Justice that Brings Peace, twenty-three recommendations were developed on community justice initiatives, developing alternatives to jails, the role of justices of the peace and healing, and
counselling and the justice system in Nunavut. *Towards Justice that Brings
Peace* (1998).

155 See, for example, Wildlife Act, S.Nu. 2003, c. 26, as amended. Colin Amega-
inek signed the guilty plea without knowing what the words 'complainant,'
'incensed,' or 'escalated' mean. He was embarrassed about not being able
to read and responded affirmatively to suggestions made by his lawyer,
Euan Mackay. Sara Minogue, 'Judge Strikes Unintentional Guilty Plea,'
Nunatsiaq News, 17 March 2006.

156 Harhoff (1992:208).

157 Harhoff (1994b:251).

158 On legal feasibility, see H.G. Jensen (1996:139–40). The quote is from Harhoff (1994b:251).

159 Commission on Greenland's Judicial System (2004:117).

160 Ibid.

161 Ibid., 118.

162 Ibid., 119.

163 See the discussion in chapter 2 above.

164 For example, a proposed federal law to eliminate the use of conditional
sentences is expected to pose a problem in Nunavut, where, statistically,

judges grant a high number of conditional sentences, allowing the Inuit to serve their sentences closer to their communities. This change could prove difficult in the territory, where the Baffin Correctional Centre is already overcrowded and existing restorative-justice programs may be challenged. 'Crime Law Changes Spark Northern Debate,' CBC News Online, 10 May 2006, www.cbc.ca; Sara Minogue, 'Overcrowded Baffin Sends Inmates to Overcrowded Ottawa-Carleton,' *Nunatsiaq News*, 5 May 2006.

165 Macklem (1993:326).

166 Ibid.

167 Macklem (1992) states that, 'By virtue of s. 25 and other provisions of the *Charter*, Parliament possesses significant constitutional flexibility to pass laws that accommodate Aboriginal aspirations for greater responsibility over the administration of criminal justice' (299). In his view, the combined effect of ss. 35(1) and 25 of the Constitution Act, 1982 authorizes legislative reform of the criminal justice system in order to 'enable Aboriginal Peoples to assume more responsibility for the administration of justice in Aboriginal communities across the country' (280).

168 Gray (1994:340) notes that in Nunavut the issue of 'recognition of customary law and the concept of a separate aboriginal justice' was not the focus of political debates, compared to other land claims discussions, which have centred on this issue.

169 See Jim Bell, 'Congratulations to Maliiganik Tukisiiniakvik' (editorial), *Nunatsiaq News*, 3 December 2004; Mr. Justice Robert Kilpatrick from a transcript by court reporter Linda Kimball 'Passing Judgment on Lack of Resources,' *Nunatsiaq News*, 17 March 2006; Jane George, 'Nunavut's Correctional System a Revolving Door,' *Nunatsiaq News*, 3 March 2006, Family Abuse Intervention Act, S.Nu. 2006, c. 18. See also Pauktuutit (2006b), outlining recommendations for the national strategy to prevent abuse in Inuit communities.

170 Elders Akisu Joamie and Emile Imaruittuq, in Oosten et al. (1999:51–2).

171 'Elders Complain about Court System,' *Nunatsiaq News*, 5 November 2004.

172 Ibid.

173 Cited in Jim Bell, 'Nunavut Courts a Scene of Ethnic Conflict: Researcher,' *Nunatsiaq News*, 3 September 2004.

174 Ibid.

175 'Furious with Justice System' (letters to the editor), *Nunatsiaq News*, 5 November 2004.

176 Jim Bell, 'Nunavut Crime Rates Keep on Soaring,' *Nunatsiaq News*, 6 August 2004; 'Nunavut Leads Nation in Violence, Sexual Assault,' *Nunatsiaq News*, 3 November 2006.

177 Frances Piugatuk, interviewed by D. Eber, quoted in Eber (1997:38–9).

178 Cohen (2002:26–31). An interview with Kelly Gallagher-Mackay, quoted in Cohen (2002:30). The program opened in September 2001 and was based in Iqaluit. In 2005 eleven Inuit students graduated with bachelor of law degrees from the University of Victoria. Aboriginal professors included Dr John Borrows and Heather Raven. It should be noted that Greenland does not have a law school program. However, possible forthcoming law and reforms to the home rule system should bring some change to further indigenous involvement in the administration of justice.

179 Greg Younger-Lewis, 'Akitsiraq Grads Bring Inuit Values to Northern Law,' *Nunatsiaq News*, 17 June 2005.

180 Ibid.

181 Crnkovich et al. (2000:6), Sanders (2007).

182 They asked Nunavut MP Nancy Karetak-Lindell to help them to resolve this issue. 'Cambridge Works to Banish Repeat Offenders,' *Nunatsiaq News*, 19 November 2004.

183 Greg Younger-Lewis, ' Elders Pitch in to Help Crime Victims,' *Nunatsiaq News*, 26 November 2004.

184 Greg Younger-Lewis, 'Video Demonstrates Elders' Approach to Dealing with Criminals,' *Nunatsiaq News*, 6 May 2005.

185 One of the options is to use alternative dispute-resolution models. For example, as a pilot project the Innusirmut Aqqusiuqtiit Mediation/Family Counselling Program was introduced in Nunavut. It incorporated 'southern-based mediation techniques with traditional Inuit approaches to problem-solving in order to deliver culturally relevant dispute resolution services to Inuit' (Johnson [2005:13]). See also Sara Minogue, 'Mediator Can Solve Family Disputes without the Courts,' *Nunatsiaq News*, 11 February 2005.

Chapter 5: Greenland and Nunavut in International Affairs

1 Jull (1998b:4–9; 1999:12–17).

2 The participation of German Länder in international cooperation and international treaty-making powers of regions and communities in Belgium might be an exception. Similarly, Canadian provinces play an increasing role in international affairs. However, there is no clear recognition of this sort of activity in international law.

3 About strategy, see J.K. Nielsen (2001:15–21). The quote is from ibid., 6. To enhance its participation in international relations, an international office was created in 1994 under the secretary of the home rule's premier. Ibid., 5.

4 *Report from the Commission on Self-Governance* (2003:78, 80).

5 J.K. Nielsen (2001:23 and 12–13) argues that, because of the challenges posed by globalized processes, Greenland 'has responded by reclaiming its foreign policies.'

6 *Report from the Commission on Self-Governance* (2003:84); Act No. 577, 24 June 2005.

7 Rothwell (1996:161) assesses the extent of the Arctic legal regime as a part of 'Arctic' international law in three areas: Arctic sovereignty, the law of the sea, and environmental protection. Though it is arguable whether the Arctic has a comprehensive legal regime, in practical terms Greenland and Nunavut fall under the jurisdiction of 'Arctic' international law, but only as subnational territories.

8 The Prime Minister's Office, 'The Greenland Home Rule Arrangement,' Copenhagen, www.stm.dk.

9 Commission on Home Rule, Résumé of the Report, in Henry and Miller (2003:70).

10 For example, Denmark ratified the International Labour Organization (ILO) Convention (No. 169) concerning Indigenous and Tribal Peoples in Independent Countries (adopted on 27 June 1989), only after receiving consent from home rule authorities. Harhoff (1994b:252).

11 Home Rule Act, s. 16(3).

12 Ibid., ss. 16 (1), (2); and Act No. 577, 24 June 2005, s. 3.

13 Act No. 577, 24 June 2005, s. 3.

14 They mostly included fisheries agreements with Norway and Iceland. Harhoff (1994b:252).

15 Ibid.

16 Ibid.

17 *Report from the Commission on Self-Governance* (2003:93).

18 Ibid., 93, 104.

19 Ibid., 93; see also Eliasen (2004c).

20 NLCA, Part 9, 'International and Domestic Interjurisdictional Agreements,' ss. 5.9.1 and 5.9.2. S. 5.9.4, specifies that 'subject to Section 5.9.1 all harvesting in the Nunavut Settlement Area shall be subject to legislation implementing those terms of an international agreement that were in existence at the date of ratification of the Agreement.'

21 NLCA, Part 11, 'Transboundary Impacts,' s. 12.11.2.

22 *Report from the Commission on Self-Governance* (2003:105).

23 Comment by an anonymous reader.

24 Ibid., 103–4.

25 There were considerations for Greenland's membership in the Council of

Europe. The Commission on Greenland's Self-Governance concluded that direct Greenlandic representation in this body is not possible. *Report from the Commission on Self-Governance* (2003:97).

26 The commission was established under terms of a Memorandum of Understanding (MOU) between the Department of Fisheries and Oceans of the Government of Canada and the Ministry of Fisheries and Hunting of the Greenland Home Rule government. The MOU applies to stocks of beluga and narwhal that migrate between Canadian and Greenlandic waters. The commission issues recommendations and provides advice on research and monitoring. See 'The Tenth Meeting of the Canada/Greenland Joint Commission on the Conservation and Management of Narwhal and Beluga,' press release. 20 April 2006, and Jane George, 'Greenland Narwhal, Beluga in Big Trouble,' *Nunatsiaq News*, 28 April 2006.

27 Nunavut became the first Canadian territory or province to cooperate with the federal government's climate change program by signing the MOU for Cooperation on Addressing Climate Change, 31 October 2003. Thus, Nunavut was able to express its concerns about the future of the Kyoto Protocol, the implementation of which was a focal point for the territory's climate change and environmental protection strategy. The internal governmental relations of Greenland and Nunavut are not explored here. See Timpson (2005:207–35). Generally, Nunavut has broader opportunities for that sort of cooperation than Greenland, because it can participate in the institutions of the Canadian federative structure, such as intergovernmental meetings (the first ministers conferences, where the premiers of the three Northern territories are invited), and can also participate in the Council of the Federation or the Canada Health Council and other institutions. Greenland is more focused on international collaboration. Regarding institutions of the Canadian federative structure, see Russell (2004:228). According to the Northern Cooperation Accord, which was first negotiated in 1999 and was renewed by Canadian Northern premiers in 2003 and in 2006, Nunavut also participates in the annual Northern Premiers' Forum. See 'The North's Place in Canada's Future,' statement by the Northern premiers, 7 November 2006, available at www.gov.nu.ca.

28 It mostly includes ties with Iceland and the Faroe Islands. See J.K. Nielsen (2001:18–19) and Bærenholdt (2002:33–55).

29 Greenlanders have participated in Danish UN delegations. For details see Eliasen (2004b:169–78).

30 The West Nordic Parliamentarian Council (since 1997 the West Nordic Council) was created in 1985 as a form of cooperation between Greenland, Iceland, and the Faroe Islands. It meets annually and issues recommenda-

tions to the governments of those territories, focusing on priorities such as health, culture, hunting, infrastructure, and language issues. Greenland home rule government appoints six representatives to the council. See www.vestnordisk.is

31 I use the term 'Norden' or Scandinavia to refer to the five Nordic countries of Northern Europe – that is, Denmark, Norway, Sweden, Iceland, and Finland. About the definition of 'Norden' and Scandinavia, see Wendt (1981:11).

32 Helsinki Treaty, 23 March 1962, as amended. According to article 40 of the treaty, 'Nordic cooperation shall take place in the Nordic Council, in the Nordic Council of Ministers, at the meetings of the Prime Ministers, at the meetings of the Foreign Ministers and those of other Ministers, in special cooperative bodies as well as between the specialized public authorities of the Nordic countries.' About Nordic cooperation, see Haagensen (2002:307); on the environmental aspects of the Nordic cooperation, see Koivurova (2002:193–205). See also www.norden.org.

33 Preamble to the Agreement (Helsinki Treaty), 29 September 1995, www.norden.org

34 For details on Greenland's involvement in Nordic cooperation, see Statistics Greenland (2001:17).

35 Anderson (1967:15–25) names the Nordic Inter-Parliamentary Union (1907), the Scandinavian Defence Alliance conferences (1949), and the Nordic Parliamentary Committee for Traffic Freedom (1951) as interparliamentary predecessors of the Nordic Council.

36 On the establishment of the Nordic Council, see Wendt (1959:103–4, 1981:33–8), Solem (1977:40–6), and Lyche (1974:37–8). Finland joined the council in 1955; Wendt (1959:104–6).

37 See Lindholm (1985:79). About the evolution of the status of autonomous territories in the Nordic Council and the Nordic Council of Ministers, see also Nauclér (2005:528–9).

38 Petersson (1994:214).

39 Helsinki Treaty, art. 47 and 48.

40 See art. 39 of the Nordic Council Rules of Procedure, Nordic Council, *Rules of Procedure*, 30 October 2001, www.norden.org. Helsinki Treaty, art. 49. Nordic Council, 'Facts on Nordic Co-operation,' Nordic Council and the Nordic Council of Ministers, 2002, 2. Greenlanders wish to have two members in the Nordic Council in their own right, but that is not yet the case. Government of Greenland, 'New Year Speech by Premier Hans Enoksen,' 8 January 2003.

41 Helsinki Treaty, art. 45. For an analysis of the council's competence, see Solem (1977:47–54); re the forms of cooperation, see Wendt (1959).

42 For a simplified outline of the Nordic Council procedures, see Nordic Coun-
    cil, 'Facts on Nordic Co-operation,' 4.
43 The consultative status of the Nordic Council was confirmed by the legal
    nature of the Helsinki Agreement: it is not a binding international treaty as it
    was established through acts of parliament of its respective signatories. See
    Baldersheim and Ståhlberg (1999:7), Koivurova (2002:193n.679).
44 Haagensen (2002:308), Helsinki Treaty, art. 60. About the Nordic Council of
    Ministers generally, see www.norden.org.
45 Helsinki Treaty, art. 61.
46 See 'The Nordic Council of Ministers,' www.norden.org.
47 For details see www.norden.org; Helsinki Treaty, art. 60, and art. 63 regard-
    ing the implications of the council's decisions for autonomous territories.
48 Eliasen (2004a:197).
49 'Greenland: We Want Our Own Delegation to the Nordic Council,' Siku Cir-
    cumpolar News Service, 1 November 2006.
50 'New West Nordic Agreement,' 2 November 2006, www.norden.org; about
    the West Nordic Council, see note 30 above.
51 Neumann (2000:247) concludes that 'the EU has crowded out the political
    space for formal Nordic cooperation of the type we have had so far' because
    states now cooperate so closely at the level of the EU that 'there is little point
    in the Nordic states continuing to co-operate formally between themselves in
    the same manners as they did in the Cold War period.' Nauclér (2005:533)
    notes that Nordic cooperation generally is tangible in fields such as educa-
    tion, culture, and language. See also Baldersheim and Ståhlberg (1999:7–
    10). Note that Norway is not a member of the EU.
52 J.K. Nielsen (2001:6).
53 In a referendum held on 2 October 1972, the majority of Danes voted for
    joining the EEC, while 71 per cent of Greenlanders voted against it. Krämer
    (1982:273). Technically Greenland joined the EEC as a part of Denmark in
    1973.
54 'Greenland,' in Henry and Miller (2003:53).
55 See Mason (1983:865); Statistics Greenland (2001:19), and Weiss
    (1985:173).
56 After 1972 the EEC invested $10 million to $25 million a year in infrastruc-
    ture and education in Greenland, but any positive image that might have
    resulted from this 'was undermined by West German trawlers fishing illegally
    off Greenland and disagreements over fishing quotas' (Johansen [1992:34]).
    Harhoff (1983:20) notes that Greenland has received considerable financial
    grants from the Regional Fund (ECU 49 million), from the Social Fund,
    (approx. ECU 28 million) and from the FEOGA (approx. ECU 2 million);

the European Investment Bank has granted loans to Greenland (approx. ECU 47 million). Furthermore, Protocol No. 4 on Greenland to the Act of the Accession to the European Communities of the Kingdom of Denmark, Ireland, the Kingdom of Norway and the United Kingdom of Great Britain and Northern Ireland, of 22 January 1972 considered special arrangements for Greenland. In addition, according to the Council Directive No. 77/805 on the value-added tax (VAT), the VAT was not collected in Greenland (ibid., 17 and 21).

57 In the words of the then premier L.E. Johansen (1992:35), 'Being a former colony, we have had our share of bad experience with regards to centralistic supranational authority. As was the case in 1972, we feel no desire to replace the yoke of Brussels.'

58 See Olsen (1983).

59 Johansen (1992:35).

60 Ibid. See also Krämer (1982:276–7).

61 Johansen (1992:34–5).

62 Harhoff (1983:22) notes that the costs of travel alone, both in terms of money and time, were burdensome.

63 Greenland's withdrawal created a legal precedent for secession from the EEC, as there had been no provision for secession within the EEC's (now EU's) legislation. Interestingly, Greenland is the only region ever to leave the EEC/EU. Nash (1996:1020) questions whether the right to secede should be built into the EU instead of requiring long renegotiations as was the case with Greenland. Because of Greenland's isolation, scarcity of resources, and low population density, its withdrawal did not threaten the economies of the member states. See Mason (1983:866, 867).

64 See Harhoff (1983:13–33), Mason (1983:865–76), Weiss (1985:173–85), Ehlermann (1983:47–51), Lachmann (1983:52–5), Olsen (1983:27–9), Krämer (1982:277–89), L.T. Rasmussen (1983b:18–19).

65 See Treaty Establishing the European Community as amended by subsequent treaties, Rome, 23 March 1957; 'Association of the Overseas Countries and Territories,' Part IV articles 182–8 (ex articles 131–6a).

66 See Treaty Amending, with regard to Greenland, the Treaties Establishing the European Communities, 13 March 1984, in force since 1 February 1985, [1985] O.J. of the European Communities (EC) L29, 1.2.1985/1.

67 These specific circumstances included the fishery industry and free trade zone principles. For details, see Mason (1983:873–5).

68 Protocol on Special Arrangements for Greenland (1985) O.J. (EC) L29, 1.2.1985, arts. 1 and 3. About fisheries protocol see note 81 below.

69 Art. 182 (ex art. 131) of the Treaty Establishing the European Community.

70 Ibid., art. 183 (ex art. 132).
71 Declaration No. 25 on the representation of the interests of the overseas countries and territories referred to in art. 299 (ex art. 227 (3) and (6) (a) and (b) of the Treaty Establishing the European Community).
72 About the Council Decision of 17 July 2006, see note 78 below. Article 63 of Council Decision on the OCTs (27 November 2001) stipulates that the decision is applicable until 31 December 2011. Regarding the principles of cooperation, dialogue, and partnership, see chapters 1–3 of this decision. Council Decision 2001/882 of 27 November 2001 on the association of the OCTs with the European Community, [2001] O.J. (EC) L.314/1.
73 Arts. 11–17; finance cooperation (Title I, arts. 18–33), economic, and trade cooperation (Title II); decision of November 2001.
74 See 'EU Programs via OCT,' www.nanoq.gl.
75 Author's interview with special adviser, Foreign Affairs Office, Secretariat to the Cabinet, Nuuk, 12 November 2002.
76 Art. 61 of the council's decision on the OCTs of 2001 stipulates the change of status. If Greenland becomes independent, the arrangements provided for in this decision may continue to apply provisionally to Greenland under conditions laid down by the council. In addition, the council reconsiders the decision periodically, which is why the change of Greenland's status, like its home rule system, is taken into consideration. Council Decision 2001/882 of 27 November 2001 on the association of the OCTs with the European Community.
77 See Commission of the European Communities, Communication from the Commission to the Council and the European Parliament: Mid-Term Review of the Fourth Fisheries Protocol between the EU and Greenland, Brussels, 3 December 2002, COM (2002) 697 final at 8 and 5. In 2003 the Council of the EU recommended the creation of proposals on broadening future relations between the EU and Greenland. See Council of the European Union, Minutes of the 2487th Session of the Council of the European Union (General Affairs and External Relations), held in Brussels on 24 February 2003, Doc. 6695/03, 2 July 2003.
78 See Commission of the European Communities, Communication from the Commission, A new comprehensive partnership with Greenland in the form of a joint declaration and a Council Decision based on Article 187 of the EC Treaty, Brussels, 20 April 2006, COM (2006)142 final/2; 2006/526/EC: Council Decision of 17 July 2006 on relations between the European Community on the one hand, and Greenland and the Kingdom of Denmark on the other (Text with EEA relevance), Brussels, 17 July 2006. Joint Declaration by the European Community, on the one hand, and the Home Rule

Government of Greenland and the Government of Denmark, on the other, on partnership between the European Community and Greenland, Luxembourg, 27 June 2006, O.J.(EC) 29.7 2006 L208/0028–34.

79 See 'EU and Greenland Initial New Fisheries Partnership Agreement,' European Commission, Fisheries, Press Corner, Brussels, 9 June 2006.

80 Ibid.

81 Agreement on Fisheries between the European Economic Community, on one Hand, and the Government of Denmark and the Local Government of Greenland, on the other, Brussels, 13 March 1984, in force since 1 February 1985 [1985] O.J. (EC) L29/9. The foundation of the EEC's policy on the fisheries agreement of 1985 is the council resolution of 3 November 1976 on the creation of a 200–mile fishing zone off the coastal areas of the North Atlantic and the North Sea. The assertion by Greenland of a 200–mile Exclusive Economic Zone in 1977 did not substantially affect Greenlanders but reduced the international fishery. Because Greenland was a part of the EEC, the rules of the latter provided concessions to Greenlandic fisherman, who 'were allocated as much of the total allowable catch as they were able to catch' (Krämer [1982:274]). Rasmussen and Hamilton (2001:44) also note that 'following the 1977 expansion of the EEZ, virtually all of the cod was reserved for Greenland.'

82 Protocol on the Conditions Relating to Fishing between the European Economic Community on the one Hand, and the Government of Denmark and the Local Government of Greenland, on the other, [1985] O.J.(EC) L 29/14, arts. 1–6. I am grateful to Peter Hopkins, from the European Commission, Directorate-General Fisheries, External Policy and Markets Bilateral Agreements, for providing me with this document.

83 Agreement on Fisheries between the European Economic Community, on one Hand, and the Government of Denmark and the local Government of Greenland, on the other,' 13 March 1984, arts. 1–2(1).

84 Ibid., art. 6.

85 According to art. 11 of the Fourth Protocol, the financial compensation during the period of the protocol is fixed at €42,820,000 per year. Fourth Protocol Laying down the Conditions Relating to Fishing Provided for in the Agreement on Fisheries between the European Economic Community, on the one Hand, and the Government of Denmark and the Home Rule Government of Greenland, on the other,' [2001] O.J. (EC) L. 209/2. On high compensation, see written question E-1672/99 by Arlindo Cunha (PPE-DE) to the commission, 22 September 1999, no. 2000/C203E/025, [2000] O.J. (EC) C.43/19. Another criticism was raised against art. 11 of the Fourth Protocol, the text of which 'does not differentiate between the part of that

amount [€42,820,000] corresponding to payment for the catch possibilities offered by Greenland and the other part intended for development cooperation.' See written question E-3443/00 by Carmen F. Estévez (PPE-DE) to the commission, 7 November 2000, no. 2001/C163E/131, [2001] O.J.(EC)C44/118–19. The financial compensation was increased, and has been considerably overestimated in light of the real catch possibilities. See question E-3444/00 by Carmen F. Estévez, [2001] O.J. (EC) C.44/119.

86 See Husebye (2001:111–18) and Heikkilä (2006).
87 'EU Northern Dimension,' Objectives, www.nanoq.gl
88 See Conclusion of the Chair, EU Ministerial Conference on the Northern Dimension, Luxembourg, April 2001. For documents, see, among others, Council of the European Union (General Affairs and External Relations), 'Northern Dimension: Action Plan for the Northern Dimension with External and Cross-border Policies of the European Union 2000–2003,' 9401/00, Feira, 14 June 2000; Council of the European Union, 'The Second Northern Dimension Action Plan, 2004–2006,' Brussels, 16–17 October 2003; Council of the European Union, 'Guidelines for the Development of a Political Declaration and a Policy Framework Document for the Northern Dimension Policy from 2007, Brussels, 21 November 2005; Commission of the European Communities, 'Commission Staff Working Document, 2005; Annual Progress Report on the Implementation of the Northern Dimension Action Plan,' 2 June 2006, SEC(2006)729.
89 See 'The Arctic Window,' www.nanoq.gl.
90 Conclusion of the Chair, EU Ministerial Conference on the Northern Dimension, Helsinki, November 1999.
91 *Greenland Report: An Arctic Window,* September 2001, www.nanoq.gl.
92 Joint host speech by Premier Jonathan Motzfeldt, 2002, www.nanoq.gl.
93 A basis for concretizing the Arctic Window 'has been established so that, for example, future EU programmes will be so structured that they will also implicate the relevance for Greenland, and so that the EU in its legislation will automatically include Arctic considerations in its consultation procedure.' Foreign Policy Statement by the Greenland Premier, 17 October 2001.
94 Author's interview with special adviser, Foreign Affairs Office, Secretariat to the Cabinet, Nuuk, 12 November 2002.
95 *The Northern Dimension of Canada's Foreign Policy* (2000). See also *Strengthening Canada's Leadership and Influence ...* (2005:31–4, 44); 'Canada–EU Joint Statement on Northern Cooperation,' Ottawa, December 1999; *Canada–EU Cooperation on Northern Issues: Progress Report,* Ottawa, June 2001; *Canada–EU Cooperation on Northern Issues: A Progress Report,* Ottawa, 19 December 2002;

'Canada–EU Joint Statement on Defence and Security,' Ottawa, December 2000.

96 *EU–Canada Partnership Agenda,* EU-Canada Summit, Ottawa, 18 March 2004.

97 Premier Jonathan Motzfeldt, quoted in 'The Arctic Window,' www.nanoq.gl.

98 Hitchins and Liander (1991:309); Young (2000:120; 1996:4–13).

99 This phenomenon can be explained by the end of the Cold War, the dissolution of the romanticized image of the Arctic, and by the creation of regional authorities (Nunavut, Greenland home rule government) with less dependency on the South. Young (2000:119–20).

100 Ibid., 121; Young (1996:14–16; 2005:9–10).

101 The Arctic Council was established on 19 September 1996 in Ottawa, with the signing of the Declaration on the Establishment of the Arctic Council. Young (2000:125) features some advantages of informal arrangements. Quoting Scrivener, he notes: 'Because they are not legally binding, the parties are often willing to reach agreement in relatively short order and to include substantive provisions of a more far-reaching nature in their agreements. Informal arrangements are comparatively easy to adjust or revise, either on the basis of experience with the operation of existing arrangements or as a response to new understandings of the problems to be solved. The transition from the Arctic Environmental Protection Strategy to the Arctic Council constitutes a striking illustration of this feature of informal arrangements.'

102 The idea originated with M. Cohen's proposition in 1971 for the creation of an Arctic body for cooperation (Pharand [1992:165]). The proposal for an Arctic Council was inspired by various Canadian NGOs, and the Arctic Council Panel was set up by the Canadian Arctic Resources Committee (CARC), the Canadian Arms Control Centre, and the ICC (Scrivener [1996:18–19]). The creation of a council of that kind had been on the Inuit political agenda since 1980s and had been suggested several times. See Canadian Arctic Resources Committee (1988a:109–59); *The North and Canada's International Relations* (1988b:58–9). The Northern Policy Working Group supported the establishment of an Arctic Basin Council; however, the signing in 1991 in Rovaniemi of the Declaration on the Protection of the Arctic Environment and the Arctic Environmental Protection Strategy (AEPS) launched the Arctic Council initiative. See Bloom (1999:712–14); Declaration on the Establishment of the Arctic Council, 19 September 1996. A detailed proposal was developed by the Arctic Council Panel chaired by Griffiths and Kuptana (1991). See also Keskitalo (2004:65–73).

For more information on participation of indigenous communities, see
Tennberg (1996:21–32).

103 See Young (1997:259–277); Heininen (2004:212–15); Declaration on the
Establishment of the Arctic Council (1996), s. 1.
104 For the text of declarations issued at ministerial meetings of the Arctic
Council, see www.arctic-council.org.
105 *Arctic Human Development Report* (2004), ACIA (2005).
106 Declaration on the Establishment of the Arctic Council (1996), s. 7. Bloom
(1999:721–2).
107 Declaration on the Establishment of the Arctic Council (1996), s. 5. Young
(2000:126).
108 For such criticism, see Young (2000:130–2), and the chapter entitled 'The
Meaning of Establishing the Arctic Council' in Tennberg (2000:112–16).
On its importance, see Young (2000:132–3).
109 Declaration on the Establishment of the Arctic Council (1996), s. 2.
110 *Arctic Council Rules of Procedure*, as adopted by the Arctic Council at the First
Arctic Council Ministerial Meeting, Iqaluit, 17–18 September 1998, General
Provisions.
111 Ibid.
112 Section 8 of the Declaration on the Establishment of the Arctic Council
(1996) notes, that the IPS established under AEPS continued its responsibilities within the Arctic Council.
113 Young (2000:122) underlines that although permanent participants 'are
not treated as formal members of the council, they are accorded virtually all
the rights and privileges enjoyed by member states.'
114 Young points out the danger of developing the Arctic Council as an attempt
of the foreign ministries of national governments to exercise control over
the circumpolar North (ibid., 134–5). During the release of the ACIA, the
ICC was disappointed by the inability of the Arctic Council to dissuade the
United States from neglecting the issue of climate change. See Jane
George, 'Arctic Council Bows to U.S. Pressure,' *Nunatsiaq News*, 19 November 2004, and Jane George, 'U.S. Objections Mold Arctic Council Policy,'
Nunatsiaq News, 26 November 2004. Despite this, the ICC, the Inuit, and
other groups have played an enormous role in education on global warming. Even remote regions have received information from the Arctic. Comment by an anonymous reader.
115 Koivurova and Heinämäki (2006:101).
116 Another example of interparliamentary cooperation along side the Nordic
Council is a Standing Committee of Parliamentarians of the Arctic Region,
which has conducted a number of conferences. See www.grida.no/parl. By

adopting declarations consisting of recommendations to the national governments on crucial issues for the Arctic region, these meetings are a forum for discussions on the most topical problems and challenges facing Northerners.

117 The term 'Inuitism' is used by Gulløv (1979:137) to describe a movement directed towards strengthening contact with other Inuit groups in the Arctic. On Pan-Inuit collaboration, see R. Petersen (1984:724–8).

118 The Memorandum of Consultations on a Programme of Cooperation between the Government of the Northwest Territories and the Greenland Home Rule Government was signed on 13 April 1989.

119 Memorandum of Understanding on Cooperation between the Government of Nunavut and the Greenland Home Rule Government, 24 October 2000. The Department of Intergovernmental and Executive Affairs of the Government of Nunavut provided this document to the author.

120 On the basis of the MOU of 2000, in April 2005 Nunavut and Greenland reached an agreement to manage shared populations of polar bears. Government of Nunavut, 'Nunavut and Greenland Agree to Manage Shared Polar Bears Populations,' news release, 28 April 2005. In July 2006 the Annex on Trade to the MOU was signed in Iqaluit (Annex on Trade to the Memorandum of Understanding on Cooperation between the Government of Nunavut and the Greenland Home Rule Government, Iqaluit, 8 July 2006.)

121 Appendix A to the Memorandum of Understanding on Cooperation between the Government of Nunavut and the Greenland Home Rule Government (2000).

122 See *Tip of the Iceberg* (2001:169–73). In 2005 Denmark opened a consulate in Iqaluit to develop Arctic cooperation and support cultural ties between Nunavut and Greenland. Kenn Harper was named the honorary consul. 'Harper Named Danish Honorary Consul,' *Nunatsiaq News*, 7 October 2005.

123 *Tip of the Iceberg* (2001:174–5).

124 See 'Inupiat under Four Flags,' Planning for the First Inuit Circumpolar Conference Barrow, Alaska, 13 June 1977, which includes the transcript of Inuit Circumpolar Pre-Conference, Barrow, Alaska, 28 March 1976, 1–41. Several authors note that the beginning of indigenous internationalism was a conference on Arctic oil and gas in le Havre, France (1973), which elaborated on the idea of organizing the Arctic Peoples' Conference. The latter conference was conducted in Copenhagen in 1973. As a follow-up of this initiative, in 1975 World Council of Indigenous Peoples was founded at a reserve near Port Alberni, British Columbia, and in 1977 the First Inuit Circumpolar Conference was held in Point Barrow, Alaska. See Kleivan

(1992:227–36); Williamson (1986:74–7); Jull (2001a:220–2); Fægteborg (1992:243).

125 The president's report, ICC, 'The Arctic: Our Common Responsibility,' Frobisher Bay, Canada, 25–31 July 1983, 6.

126 ICC Charter, adopted 29 June 1980.

127 Simon (1997:16),

128 The scope of activities is well documented in the chair's reports, annual reports on activities, resolutions, and numerous publications. The Canadian branch publishes the quarterly magazine *Silarjualiriniq* (Inuit in global issues). It contains a great deal of information about the ICC's platform and activities. See www.inuitcircumpolar.com and www.inuit.org. In 1991 and 1995 the ICC organized the first and the second Arctic Leaders' Summits, a forum where indigenous leaders of the Arctic region meet to discuss their common concerns. See Fægteborg (1993), Fægteborg and Prakhova (1995).

129 In 1992 the ICC adopted *Principles and Elements for a Comprehensive Arctic Policy* (ICC, 1992). This report is still useful for looking at a working manual of the Inuit's vision of a course of action in the Arctic.

130 Jane George, '"Climate Warrior" Plots Strategy on Behalf of Inuit,' *Nunatsiaq News*, 18 November 2005. The petition was submitted to the IACHR on behalf of all Inuit in the Arctic regions of Canada and the United States: Petition to the Inter American Commission on Human Rights Seeking Relief from Violations Resulting from Global Warming Caused by Acts and Omissions of the United States, 7 December 2005. In December 2006 the IACHR refused to proceed with the petition but in February 2007 decided to hold a hearing. The petition itself brought international attention to the Inuit situation and contributed to the development of legal and academic discourse on the rights of indigenous peoples in international environmental law. See Jane George, 'ICC Climate Change Petition Rejected,' *Nunatsiaq News*, 15 December 2006; 'Human Rights Body Reconsiders Inuit Climate Change Petition,' CBC News, 6 February 2007.

131 See L.T. Rasmussen (1983a:3). Article 71 of the UN Charter allows the Economic and Social Council to make suitable arrangements for consultation with the NGOs that are concerned with matters within its jurisdiction. ECOSOC resolution 1296 (XLIV), 23 May 1968, revised in its resolution 1996/31, 25 July 1996, regulates such arrangements.

132 Category II allows the ICC to express concerns only in a few areas considered to be within the purview of the ICC. See www.unog.ch (UN and the NGOs).

133 In July 2000 ECOSOC adopted resolution E/RES/2000/22 on the Establish-

ment of a Permanent Forum on Indigenous Issues. The Permanent Forum is an advisory body to ECOSOC with a mandate to discuss indigenous issues related to economic and social development, culture, the environment, education, health, and human rights. As an NGO, the ICC may participate in this forum as an observer. See the website of the UN Permanent Forum on Indigenous issues, www.un.org/esa/socdev/unpfii/. See also Arctic Indigenous Peoples' Declaration on the Establishment of a Permanent Forum for Indigenous Peoples within the United Nations (1998), in García-Alix (1999:109–11). Since 1984 the ICC has actively participated in the UN Working Group on Indigenous Peoples, reviewing the developments and conditions of indigenous peoples, and drafting a Universal Declaration on Indigenous Peoples' Rights. Sambo (1992:27–32). The declaration was adopted by the UN Human Rights Council on 29 June 2006.

134 Clark and Dryzek (1986:215–20).
135 On the ICC as a transnational NGO, see Saladin d'Anglure and Morin (1991:7–11).
136 Aqqaluk Lynge, 'A Message from ICC's President,' ICC, Kuujuaq, August 2002.
137 Simon (1985:33).
138 Espersen (2004:10) gives an example of such neglect on the part of the Danish delegation and non-consideration of Greenland as internationally important. During 2001 reporting on the UN Convention on the Rights of the Child, representatives of Greenland were not even invited to present their opinion before the UN Committee, despite the fact that the island has a high rate of infant and maternal mortality.
139 *Report from the Commission on Self-Governance* (2003:105). Re international trade in Greenland, see Lyck (1999).
140 Eliasen (2004a:183–5).
141 Henriksen (2001:10). See also The Draft Nordic Saami Convention, 16 November 2005. An unofficial English translation of the convention is provided in (2006 No. 4) *Gáldu Čála: Journal of Indigenous Peoples Rights* (Annex:41–7).
142 Chaturvedi (1996:1–11); Huebert (1999:203–29); see also 'Post–Cold War Cooperation in the Arctic: From Interstate Conflict to New Agendas for Security,' in *Canada and the Circumpolar World* (1997:77–100).
143 *Report from the Commission on Self-Governance* (2003:83–91).
144 See Huebert (2000:101–4). F. Griffiths (1999b:104) notes, 'As of the late 1990s, Canadians speak with varying degrees of knowledgeability and frequency about civil, collective, common, comprehensive, cooperative, cultural, demographic, ecological, economic, energy, food, global, human,

military, national, personal, political, regional, shared, and subregional as well as environmental security.'

145 Østreng (1992:30).

146 F.Griffiths (1999b:107). Griffiths further states that 'remoteness from the scene of warfare, comparative military inability, tension between two founding peoples, and the presence of an adjacent and friendly but potentially overwhelming superpower have all conspired to prevent Canadians from becoming resolutely attached to a military view of security.'

147 See Eyre (1981) and Diubaldo (1981:93–110).

148 Comment by an anonymous reader.

149 N. Petersen (1988:39).

150 *Report from the Commission on Self-Governance* (2003:91).

151 Comment by an anonymous reader. For a historical account, see Grant (1988). Regarding the sovereignty concerns in the High Canadian Arctic (a case study on Ellesmere Island), see Langlais (1995:110–15).

152 In N. Petersen (1988:63).

153 The Commission on Self-Governance underlines this element of security policies. *Report from the Commission on Self-Governance* (2003:85–6).

154 Some may argue, however, that in practice they are ignored.

155 See Simon (1989:35–6).

156 Sambo (1993:62) defines the following elements of sustainable security in Inuit tradition: 'initiatives based on the principle of self-determination; full respect for land and resource rights; recognition of the right to development and the right to peace; direct participation in international, national, and regional processes that affect indigenous communities and peoples; respect and recognition of indigenous values; recognition as distinct societies; security in hunting and fishing rights; the right to a safe and healthy environment; and removal of the threat of environmental destruction.'

157 The last point is particularly emphasized by Greenland's Commission on Self-Governance. See *Report from the Commission on Self-Governance* (2003:84). It is also relevant for potential Nunavut interests.

158 Ibid., 83.

159 Regarding the linkages between security and environment in the Canadian Arctic, see Huebert (2000:101–17).

160 For an analysis of Greenland during the Second World War, see Taagholt and Hansen (2001:21–6). See also Archer (1985:10–22).

161 Quoted in Archer (1988:124).

162 The form and validity of this agreement are questionable. For details, see Briggs (1941:506–13). The quote is from *Greenland during the Cold War* (1997:11).

163 Archer (1988:124).
164 John J. Miller, 'The U.S. Should Buy Greenland: What Better Way to Ensure Missile Defence Takes Off?' *National Post*, 16 May 2001, A14. See also Archer (1985:11–12).
165 For details, see *Greenland during the Cold War* (1997:12–17).
166 Agreement between the Government of the United States of America and the Government of the Kingdom of Denmark, pursuant to the North Atlantic Treaty, concerning the defence of Greenland, Copenhagen, 27 April 1951, entered into force 8 June 1951. I am grateful to Greenland's former deputy minister of foreign affairs Mikaela Engell for providing me with this document. See also Taagholt and Hansen (2001:29).
167 1951 Agreement, see arts. 14 and 1–3.
168 The agreement of 1951 was revised in 2004. See Agreement between the Government of the United States of America and the Government of the Kingdom of Denmark, including the Home Rule Government of Greenland, to amend and supplement the Agreement of 27 April 1951 pursuant to the North Atlantic Treaty between the Government of the United States of America and the Government of the Kingdom of Denmark concerning the Defence of Greenland (Defence Agreement) including relevant subsequent agreements related thereto, 25 May 2004.
169 N. Petersen (1988: 42–3); Archer (1988:128–9); *Greenland during the Cold War* (1997:17–18).
170 For more information, see Taagholt and Hansen (2001:31–53); Zimmerman (1987:9–11); Fischer (1993:7–20).
171 'Denmark and Greenland Ultima Motives' (2001:55).
172 H. Rasmussen (2001:76).
173 Excerpts from a letter from President George W. Bush to the Premier of Greenland, Jonathan Motzfeldt, 22 January 2001, quoted in ibid.
174 See Eric Schmidt, 'Antimissile System, in a Limited Form, Is Ordered by Bush,' *New York Times*, 18 December 2002; Suzanne Goldenberg, 'America Announces Premature Birth of Son of Star Wars: Rumsfeld Says Defences Will Be Put in Place before They Work but Will Deter Attacks,' *Guardian*, 18 December 2002; Andrew Buncombe, 'The Day Fantasy Became Reality: Bush Gives the Order for "Son of Star Wars" to Be Deployed,' *Independent*, 18 December 2002.
175 ICC news, Information submitted by the chairman of the new Landstinget's Foreign Affairs and Security Policy Committee, A. Lynge, December 2002.
176 Ibid.
177 Agreement between the Government of the United States of America and

the Government of the Kingdom of Denmark ..., 25 May 2004. See also, 'Historic Day for Greenland in Igaliku,' 6 August 2004, www.dk.nanoq.gl.

178 Opening Statement by Executive Deputy Minister Kaj Kleist at the first meeting of the Joint Committee, 6 October 2004, www.dk.nanoq.gl; and 'Fact Sheet: The New Partnership between the United States and Greenland and Denmark,' U.S. Department of State, Bureau of European and Eurasian Affairs, Washington, 24 May 2005.

179 One reason is connected with the legitimacy of the Danish accession to the Thule district in 1937. For details, see Brøsted (1988:259–5).

180 For a detailed analysis of the relocation, see Brøsted and Fægteborg (1985:221, 229; 1986:14–16).

181 N. Nielsen (1986:79); Brøsted and Fægteborg (1985:215).

182 A. Lynge (2002:27).

183 'Appendix: The Eastern High Court Reasons and Ruling,' an English translation from section 7 of the Court's Reasons and Ruling, in A. Lynge (2002:77, 76).

184 See Greenland, in Indigenous World (1999–2000:31).

185 A. Lynge (2002:49).

186 The ILO Committee of Experts on the Application of Conventions and Recommendations delivered its report on the matter in March 2001. See ILO (2001). In September 2003 the Thule hunters could not continue their case against the Danish government as their lawyer said that he could not afford to represent the hunters any longer because of the low pay. 'Thule Case Dropped,' *Nunatsiaq News*, 5 September 2003. However, the hearing at the Supreme Court started on 2 November 2003, and the ruling was rendered on 28 November 2003.

187 Transcript of the Record of Judgments of the Supreme Court in the case of *Hingitaq 53, acting for the Thule tribe, v. the Danish Government,* judgment delivered by the Supreme Court, 28 November 2003 in cases 489/1999 and 490/1999, 1st Division, www.dk.nanoq.gl.

188 Ibid., 19.

189 Ibid., 20.

190 Ibid., 21.

191 Ibid., 24.

192 'Displaced Greenland Inuits Lodge Complaint at European Rights Court,' Agence France Presse, 25 May 2004.

193 'A Loud No to Agreement,' 24 February 2003, information provided by the ICC Greenland.

194 The ICC Greenland, Hingitaq 53, and Inuit Youth International were among the protesters. DeNeen L. Brown, 'Trail of Frozen Tears: The Cold

War Is Over, but to Native Greenlanders Displaced by It, There's Still No Peace,' *Washington Post,* 22 October 2002.

195 Steve Boggan, 'Evicted by the US Military, the Inuit Prepare to Fight Star Wars,' *Independent,* 8 October 2001.

196 Oreskov (1995:54). Those who participated in the clean-up after the crash sought financial compensation from the state. However, 'the hearing committee did not find sufficient evidence of a connection between the many health problems suffered by the Thule workers and Inughuit hunters and their participation in the clean-up.' The government decided to pay approximately US$9,000 to everyone (including surviving relatives) able to document their presence and involvement in this incident. Thomsen (1995–96:32).

197 Boggan, 'Evicted by the US Military.' Qujaakitsoq said: 'We are finding many deformed animals – musk oxen with deformed hooves and seals with no hair. We believe a lot of the pollution must be coming from the base, perhaps from the missing plutonium.' Ibid. In 2005 a new report was released with evidence of plutonium contamination on dry land 15 km from the Thule air base. 'Plutonium Found Near Thule,' Siku Circumpolar News Service, 8 October 2005.

198 For details of the U.S. stationing of nuclear weapons in Greenland and the Danish attitudes towards it, see *Greenland during the Cold War* (1997:17–51).

199 Among numerous complaints, there are concerns about the control exercised by military authorities over the traffic in the Thule area. This blocks the development of tourism and mineral resources.

200 Interestingly, the issue of demilitarization has been raised in a number of ICC resolutions since 1977. It was an issue in Greenland's parliamentary debates. Archer (1985:32–3). For example, in 1984 the Landsting declared Greenland as a nuclear-weapons-free zone (ibid., 33). However, these steps did not result in any changes, as the demilitarization of the Arctic or making Greenland a nuclear-weapons-free zone seemed not to be feasible in the context of the Cold War. The situation is not much different now.

201 'U.S. Presses Danes on Thule Base,' *Nunatsiaq News,* 13 February 2004.

202 Quoted in Jane George, 'Thule Base Key to Greenland's Independence,' *Nunatsiaq News,* 10 September 2004.

203 See Eyre (1981:211–55), ch. 8, 'Nation Building: The Post War Years: 1945–1964.' For U.S.–Canadian military activity in Canada's Arctic, see Eyre (1987:292–9).

204 Canada, House of Commons, *Debates,* 12 February 1947, 345–8, cited by Diubaldo (1981:93).

205 Ibid.

206 Eyre (1981:295). About the U.S. presence in the Canadian North, see Diubaldo (1981:100–10).

207 Establishment of a Distant Early Warning System: Agreement between Canada and the United States of America, effected by exchange of notes signed at Washington, 5 May 1955 (DEW agreement). See also Myers and Munton (2000:120–2). For details on the location of the DEW Line in Greenland, see Archer (1988:131–3) and N. Petersen (1988:43–9).

208 DEW agreement, 1955, s. 13. For original information regarding interactions of the Inuit with the U.S. military, see Gagnon and Iqaluit Elders (2002).

209 DEW agreement, s. 13(f).

210 If the Thule base had not been available to the United States, the question of constructing such a base in the Canadian Arctic would have arisen. Sutherland (1966:259).

211 Amagoalik, then the president of the Inuit Tapirisat of Canada, said 'in 1953 the Government of Canada, through the RCMP, came to our little camps in northern Quebec and persuaded my parents that it would be best for them to relocate to a new place where there was better hunting, more opportunities for wage employment ... It was only years later we found out the real reason behind that move was to assert Canadian sovereignty.' J. Amagoalik, quoted in Abele (1989:181). About U.S. threats to Canada's sovereignty, see Bankes (1987:285–91), who notes, 'This paper might have been subtitled "The enemy within," for during the last 40 years the greatest practical threat to Canadian aspirations in the Arctic has been posed, curiously enough, by its formidable ally in the south, the United States of America' (285). The threats to Canadian sovereignty are often traced to the voyage of the U.S. oil tanker *Manhattan* in Canadian waters in 1969–70 without the authorization of Canadian authorities, and a similar incident in 1985, when the *Polar Sea*, a U.S. coastguard icebreaker, traversed the Northwest Passage. See Lenarcic and Reford (1989:161–3); Kirton and Munton (1987:67–97); Franckx (1993:75–134). Other facts are related to the U.S. refusal to recognize Canada's sovereignty in Canadian waters according to the sector theory. See Pharand (1981:111–30; 1984:742–99; 1988; 1989:145–58); VanderZwaag and Pharand (1983:53–84); Pharand with Legault (1984).

212 Eyre (1981:301). Sutherland (1966:270) emphasizes that, as a result of the creation of the DEW Line, Canadian firms have acquired great experience in construction, air transportation, and aerial surveying. There were economic benefits from the U.S. presence (e.g., employment of the Inuit at U.S. military facilities, the civilian use of former U.S. airdromes). Archer

(1985:25–6) notes that an important source of Greenland's revenue in the 1980s was tax paid by the Danes employed at the U.S. bases.

213 A. Lynge said in one of his interviews that 'we don't like that superpower attitude that says, "We can do what we want with our air bases."' Quoted in James Brooke, 'Greenlanders Wary of a New Role in U.S. Defences,' *New York Times*, 18 September 2000, A6. Greenland has never left NATO, as it had in the case with the EEC. However, there have been 'fluctuations' in the opinions of Greenlandic politicians as to what benefits to seek from U.S. presence on the island. As Archer (1985:55) puts it, often the question of the U.S. bases arose when the Greenlandic exchequer was short of money. Thus, the question of U.S. payments for the use of Greenland's territory and other requirements has also been raised. See N. Petersen (1988:65–6).

214 In 1996 the Canada–U.S. Military Bases Clean-up Agreement was signed after long efforts on behalf of the Canadian government. This agreement covers only half of the original DEW Line sites in Canada and leaves Ottawa with substantial financial responsibility for the DEW stations returned to Canada by the 1970s. For a detailed analysis of this agreement and problems connected with environmental contamination, see Myers and Munton (2000:119–34).

215 See table 1, 'Location and Status of Site Remediation at Former DEW Line Sites,' in ibid., 127, 128–9. Four sites have been cleaned up and the rest are expected to be dealt with by 2012. The clean up began in 1998 after conclusion of an agreement with the NTI. About 70 per cent of those doing this job are Inuit. See John Thomson, 'DEW Line Sites Leaking Contaminants,' *Nunatsiaq News*, 16 September 2005.

216 Agreement between the Government of the Kingdom of Denmark and the Government of Canada relating to the Delimitation of the Continental Shelf between Greenland and Canada, 17 December 1973.

217 See Adrian Humphreys, 'Canada–Danish Spat Erupts over Island,' *National Post*, 25 March 2004, A8; Jim Bronskill, 'Pact to End Tiff over Island,' *Toronto Star*, 19 September 2005, A2.

218 Poul E.D. Kristensen, 'Let Law Decide on Hans Island,' *Toronto Star*, 13 July 2005, A17.

219 Jim Bronskill, 'Hans Island Deal Struck with Danes,' *Globe and Mail*, 19 September 2005, A4. Joint Statement by the Ministers of Foreign Affairs of Canada and Denmark, Agreed to disagree about Hans Island, 19 September 2005, New York, www.nanoq.gl.

220 Adrian Humphreys, 'Troops Capture Danish Flags from Hans Island,' *National Post*, 9 November 2005, A1. 'Prospector's Permit Gives Man

Exclusive Rights to Hans Island for Five Years,' *National Post*, 15 August 2006.

221 Nathan Vanderklippe, 'Sovereignty Spat Keeps Scientist off Arctic Island: Both Canada and Denmark Lay Claim to Hans Island Near Greenland,' *Edmonton Journal*, 13 September 2006.

222 'Hans Island Belongs to Canadian Inuit,' *Nunatsiaq News*, 7 May 2004; 'Greenlandic Hunting Grounds at Stake in Hans Island Dispute,' *Nunatsiaq News*, 12 August 2005.

223 'Greenland Sees U.N. Settling Dispute with Canada,' Reuters. 28 April 2006.

224 Jane George, 'Ottawa Affirms Commitment to Missile Defence Talks,' *Nunatsiaq News*, 27 February 2004. On 24 February 2005 the Canadian prime minister announced that Canada 'will not take part in the proposed [U.S.] ballistic missile defence system,' Colby Cosh, 'Loaded Weapons, Hollow Debate: Comment,' *National Post*, 25 February 2005, A1. On Canada–U.S. security cooperation, see W. Graham, 'Text of the Canada–U.S. Security Cooperation Agreement,' Department of Foreign Affairs, 9 December 2002. In August 2004 Canada agreed to amendments to the NORAD agreement that allow Canada to transmit information and warnings to the U.S.-based commanders responsible for fulfilment of the missile defence program. Sean Gordon, 'Ottawa to Co-Operate on Shield: Canada Agrees to Link NORAD to Missile Plan,' *National Post*, 5 August 2004, A1. The NORAD treaty was originally signed on 12 May 1958 and has been renewed for different periods since that time. The text of a new NORAD agreement was signed in Ottawa on 28 April 2006. It expands NORAD to include maritime surveillance. There are concerns that this new deal will increase Canada's integration with the U.S. military, especially over the controversial anti-missile defence shield program. See Martin Sieff, 'NORAD Renewal Good News for U.S,' Intelligence and Terrorism Features, 10 May 2006. Jim Bell, 'NTI Wants in on Missile Defence Shield Talks,' *Nunatsiaq News*, 7 May 2004; 'Prominent Canadians Protest Missile Defence,' *Nunatsiaq News*, 26 March 2004.

225 Jane George, 'U.S. Defence Researchers Eye High Arctic,' *Nunatsiaq News*, 5 March 2004; George, 'Ottawa Affirms Commitment to Missile Defence Talks.'

226 Jane George, 'Northern Premiers Want Involvement in Missile Defense,' *Nunatsiaq News*, 12 September 2003; Jane George, 'Canada, United States Near Missile Defence Pact' *Nunatsiaq News*, 16 January 2004.

227 Quoted in Jane George, 'Nunavut Stays out of Ballistic Missile Debate,' *Nunatsiaq News*, 23 April 2004.

228 Ibid.

229 Ibid.

230 These include Ranger patrols, Operations Narwhal, Nunalivut ('land which is ours'), and Lancaster. Re the Ranger patrols, see Greg Younger-Lewis, 'National Defence Seeks Bigger Presence in the North,' *Nunatsiaq News*, 16 April 2004. Re Operations Narwhal, Nunalivut, and Lancaster, see Sara Minogue, 'Pangnirtung Awaits Army Exercise,' *Nunatsiaq News*, 25 June 2004; Adrian Humphreys, 'Forces Plan Arctic "Land Is Ours" Mission,' *National Post*, 9 February 2006, A6; John Thompson, 'Sovereignty Patrol Goes Where Most Fear to Travel,' *Nunatsiaq News*, 7 April 2006; Phinjp Gombu, 'Arctic Trek Shows Canada's Sovereignty,' *Toronto Star*, 10 April 2006; Bob Weber, 'Forces' Arctic Patrol More Than Just an Exercise,' *Globe And Mail*, 20 August 2006. Re military exercises in the High Arctic, see Adrian Humphreys, 'Canada's Troops to Reclaim the Arctic,' *National Post*, 25 March 2004, A1; Katherine Harding, 'A Show of Sovereignty on the Top of the World,' *Globe and Mail*, 18 April 2006, A8; John Thompson, 'Skidoo Tracks in the Snow Mark Canadian Land,' *Nunatsiaq News*, 14 April 2006.

231 Greg Younger-Lewis, 'National Defence Seeks Bigger Presence in the North,' *Nunatsiaq News*, 16 April 2004; see also the following articles by Younger-Lewis: 'Armed Forces Win Narrow Victory over Nunavut Weather,' *Nunatsiaq News*, 27 August 2004; 'Military Pledges to Carry Survival Gear,' *Nunatsiaq News*, 22 October 2004; 'Military Brass Push for Heightened Disaster Preparedness,' *Nunatsiaq News*, 26 November 2004; 'Military Fails Disaster Response Test,' *Nunatsiaq News*, 22 April 2005. Ranger Donald Ittuksardjuat stated that the concept of sovereignty is foreign to Inuit culture, and thus the land belongs to everybody. Greg Younger-Lewis, 'National Defence Seeks Bigger Presence.'

232 Greg Younger-Lewis, 'Inuit Took on "Immeasurable" Role in Rangers Patrol,' *Nunatsiaq News*, 16 April 2004. Inuit were critical of the Inuit Rangers' limited involvement in military exercises. Greg Younger-Lewis, 'Senior Rangers Critical of Armed Forces,' *Nunatsiaq News*, 27 August 2004.

233 Greg Younger-Lewis, 'Rangers Get Enhanced Status in New Defence Policy,' *Nunatsiaq News*, 29 April 2005. According to Canada's defence policy the Rangers' role is becoming more important. See Canada, Department of National Defence (2005:10 and 20).

234 *Report from the Commission on Self-Governance* (2003:85). Station Nord was opened in 1952–3; the current Sirius Patrol was established in 1950. See Taagholt and Hansen (2001:32–3). For a primary source on the Danish Sirius organization, which was originally created to provide effective occupancy in Northeast Greenland by means of conduct of sledge journeys,

showing the flag and maintaining surveillance in the area in the light of a
dispute between Norway and Denmark, and then the formal establishment
of the patrol and its activities after the Second World War and during the
Cold War, see Mikkelsen (2005). For activities of the patrol during the Second World War, see also Howarth (2001).

235 *Report from the Commission on Self-Governance* (2003:87–8). The commission
also suggested the introduction of combined 'compulsory military service
and a civil societal obligation (CSP) for Greenlandic youth.' Ibid, at 88–9.

236 F. Griffiths (1993:138–9, 1999b:280–309).

237 Jim Bell, 'A Better Way' (editorial), *Nunatsiaq News*, 3 September 2004.

238 Canada's Joint Task Force North declared that the Canadian military will
refer to the Northwest Passage as Canadian internal waters. Nathan Vander-
Klippe, 'Northwest Passage Gets Political Name Change, "Internal Waters"
Hoped to Bolsters Canada's Case,' CanWest News Service, 9 April 2006. Re
some legal and political considerations on the Canadian policy of the
Northwest Passage, see Johnston (2002:145–64), Levon Sevunts, 'Northwest
Passage Redux,' *Washington Times*, 12 June 2005; Michael Byers, 'The Need
to Defend Our New Northwest Passage,' 30 January 2006, http://
thetyee.ca/Views/2006/01/30/DefendNorthwestPassage/; Michael Byers
and Suzanne Lalonde, 'Who Controls the Northwest Passage,' a discussion
paper presented in advance of a conference Canada's Arctic Waters in
International Law and Diplomacy, Ottawa, 14 June 2006; MacNeil (2006);
Doug Struck, 'Dispute over NW Passage Revived: U.S. Asserts Free Use by
All Ships, Canada Claims Jurisdiction,' *Washington Post*, 6 November 2006.

239 'On Thinning Ice' (2002); Huebert (1999); Michael Byers, 'Canada Must
Seek Deal with U.S.: Vanishing Ice Puts Canadian Sovereignty in the Far
North at Serious Risk,' *Toronto Star*, 27 October 2006. The quote is from
Huebert (2001:86); see also Huebert (2003:295–308).

240 F. Griffiths (2003:257–82); Griffiths, 'Our Arctic Sovereignty Is Well in
Hand,' *Globe and Mail*, 8 November 2006, A25. Others argue that sover-
eignty is in jeopardy: Huebert (2003); Michael Byers and Suzanne Lalonde,
'Our Arctic Sovereignty Is on Thin Ice,' *Globe and Mail*, 1 August 2005, A11;
Donat Pharand, 'Our Sovereignty Is Melting: Canada Has a Solid Claim to
Its Arctic Waters; But We Must Work Hard to Keep It from Slipping Away,'
Ottawa Citizen, 23 August 2006. For further legal considerations, see McRae
(1994–5). Charron (2005:833, 848) argues that Canada's sovereignty is not
floating away.

241 F. Griffiths, 'Our Arctic Sovereignty Is Well in Hand,' A25. See also Griffiths
(1999a:201–2).

242 The term 'Panama Canal North' is used by Usha Lee McFarling, 'Melting

Ice, Winds of Change: The Northwest Passage Is Thawing, Which Carries Major Implications for Shipping, the Environment and the Inuit Way of Life,' *Los Angeles Times*, 19 January 2003. See also Rebecca Dube, 'As Ice Melts, Debate over Northwest Passage Heats,' *USA Today*, 4 April 2006. On the effect of climate change on traditional Inuit culture, see Fenge (2001:79–85). Table 1, 'Regional Environmental Changes Observed by Inuit and Cree in the Hudson Bay Bio-region' shows drastic changes in the atmosphere, sea level, fish, and animal patterns caused by climate change (83–4). On the challenges of climate change for Nunavut authorities, see McFarling, 'Melting Ice, Winds of Change.'

243 For instance, in early 1980s, there was a strong Greenlandic opposition to the Canadian Arctic Pilot Project, launched by Petro-Canada for commercial natural gas transportation (year-round navigation) in the waters between Greenland and Labrador (Baffin Bay and Davis Strait). See L.T. Rasmussen (1987:149–55). About the APP, see Lewington (1987:163–80).

244 Comment by an anonymous reader.

245 'Coordinated Efforts in Arctic,' *Sermitsiaq News*, 22 August 2006. There is a security group consisting of representatives from the federal and territorial government departments, including the NTI. The group meets twice a year to discuss security matters. Jane George, 'Security Group Trains for Arctic Ship Disaster,' *Nunatsiaq News*, 28 November 2003; Paul Kaludjak, 'What Inuit Can Do for Arctic Sovereignty,' *Globe and Mail* on-line, 17 November 2006. Honourable Paul Okalik, Premier of Nunavut, 'Devolution and Nation Building in Canada's North,' Speech to the Public Policy Forum Seminar on Economic Transformation, North of 60, Ottawa, 13 December 2006, www.gov.nu.ca.

246 F. Griffiths (2004:15).

247 F. Griffiths (2003:279, 281–2). See also art. 15, part 1, s. 15.1.1(c) of the NLCA, which affirms Canada's sovereignty in the waters of the Arctic archipelago on the basis of Inuit land use and occupancy.

248 Comment by an anonymous reader.

Conclusion

1 For more on the concept of autonomy in legal scholarship, see Loukacheva (2005), Skurbaty (2005).

2 Starting in 2008 Greenlanders will have their own currency. This development is important for support of Greenland's national symbols and Greenlandic identity. 'Greenland to Get Own Currency,' *Nunatsiaq News*, 21 April 2006. In a similar vein, Greenland is branding a new logo internationally to ensure its

image. 'Greenland Looking for a New Image,' *Nunatsiaq News*, 28 April 2006. In 2004 a working group was established by the home rule government to design an international branding strategy. 'Background Information about Branding Greenland,' Home Rule of Greenland webpage www.nanoq.gl.

3 Comment by an anonymous reader.

4 For example, in 2005 the Inuit Relations Secretariat was established as a part of the INAC. The secretariat started its activities on 1 April 2005; see also the Partnership Accord between the Inuit of Canada as represented by Inuit Tapiriit Kanatami and Her Majesty the Queen in Right of Canada as represented by the Minister of Indian Affairs and Northern Development, 31 May 2005. The federal government in cooperation with Canada's Northern territories is developing the Northern Vision Strategy, which was formerly known as the Northern Strategy.

Bibliography

Documents and Reports

ACIA. 2005. *Arctic Climate Impact Assessment.* Cambridge: Cambridge University Press.

Arctic Human Development Report. 2004. Akureyri: Stefansson Arctic Institute.

Berger, Thomas R. 2006. *Nunavut Land Claims Agreement Implementation Contract Negotiations for the Second Planning Period 2003–2013. 'The Nunavut Project.'* Conciliator's Final Report. 1 March. Available at www.ainc-inac.gc.ca/pr/agr/nu/lca/index_e.html.

Blaustein, Albert P. and Gisbert H. Flanz, eds. 2003. *The Constitutions of the Countries of the World.* Dobbs Ferry, NY: Oceana Publications.

Building Nunavut through Decentralization: Evaluation Report. 2002. Evaluation and Statistics Division, Department of Executive and Intergovernmental Affairs, Government of Nunavut. Iqaluit, February.

Canada. Department of Indian Affairs and Northern Development. 1995. *Federal Policy Guide. Aboriginal Self-Government: The Government of Canada's Approach to Implementation of the Inherent Right and the Negotiation of Aboriginal Self-Government.* Ottawa: Minister of Public Works and Government Services Canada.

Canada. Department of Justice. 1997. *Inuit Visions of Justice: An Analysis of the Inuit Testimony Given to the Royal Commission on Aboriginal Peoples.* Ottawa: Department of Justice.

Canada. Department of National Defence. 2005. *Canada's International Policy Statement. A Role of Pride and Influence in the World. Defence.* Ottawa: Government of Canada.

Canada and the Circumpolar World: Meeting the Challenges of Cooperation into the Twenty-First Century. 1997. Report of the House of Commons Standing Committee on Foreign Affairs and International Trade, April 1997, Bill Graham,

MP, chair. In *Minutes of Proceedings of the Standing Committee on Foreign Affairs and International Trade House of Commons.* Issue No. 13, Meetings Nos. 79–81, April.

Canadian Arctic Resources Committee. 1988a. 'Canada's Interests in the International Arctic.' In *Changing Times, Challenging Agendas: Economic and Political Issues in Canada's North.* National Symposium on the North, 30–31 October 1986. Gordon Robertson, chair. Ottawa: Canadian Arctic Resources Committee.

– 1988b. *The North and Canada's International Relations.* Report of a Working Group of the National Capital Branch of the Canadian Institute of International Affairs. Gordon Robertson, chair. Ottawa: Canadian Arctic Resources Committee.

Clinton, Graeme, and Stephen Vail. 2005. *2005 Nunavut Economic Outlook: Update on Five Years of Progress.* Final Report. Prepared for the Nunavut Economic Forum. Iqaluit: Nunavut Economic Forum, October.

Commission on Greenland's Judicial System. 2004. *Report on Greenland's Judicial System. Summary.* Report No. 1442/2004, Nuuk and Copenhagen: www.jm.dk

Crnkovich, Mary, Lisa Addario, and Linda Archibald. 2000. *Inuit Women and the Nunavut Justice System 2000-8e.* Research Report. Ottawa: Department of Justice Canada, March.

Dussault, René, and Georges Erasmus. 1994. *The High Arctic Relocation: A Report on the 1953–55 Relocation.* Ottawa: Royal Commission on Aboriginal Peoples, Canada Government Publishing.

Fraser, Sheila. 2005. *Report of the Auditor General of Canada to the Legislative Assembly of Nunavut – 2005.* Ottawa: Office of the Auditor General of Canada.

García-Alix, Lola, ed. 1999. *The Permanent Forum for Indigenous Peoples: The Struggle for a New Partnership.* IWGIA Doc. 91. Copenhagen: IWGIA.

Giff, Naomi. 2000. *Nunavut Justice Issues: An Annotated Bibliography.* 2000-7e. Ottawa: Department of Justice Canada. 31 March.

Government of Nunavut. 1999a. *Report from the September Inuit Qaujimajatuqangit Workshop.* Iqaluit: Department of Culture, Language, Elders, and Youth, Government of Nunavut Printing Office.

– 1999b. *The Bathurst Mandate: Pinasuaqtavut. That Which We've Set Out to Do: Our Hopes and Plans for Nunavut.* Iqaluit: Government of Nunavut.

– 2002a. *The First Annual Report of the Inuit Qaujimajatuqanginnut (IQ) Task Force.* Iqaluit: Department of Culture, Language, Elders, and Youth, Government of Nunavut Printing Office.

– 2002b. The Naujaat Challenge: Working Together – A Framework for Discussion about an Economic Development Strategy for Nunavut. Iqaluit: Government of Nunavut.

- 2003. *Nunavut Economic Development Strategy.* Sivummut Economic Developments Strategy Group, June.
- 2004. *Pinasuaqtavut, 2004–2009: Our Commitment to Building Nunavut's Future.* Iqaluit: Government of Nunavut.
Greenland Criminal Code (1954). 1970. The American Series of Foreign Penal Codes No. 16. Greenland. London: Sweet and Maxwell.
Henry, Roxann E., and Kenneth E. Miller. 2003. *Denmark, including Greenland and Faroe Islands.* Official translations, issued February 1985. Edited by Paul Boeg. In *The Constitutions of the Countries of the World* (1985), ed. Albert P. Blaustein and Gisbert H. Flanz. Dobbs Ferry, NY: Oceana Publications; reprinted in volume 5 of 2003 edition.
ICC. 1992. *Principles and Elements for a Comprehensive Arctic Policy.* Montreal: Centre for Northern Studies and Research, McGill University.
ILO. 2001. *Report of the Committee Set Up to Examine the Representation Alleging Non-Observance by Denmark of the Indigenous and Tribal Peoples Convention, 1989.* No.169, made under article 24 of the ILO Constitution by the National Confederation of Trade Unions of Greenland – Sulinermik Inuussutissarsiuteqartut Kattuffiat, SIK. Doc. GB.280/18/5, March.
Inuit Tapirisat of Canada. 1994a. *Justice Needs Assessment: Final Report to the Ministry of Justice.* Ottawa: Inuit Tapirisat of Canada.
- 1994b. *Submission of the Inuit Tapirisat of Canada to the Royal Commission on Aboriginal Peoples.* Ottawa: Inuit Tapirisat of Canada, 31 March.
Iqqanaijaqatigiit: Government of Nunavut and Nunavut Tunngavik Incorporated Working Together. 2004. Nunavut Tunngavik Incorporated and the Government of Nunavut. 28 May.
Iqqanaijaqatigiit: 2004–2005 Annual Review of Priorities. 2005. Nunavut Tunngavik Incorporated and the Government of Nunavut. 28 May.
Johnson, Charlene. 2005. 'Family Support Office,' In *Nunavut Court of Justice Annual Report.* Iqaluit: Nunavut Court of Justice.
Joint Review of the Clyde River Protocol. 2000. *CRP Joint Review: Finding Our Way – Year One – 1999–2000.* Iqaluit: Nunavut Tunngavik Incorporated and the Government of Nunavut.
Justice that Brings Peace. 1997. Report on the Consultation Meeting on Justice in Nunavut, Iqaluit, 18–19 November.
Kublu, Alexina, and Neil A. Sharkey. 2003. 'Justice of the Peace Program.' In *Nunavut Court of Justice Annual Report.* Iqaluit: Nunavut Court of Justice.
Legal Status of Eastern Greenland. 1933. Publications of the Permanent Court of International Justice. Series A./B, No. 53. Collection of Judgments, Orders and Advisory Opinions. Leyden: A.W.Sijthoff's Publishing.

Martin's Annual Criminal Code of Canada 2004. 2004. Annotated by Edward Greenspan and Marc Rosenberg. Aurora, ON: Canada Law Book.

The Northern Dimension of Canada's Foreign Policy. 2000. Ottawa: Department of Foreign Affairs and International Trade.

Nunavut. Legislative Assembly. 2000. Standing Committee *Ajauqtiit. Review of the Report of the Chief Electoral Officer of Nunavut: Election of the First Legislative Assembly of Nunavut –1999: A New Beginning.* October.

– 2001. *Statement of the Regular Members on the Midterm Leadership Review.* 15–17 November. Iqaluit: Legislative Assembly.

Nunavut Consulting and Ekho Inuit Originals. 1999. *Report on the Social Impact Study of the Decentralization in Nunavut.* Iqaluit: Nunavut Consulting and Ekho Inuit Originals, January.

Nunavut Electoral Boundaries Commission. 2006. *Final Report.* Iqaluit: Nunavut Electoral Boundaries Commission. 6 November.

Nunavut Implementation Commission (NIC). 1994. *Discussion Paper Concerning the Development of Principles to Govern the Design and Operation of the Nunavut Government.* Iqaluit: NIC, 23 June.

– 1995a. *Footprints in New Snow: A Comprehensive Report from the Nunavut Implementation Commission to the Department of Indian Affairs and Northern Development, Government of the Northwest Territories and Nunavut Tunngavik Incorporated Concerning the Establishment of the Nunavut Government.* Iqaluit: NIC, 31 March.

– 1995b. *Two-Member Constituencies and Gender Equality: A 'Made in Nunavut' Solution for an Effective and Representative Legislature.* Discussion Paper released by the Nunavut Implementation Commission. Revised version. 15 February.

– 1995c. *Nunavut Telecommunication Needs: Community Tele-service Centres.* A Supplementary Report of the NIC. Iqaluit: NIC, 18 August.

– 1995d. *An Interim Commissioner for Nunavut.* Iqaluit: NIC, 18 August.

– 1995e. *Choosing a Capital: A Supplementary Report of the NIC.* Iqaluit: NIC, 30 June.

– 1995f. *Education and Training: A Supplementary Report of the NIC.* Iqaluit: NIC, 30 August.

– 1995g. *Infrastructure Requirements of the Nunavut Government: A Supplementary Report of the NIC.* Iqaluit: NIC, 8 September.

– 1995h. *Staff Housing: Nunavut Government: A Supplementary Report of the NIC.* Iqaluit: NIC, 14 September.

– 1996a. *Footprints 2: A Second Comprehensive Report from the Nunavut Implementation Commission to the Department of Indian Affairs and Northern Development, Government of the Northwest Territories and Nunavut Tunngavik Incorporated Concerning the Establishment of the Nunavut Government.* Iqaluit: NIC, 21 October.

– 1996b. *Nunavut's Legislature, Premier and First Election.* Iqaluit: NIC, 23 December.

– 1996c. *Selection of a Premier in Nunavut and Related Issues.* Report of the Nunavut Implementation Commission Iqaluit: NIC, 10 July.

– 1997. *Integrating Inuit Rights and Public Law in Nunavut: A Draft Nunavut Wildlife Act.* Iqaluit: NIC, 17 October.

– 1998. *Direct Election of the Nunavut Premier: Schemes for Legislative Enactment.* Iqaluit: NIC, 15 October.

Nunavut Tunngavik Incorporated. 1999. *Taking Stock: A Review of the First Five Years of Implementing the Nunavut Land Claims Agreement.* Iqaluit: NTI.

– 2004. *Tukisittiarniqsaujumaviit? A Plain Language Guide to the Nunavut Land Claims Agreement.* Iqaluit: NTI.

Report from the Commission on Self-Governance. 2003. Trans. Marianne Stenbæk. Nuuk, Greenland: Greenland Home Rule, March.

Report of the Nunavut Electoral Boundaries Commission. 1997. Iqaluit: Nunavut Electoral Boundaries Commission. 30 June.

Royal Commission on Aboriginal Peoples. 1993a. *Aboriginal Peoples and the Justice System: Report of the National Round Table on Aboriginal Justice Issues.* Ottawa: Minister of Supply and Services Canada.

– 1993b. *Partners in Confederation. Aboriginal Peoples, Self-Government, and the Constitution.* Ottawa: Minister of Supply and Services Canada.

– 1996a. Restructuring the Relationship. Report of the Royal Commission of Aboriginal Peoples. Volume 2. Ottawa: Minister of Supply and Services Canada.

– 1996b. *Bridging the Cultural Divide: A Report on Aboriginal People and Criminal Justice in Canada.* Ottawa: Minister of Supply and Services Canada.

Sharkey, Neil. 2000. 'Justice of the Peace Court.' In *Nunavut Court of Justice, Annual Report.* Iqaluit: Nunavut Court of Justice.

Statistics Canada. 2006. *Provincial and Territorial Economic Accounts Review, 2005. Preliminary Estimates.* Vol. 2, no. 1.Catalogue no. 13-016-XIE. Ottawa: Minister of Industry, April.

Strengthening Canada's Leadership and Influence in the Circumpolar World: Summative Evaluation of the Northern Dimension of Canada's Foreign Policy. 2005. Aboriginal and Circumpolar Affairs Division, Global Issues Bureau, Final Report. Ottawa: Foreign Affairs Canada, Office of the Inspector General, Evaluation Division. May.

'Summary of the Commission's Proposals on the Future of the System of Correctional Institutions and Probation in Greenland.' 2001. 25 *Meddelelser om Grønland / Man and Society* Annexe 3:132.

Towards Justice That Brings Peace. 1998. Nunavut Social Development Council Justice Retreat and Conference. Rankin Inlet. 1–3 September. Igloolik: Nunavut Social Development Council.

Vail, Stephen and Graeme Clinton. 2001. *Nunavut Economic Outlook: An Examination of the Nunavut Economy.* Prepared for the Conference Board of Canada. Ottawa: Conference Board of Canada, May.

Venne, Sharon. 1981. *Indian Act and Amendments, 1868–1975.* Saskatoon: University of Saskatchewan, Native Law Centre.

Vertes, Louise, David M.H. Connelly, and Bruce A.S. Knott. 2000. *Implementation of the Nunavut Land Claims Agreement: An Independent 5-Year Review, 1993 to 1998.* Yellowknife: Ile Royale Enterprises.

Yabsley, Gary R. 1984. *Nunavut and Inuit Customary Law.* Report to the Nunavut Constitutional Forum. Yellowknife, NWT.

Books, Articles, Theses

Abele, Frances. 1989. 'Confronting "Harsh and Inescapable Facts": Indigenous Peoples and the Militarization of the Circumpolar Region.' In Edgar J. Dosman, ed., *Sovereignty and Security in the Arctic.* London and New York: Routledge.

Aikio, Pekka, and Martin Scheinin, eds. 2000. *Operationalizing the Right of Indigenous Peoples to Self-Determination.* Turku/Åbo, Finland: Åbo Akademi University.

Alfred, Taiaiake. 2005. *Wasáse Indigenous Pathways of Action and Freedom.* Peterborough, ON: Broadview Press.

Alfreðsson, Guðmundur S. 1982a. 'Greenland and the Law of Political Decolonisation.' 20:25 *German Yearbook of Internation Law* 290.

– 1982b. 'Greenland and the Right to External Self-Determination.' SJD thesis, Harvard Law School.

– 1999. 'The Rights of Indigenous Peoples with a Focus on the National Performance and Foreign Policies of the Nordic Countries.' 59:2 *Zeitschrift für äuslandisches öffentliches Recht und Völkerrecht* 529.

– 2003. 'The Greenlanders and Their Human Rights Choices.' In Morten Bergsmo, ed., *Human Rights and Criminal Justice for the Downtrodden: Essays in Honour of Asbjørn Eide.* Leiden: Martinus Nijhoff.

– 2004. 'Greenland under Chapter XI of the United Nations Charter: A Continuing International Law Dispute.' In Sjúrður Skaale, ed., *The Right to National Self-Determination: The Faroe Islands and Greenland.* Nijhoff Law Specials 60. Leiden: Martinus Nijhoff.

Amagoalik, John. 1994. 'Canada's Nunavut: An Indigenous Northern Territory.' In Peter Jull et al., eds., *Surviving Columbus: Indigenous Peoples, Political Reform and Environmental Management in North Australia.* Darwin: North Australia Research Unit, Australian National University.

Anawak, Jack. 1993. 'The Nunavut Bills: What Our Parliamentarians Said.' 21:3 *Northern Perspectives* 8.

Anaya, S. James. 2004. *Indigenous Peoples in International Law.* 2nd ed. Oxford: Oxford University Press.

Anderson, Stanley V. 1967. *The Nordic Council: A Study of Scandinavian Regionalism.* Stockholm: Svenska Bokförlaget/Norstedts.

Anderson, W.W. 1974–5. 'Song Duels of the Kobuk River Eskimo.' 16–17 *Folk* 73.

Archer, Clive. 1985. *Greenland and the Atlantic Alliance.* Occasional paper of Centre for Defence Studies. Aberdeen: University of Aberdeen.

– 1988. 'The United States Defence Areas in Greenland.' 23:3 *Cooperation and Conflict* 123.

Arnakak, Jaypetee. 2001. 'Northern IQ.' 12:1 *Public Sector Management* 17.

Ashlee, Jette Elsebeth. 1984. 'Inuit Integration with Denmark and Canada. A Comparative Study of Colonialism in Greenland and the Northwest Territories.' PhD diss., University of Cambridge.

Atsainak, Akeeshoo. 1993. 'Legal Interpreting in Canada's Eastern Arctic.' 38:1 *Meta* 35.

Bærenholdt, Jørgen Ole. 2002. 'The Significance of Transnational Cooperation in Nordic Atlantic Regions.' Fróðskaparrit 50, bók: 33.

Baldersheim, Harald, and Krister Ståhlberg. 1999. 'Transborder Region-Building: Cement or Solvent in Nordic Co-operation?' In Harald Baldersheim and Krister Ståhlberg, eds., *Nordic Region-Building in a European Perspective.* Aldershot, UK, and Brookfield, VT: Ashgate.

Balikci, Asen. 1970. *The Netsilik Eskimo.* Garden City, NY: Natural History Press.

Bankes, Nigel D. 1987. 'Forty Years of Canadian Sovereignty Assertion in the Arctic, 1947–87.' 40:4 *Arctic* 285.

Bartmann, Barry. 1996. 'Footprints in the Snow. Nunavut: Self-Determination and the Inuit Quest for Dignity.' In Lise Lyck and V. Boyko, eds., *Management, Technology and Human Resources Policy in the Arctic (the North).* Dordrecht: Kluwer.

Baunbæk, Lene, ed. 2005. *Greenland in Figures, 2005.* Nuuk: Statistics Greenland.

Bayly, John U. 1985. 'Toward the Development of a Northwest Territories Law Reform Capability to Enable the Development of Proposals for New Legislation to Meet the Special Needs and Circumstances of Northern Peoples.' In Anthony Allot and Gordon R. Woodman, eds., *People's Law and State Law.* Dordrecht, Netherlands: Foris Publications.

Bentzon, Agnete Weis. 1966. 'The Structure of the Judicial System and Its Function in a Developing Society.' 10:1–2 *Acta Sociologica* 121.

– 1986. 'Law and Legislation in Greenland during the Transition from Colonial Status to Home Rule Status (1945–1980).' 1 *Law and Anthropology* 199.

– 1996. 'JUREX Reconsidered: A Confessional Tale about the Juridical Expedition (Jurex) to Greenland in 1948–49 and the Greenlanders' Customary Law.' In Henrik G. Jensen and Torben Agersnap, eds., *Crime, Law and Justice in Greenland.* Copenhagen: New Social Science Monographs.

– 1999. 'The Role of Social Science in the Administration of Sustainable Democracy.' In *Dependency, Autonomy, Sustainability in the Arctic,* ed. Hanne Petersen and Birger Poppel. Aldershot, UK, and Brookfield, VT: Ashgate.

Bentzon, Agnete Weis, and Henning Brøndsted. 1983. 'Recognition, Repression and Transformation of Customary Law in Greenland During the Last Forty Years of Transition to Capitalism.' In Harald W. Finkler, ed., *Papers of the Symposia on Folk Law and Legal Pluralism, XIth International Congress of Anthropological and Ethnological Sciences.* Vancouver: Commission on Folk Law and Legal Pluralism.

Berlin, Knud. 1932. *Denmark's Right to Greenland: A Survey of the Past and Present Status of Greenland, Iceland and the Faroe Islands in Relation to Norway and Denmark.* Trans. P.T. Federspiel. London: Humphrey Milford, Oxford University Press; Copenhagen: NYT Nordisk Forlag, Arnold Busk.

Birket-Smith, Kaj. 1929. *The Caribou Eskimos: Material and Social Life and Their Cultural Position.* Report of the Fifth Thule Expedition 1921–4. Volume 5. Copenhagen: Nordisk Forlag.

– 1959 [1936]. *The Eskimos.* London: Methuen.

Bloom, Evan T. 1999. 'Current Developments. Establishment of the Arctic Council.' 93 *American Journal of International Law* 712.

Breinholt-Larsen, Finn. 1992. 'The Quiet Life of a Revolution: Greenlandic Home Rule 1979–1992.' 16:1–2 *Études/Inuit/Studies* 199.

– 1996. 'Interpersonal Violence among Greenlandic Inuit: Causes and Remedies.' In Henrik G. Jensen and Torben Agersnap, eds., *Crime, Law and Justice in Greenland.* Copenhagen: New Social Science Monographs.

Brice-Bennet, Desmond. 1997. *Legal Glossary/Glossaire juridique.* Iqaluit: Nunavut Arctic College.

Briggs, Herbert W. 1941. 'The Validity of the Greenland Agreement.' 35:3 *American Journal of International Law* 506.

Brochmann, Helene. 2001. 'Detention in Greenland: Night-time Correctional Institutions, Probation and Hostels for Juvenile Offenders as Seen by Inmates and Staff.' 25 *Meddelelser om Grønland / Man and Society* 1.

Brody, Hugh. 2000. *The Other Side of Eden: Hunters, Farmers and the Shaping of the World.* Vancouver and Toronto: Douglas and McIntyre.

Brøndsted, Henning. 1973. 'Ruling in Greenland and Forms of Integration into

Denmark: The Established Legal Components.' In Jean Malaurie, ed., *The Eskimo People To-day and To-morrow*. Paris: Mouton.

– 1996. 'The Historical Development of the Greenlandic Judicial System.' In Henrik G. Jensen and Torben Agersnap, eds., *Crime, Law and Justice in Greenland*. Copenhagen: New Social Science Monographs.

Brøsted, Jens. 1988. 'Danish Accession to the Thule District, 1937.' 57:3 *Nordic Journal of International Law* 259.

Brøsted, Jens, and Mads Fægteborg. 1985. 'Expulsion of the Great People: When U.S. Air Force Came to Thule. An Analysis of Colonial Myth and Actual Incidents.' In Jens Brøsted et al., eds., *Native Power: The Quest for Autonomy and Nationhood of Indigenous Peoples*. Bergen and Oslo: Universitetsforlaget AS.

– 1986. 'Civil Aspects of Military Installations in Greenland.' *Information North* (Winter) 14.

Cameron, Kirk, and Graham White. 1995. *Northern Governments in Transition: Political and Constitutional Development in the Yukon, Nunavut and the Western Northwest Territories*. Montreal: Institute for Research on Public Policy.

Carswell, Margaret. 1984. 'Social Controls among the Native Peoples of the Northwest Territories in the Pre-contact Period.' 22:2 *Alberta Law Review* 303.

Caulfield, Richard A. 2000. 'The Kalaallit of West Greenland.' In Milton M.R. Freeman, ed., *Endangered Peoples of the Arctic: Struggles to Survive and Thrive*. Westport, CT: Greenwood Press.

Charron, Andrea. 2005. 'The Northwest Passage. Is Canada's Sovereignty Floating Away?' 60:3 *International Journal* 831.

Chaturvedi, Sanjay. 1996. *The Polar Regions: A Political Geography*. Chichester, NY, and Toronto: John Wiley and Sons.

Chemnitz, Laila. 2005. 'Danish-speaking Students in Denmark: Language and Identity Conflicts.' 3–4 *Indigenous Affairs* 54.

Clark, Margaret L., and John Dryzek. 1986. 'The Inuit Circumpolar Conference as an International Nongovernmental Actor.' In Marianne Stenbæk, ed., *Arctic Policy: Papers Presented at the Arctic Policy Conference, September 19–21, 1985*. Montreal: Centre for Northern Studies and Research, McGill University.

Cohen, Gail J. 2002. 'Northern Promise: Canada's First Arctic Law School.' 26:5 *Canadian Lawyer* 26.

Cook, Curtis, and Juan D. Lindau, eds. 2000. *Aboriginal Rights and Self-Government: The Canadian and Mexican Experience in North American Perspective*. Montreal and Kingston: McGill-Queen's University Press.

Craig, Donna, and Steven Freeland. 1999. *Indigenous Governance by the Inuit of Greenland and the Sámi of Scandinavia*. Discussion Paper 8. Governance Structures for Indigenous Australians on and off Native Title Lands. Sydney: University of New South Wales and Murdoch University.

Creery, Ian. 1993. 'The Inuit (Eskimo) of Canada.' 3 *Minority Rights Group Report* 6.

Curran, Vivian Grosswald, ed. 2002. *Comparative Law: An Introduction*. Durham, NC: Carolina Academic Press, Comparative Law Series.

Dahl, Jens. 1985. 'New Political Structure and Old Non-Fixed Structural Politics in Greenland.' In Jens Brøsted et al., eds., *Native Power the Quest for Autonomy and Nationhood of Indigenous Peoples*. Bergen and Oslo: Universitetsforlaget AS.

– 1986a. *Arktisk selvstyre: Historien bag og rammerne for det Grønlandske hjemmestyre* [Arctic Self-Government: The History and Scope of Greenland Home Rule]. Copenhagen: Akademisk Forlag.

– 1986b. 'Greenland: Political Structure of Self-Government.' 23:1-2 *Arctic Anthropology* 315.

– 1988a. 'Self-Government, Land Claims and Imagined Inuit Communities.' 30 *Folk* 73.

– 1988b. 'From Ethnic to Political Identity.' 57:3 *Nordic Journal of International Law* 312.

– 1997. 'Gender Parity in Nunavut?' 3–4 *Indigenous Affairs* 42.

– 2005a. 'Greenland.' *Indigenous World* 31.

– 2005b. 'The Greenlandic Version of Self-Government.' In Kathrin Wessendorf, ed., *An Indigenous Parliament? Realities and Perspectives in Russia and the Circumpolar North*. IWGIA Doc. 116. Copenhagen: IWGIA.

– 2006. 'Greenland.' *Indigenous World* 33.

'Denmark and Greenland Ultima Motives.' 2001. *Economist*, 17 February, 55.

Dinstein, Yoram, ed. 1981. *Models of Autonomy*. New Brunswick, NJ: Transaction Press.

Diubaldo, Richard J. 1981. 'The Role of the Arctic Islands in Defence.' In Morris Zaslow, ed., *A Century of Canada's Arctic Islands 1880–1980*. Ottawa: Royal Society of Canada.

Duffy, R. Quinn. 1988. *The Road to Nunavut: The Progress of the Eastern Arctic Inuit since the Second World War*. Montreal and Kingston: McGill-Queen's University Press.

Dybbroe, Susanne. 1988. 'Participation and Control: Issues in the Debate on Women and Development – A Greenlandic Example.' 30 *Folk* 111.

Eber, Dorothy Harley. 1997. *Images of Justice: A Legal History of the Northwest Territories as Traced through the Yellowknife Courthouse Collection of Inuit Sculpture*. Montreal and Kingston: McGill-Queen's University Press.

Eckert, Penelope, and Russell Newmark. 1980. 'Central Eskimo Song Duels: A Contextual Analysis of Ritual Ambiguity. *Ethnology* 191.

Ehlermann, C.-D. 1983. 'Constitutional Problems of a Change of Status of

Greenland in Community Law.' In Hjalte Rasmussen, ed., *Greenland in the Process of Leaving the European Communities*. Copenhagen: Forlaget Europa.

Eliasen, Bogi. 2004a. 'Non-Sovereign Polities and Their Access to the International Community.' In Sjúrður Skaale, ed., *The Right to National Self-Determination: The Faroe Islands and Greenland*. Nijhoff Law Specials, vol. 60. Leiden and Boston: Martinus Nijhoff.

– 2004b. 'The Faroes and Greenland in UN Documents.' In Sjúrður Skaale, ed., *The Right to National Self-Determination: The Faroe Islands and Greenland*. Nijhoff Law Specials, vol. 60. Leiden and Boston: Martinus Nijhoff.

– 2004c. 'The Danish Realm and Developments in the EU.' In Sjúrður Skaale, ed., *The Right to National Self-Determination: The Faroe Islands and Greenland*. Nijhoff Law Specials, vol. 60. Leiden and Boston: Martinus Nijhoff.

Espersen, Ole. 2004. 'Summary and Main Conclusions.' In Sjúrður Skaale, ed., *The Right to National Self-Determination: The Faroe Islands and Greenland*. Nijhoff Law Specials, vol. 60. Leiden and Boston: Martinus Nijhoff.

Ewald, William. 1998. 'The Jurisprudential Approach to Comparative Law: A Field Guide to "Rats."' 46:4 *American Journal of Comparative Law* 701.

Eyre, Kenneth Charles. 1981. 'Custos Borealis: The Military in the Canadian North.' PhD diss., University of London.

– 1987. 'Forty Years of Military Activity in the Canadian North, 1947–1987.' 40:4 *Arctic* 292.

Fægteborg, Mads. 1992. 'Inuit Circumpolar Conference: An Indigenous Organization as an Instrument of Influence.' In Lise Lyck, ed., *Nordic Arctic Research on Contemporary Arctic Problems: Proceedings from Nordic Arctic Research Forum Symposium 1992*. Ålborg: Ålborg University Press.

– 1993. *Towards an International Indigenous Arctic Policy: Arctic Leaders' Summit with an English–Russian Conference Dictionary*. Copenhagen: Arctic Information.

Fægteborg, Mads, and Anna Prakhova, eds. 1995. *Arctic Leaders' Summit II with an English–Russian Arctic Dictionary*. Copenhagen: Arctic Information.

Fenge, Terry A. 2001. 'The Inuit and Climate Change.' 2:4 *Isuma* 79.

Finkler, Harald W. 1975. 'Inuit and the Administration of Criminal Justice in the Northwest Territories: The Case of Frobisher Bay.' Montreal: Centre international de criminologie comparée, Université de Montréal.

– 1985a. 'Inuit and the Criminal Justice System: Future Strategies for Socio-Legal Control and Prevention.' 9:2 *Études/Inuit/Studies* 141.

– 1985b. 'The Role of Traditional Inuit Measures for Social Control in Correctional Policy and Administration.' In Anthony Allott and Gordon R. Woodman, eds., *People's Law and State Law*. Bellagio Papers. Dordrecht: Foris Publications.

– 1990. 'The Political Framework for Aboriginal Criminal Justice in Northern Canada.' 5 *Law and Anthropology* 113.

Fischer, Kristian. 1993. 'The Modernization of the U.S. Radar Installation at Thule, Greenland.' 30:1 *Journal of Peace Research* 7.

Fitzhugh, William W., and Elizabeth I. Ward, eds. 2000. *Vikings: The North Atlantic Saga*. Washington and London: Smithsonian Institution Press in association with the National Museum of Natural History.

Foighel, Isi. 1980. 'Home Rule in Greenland.' 1 *Meddelelser om Grønland / Man and Society* 3.

– 2005. 'The Right of a People to Exercise Their Culture: A Scandinavian Model.' In Zelim A. Skurbaty, ed., *Beyond a One-Dimensional State: An Emerging Right to Autonomy?* Raoul Wallenberg Institute Human Rights Library, vol. 19. Leiden and Boston: Martinus Nijhoff.

Fossett, Renée. 2001. *In Order to Live Untroubled: Inuit of the Central Arctic, 1550–1940*. Winnipeg: University of Manitoba Press.

Franckx, Erik. 1993. *Maritime Claims in the Arctic: Canadian and Russian Perspectives*. Dordrecht: Martinus Nijhoff.

Frideres James S., and René R. Gadacz, eds. 2001. *Aboriginal Peoples in Canada: Contemporary Conflicts*. 6th ed. Toronto: Prentice Hall.

Gad, Ulrik Pram. 2005. *Dansksprogede grønlænderes plads i et Grønland under grønlandisering og modernisering. En diskursanalyse af den grønlandske sprogdebat-læst som identitetspolitisk forhandling.* (The place of Danish speaking Greenlanders in Greenland under greenlandization and modernization. A discourse analysis of the Greenlandic debate on language – read as political negotiation about identity). Copenhagen: University of Copenhagen, Department of Eskimology and Arctic Studies, Papers in Eskimology No 19.

Gagnon, Mélanie, and Iqaluit Elders. 2002. *Inuit Recollections on the Military Presence in Iqaluit: Memory and History in Nunavut*. Vol. 2. Iqaluit: Nunavut Arctic College.

Gallagher-Mackay, Kelly. 2000. 'Rule of Law and Aboriginal Government: The Case of Nunavut.' LLM thesis, Osgoode Hall Law School, York University.

Goldschmidt, Verner. 1956. 'The Greenland Criminal Code and Its Sociological Background.' 1 *Acta Sociologica* 217.

– 1963. 'New Trends in Studies on Greenland Social Life: Criminal Law in Changing Greenland.' 5 *Folk* 113.

Gombay, Nicole. 2000. 'The Politics of Culture: Gender Parity in the Legislative Assembly of Nunavut.' 24:1 *Études/Inuit/Studies* 125.

Graburn, Nelson H. 1969. 'Eskimo Law in Light of Self- and Group-Interest.' 4:1 *Law and Society Review* 45.

Grant, Shelagh D. 1988. *Sovereignty or Security? Government Policy in the Canadian North, 1936–1950.* Vancouver: UBC Press.
– 1991. 'A Case of Compounded Error: The Inuit Resettlement Project (1953), and the Government Response, 1990.' 19:1 *Northern Perspectives* 3.
– 2002. *Arctic Justice: On Trial for Murder, Pond Inlet, 1923.* Montreal and Kingston: McGill-Queen's University Press.
Gray, Kevin. 1994. 'The Nunavut Land Claims Agreement and the Future of the Eastern Arctic: The Uncharted Path to Effective Self-Government.' 52:2 *University of Toronto Faculty of Law Review* 300.
'Greenland.' In 1999–2000 *Indigenous World* 28.
'Greenland.' In 2000–1 *Indigenous World* 26.
Greenland during the Cold War: Danish and American Security Policy, 1945–68. 1997. Summary. Trans. Henry Myers. Copenhagen: Danish Institute of International Affairs.
Griffiths, Curt Taylor. 1996. 'Crime, Law and Justice in the Circumpolar North: The Greenlandic Experience in a Comparative Context.' In Henrik G. Jensen and Torben Agersnap, eds., *Crime, Law and Justice in Greenland.* Copenhagen: New Social Science Monographs.
Griffiths, Curt Taylor, et al. 1995a. Crime, Law and Justice in the Baffin Region, NWT, Canada: Final Report. Burnaby, BC: Criminology Research Centre, Simon Fraser University.
Griffiths, Curt Taylor, et al. 1995b. 'Crime, Law and Justice in the Baffin Region: Preliminary Findings from a Multi-year Study.' In Kayleen M. Hazlehurst, ed., *Legal Pluralism and the Colonial Legacy: Indigenous Experiences of Justice in Canada, Australia and New Zealand.* Aldershot, UK, and Brookfield, VT: Avebury.
Griffiths, Franklyn. 1993. 'Defence, Security and Civility in the Arctic Region.' *Arctic Challenges.* Report from the Nordic Council's Parliamentary Conference in Reykjavik, 16–17 August.
– 1999a. 'The Northwest Passage in Transit.' 54:2 *International Journal* 189.
– 1999b. 'Environment and Security in Arctic Waters: A Canadian Perspective.' In Willy Østreng, ed., *National Security and International Environmental Cooperation in the Arctic: The Case of the Northern Sea Route.* Environment and Policy, vol. 16. Dordrecht: Kluwer Academic Publishers.
– 2003. 'The Shipping News: Canada's Arctic Sovereignty Not on Thinning Ice.' 58:2 *International Journal* 257.
– 2004. 'Pathetic Fallacy: That Canada's Arctic Sovereignty Is on Thinning Ice.' 11:3 *Canadian Foreign Policy* 1.
Griffiths, Franklyn, and Rosemarie Kuptana. 1991. *To Establish an International Arctic Council: A Framework Report.* Ottawa: Canadian Arctic Resources Committee.

Grinde, Donald. A., Jr., and Bruce E. Johansen. 1991. *Exemplar of Liberty: Native America and the Evolution of Democracy.* Los Angeles: American Indian Studies Center, University of California.

Gulløv, Hans Christian. 1979. 'Home Rule in Greenland.' 3:1 *Études/Inuit/Studies* 131.

Haagensen, Klaus M., ed. 2002. *Nordic Statistical Yearbook, 2002.* Vol. 40. Copenhagen: Statistics Denmark, Nord.

Hallendy, Norman, with Osuitok Ipeelee, Annie Manning, Pauta Saila, and Pitaloosie Saila. 1994. 'The Last Known Traditional Inuit Trial on Southwest Baffin Island in the Canadian Arctic.' August 1991. Background Paper No. 2 for *Places of Power and Objects of Veneration in the Canadian Arctic.* Paper presented at the World Archaeological Congress III, Ottawa.

Hannikainen, Lauri. 1996. 'The Status of Minorities, Indigenous Peoples and Immigrant and Refugee Groups in Four Nordic States.' 65:1 *Nordic Journal of International Law* 1.

Hannikainen, Lauri, and Frank Horn, eds. 1997. *Autonomy and Demilitarization in International Law: The Åland Islands in a Changing Europe.* The Hague: Kluwer Academic Publishers.

Hannum, Hurst. 1993. *Documents on Autonomy and Minority Rights.* Dordrecht: Martinus Nijhoff.

– 1996. *Autonomy, Sovereignty, and Self-Determination: The Accommodation of Conflicting Rights.* Philadelphia: University of Pennsylvania Press.

Harhoff, Frederik. 1983. 'Greenland's Withdrawal from the European Communities.' 20 *Common Market Law Review* 13.

– 1986. 'Institutions of Autonomy.' 55:1–2 *Nordic Journal of International Law* 31.

– 1992. 'Constitutional Relations between Denmark, the Faroe Islands and Greenland.' In Lise Lyck, ed., *Nordic Arctic Research on Contemporary Arctic Problems: Proceedings from Nordic Arctic Research Forum Symposium 1992.* Ålborg: Ålborg University Press.

– 1993. *Rigsfællesskabet.* [*The Community of the Danish Realm* (summary in English)]. Århus: Forlaget Klim.

– 1994a. 'National Practice and International Standards.' In Peter Jull et al., eds., *Surviving Columbus: Indigenous Peoples, Political Reform and Environmental Management in North Australia.* Darwin: North Australia Research Unit, Australian National University.

– 1994b. The Status of Indigenous Peoples under International Law: Greenland and the Right to Self-Determination.' 32 *Canadian Yearbook of International Law* 243.

– 1994–5. 'Palestinian Self-Government Viewed from a Distance: An Interna-

tional Legal Comparison between Palestinian Self-Government and Greenland's Home Rule.' 8 *Palestine Yearbook of International Law* 56.

Haysom, Veryan, and Jeffrey Richstone. 1987. 'Customizing Law in the Territories: Proposal for a Task Force on Customary Law in Nunavut.' 11:1 *Études/
Inuit/Studies* 91.

Heikkilä, Markku. 2006. *The Northern Dimension.* Trans. Lionbridge Oy. Helsinki:
Europe Information and Ministry of Foreign Affairs of Finland.

Heininen, Lassi. 2004. 'Circumpolar International Relations and Geopolitics.'
In *Arctic Human Development Report.* Akureyri: Stefansson Arctic Institute.

Henderson, Ailsa. 2004. 'Northern Political Culture? Political Behaviour in
Nunavut.' 28:1 *Études/Inuit/Studies* 133.

– 2005. *Inuit Qaujimajatuqangit.* In Mark Nuttall, ed., *Encyclopedia of the Arctic.*
Vol. 2. New York and London: Routledge.

Henriksen, John. 2001. 'Implementation of the Right to Self-Determination of
Indigenous Peoples.' 3 *Indigenous Affairs* 6.

Hicks, Jack, and Graham White. 2000. 'Nunavut: Inuit Self-Determination
through a Land Claim and Public Government?' In Jens Dahl, Jack Hicks, and
Peter Jull, eds. *Nunavut: Inuit Regain Control of Their Lands and Their Lives.*
IWGIA Doc. 102. Copenhagen: IWGIA.

– 2005. 'Building Nunavut through Decentralization or Carpet-Bombing It into
Near-total Dysfunction? A Case Study in Organizational Engineering.' Paper
presented at the annual meeting of the Canadian Political Science Association, University of Western Ontario, June.

Hitchins, Diddy R.M., and Bertil Liander. 1991. 'Cooperation, Conflict or Compromise? Superpower Responses to Canadian and Nordic Policies in the Arctic.' In Per Seyersted, ed., *The Arctic: Canada and the Nordic Countries.* NACS
Text Series, vol. 6. Lund, Sweden: Nordic Association for Canadian Studies.

Hoebel, E. Adamson. 1940–1. 'Law-ways of the Primitive Eskimos.' 31 *Journal of
the American Institute of Criminal Law and Criminology* 663.

– 1967. 'Song Duels among the Eskimo.' In Paul J. Bohannan, ed., *Law and
Warfare Studies in the Anthropology of Conflict.* New York: Natural History
Press.

– 1968 [1954]. *The Law of Primitive Man: A Study in Comparative Legal Dynamics.*
Reprint, New York: Atheneum; Cambridge, MA: Harvard University Press.

Høegh, Erling. 1973. 'The Historic Development of Political Institutions in
Greenland.' In Jean Malaurie, ed., *The Eskimo People To-day and To-morrow.*
Paris: Mouton.

Holtved, Erik. 1974–5. 'Myth Collecting in Greenland and Alaska.' 16–17 *Folk* 15.

Howarth, David. 2001. *The Sledge Patrol: A WWII Epic of Escape, Survival, and Victory.* New York: Lyons Press.

Huebert, Robert. 1999. 'Canadian Arctic Security Issues: Transformation in the Post–Cold War Era.' 54:2 *International Journal* 203.

– 2000. 'Security and the Environment in the Post–Cold War Arctic.' 4 *Environment and Security* 101.

– 2001. 'Climate Change and Canadian Sovereignty in the Northwest Passage.' 2:4 *Isuma* 86.

– 2003. 'The Shipping News Part II: How Canada's Arctic Sovereignty Is on Thinning Ice.' 58:3 *International Journal* 295.

Husa, Jaakko. 2000. 'Guarding the Constitutionality of Laws in the Nordic Countries: A Comparative Perspective.' 48:3 *American Journal of Comparative Law* 345.

Husebye, Sylvi Jane. 2001. 'Implementation of the European Union's Northern Dimension: The Arctic Area.' In *North Meets North: Proceedings of the First Northern Research Forum Akureyri and Bessastaðir.* 4–6 November 2000. Akureyri, Iceland: Stefansson Arctic Institute and University of Akureyri.

Hyde, Charles Cheney. 1933. 'The Case Concerning the Legal Status of Eastern Greenland.' 27:4 *American Journal of International Law* 732.

Inuaraq, Susan. 1995. 'Traditional Justice among the Inuit.' In Anne-Victoire Charrin, Jean-Michel Lacroix, and Michèle Therrien, eds., *Peuples des Grands Nords: Traditions et transitions.* Paris: Sorbonne Press.

Inuit Committee on National Issues. 1987. *Completing Canada: Inuit Approaches to Self-Government.* Position paper. Aboriginal Peoples and Constitutional Reform. Inuit Committee on National Issues. Kingston, ON: Institute of Intergovernmental Relations, Queen's University.

Isaac, Thomas. 1992. 'The Nunavut Agreement-in-Principle and Section 35 of the *Constitution Act, 1982.*' 21:2 *Manitoba Law Journal* 390.

Ittinuar, Peter. 1985. 'The Inuit Perspective on Aboriginal Rights.' In Menno Boldt and J. Anthony Long in association with Leroy Little Bear, eds., *The Quest for Justice: Aboriginal Peoples and Aboriginal Rights.* Toronto: University of Toronto Press.

Jenness, Diamond. 1964. *Eskimo Administration.* Volume 2. *Canada.* Technical Paper No. 14. Montreal: Arctic Institute of North America.

– 1967. *Eskimo Administration.* Volume 4. *Greenland.* Technical Paper No. 19. Montreal: Arctic Institute of North America.

– 1968. *Eskimo Administration.* Volume 5. *Analysis and Reflections.* Technical Paper No. 21. Montreal: Arctic Institute of North America.

Jensen, Henrik Garlic. 1992. 'Justice in Greenland.' In Curt Taylor Griffiths, ed., *Self-Sufficiency in Northern Justice Issues.* Burnaby: Simon Fraser University for the Northern Justice Society.

– 1996 'Contemporary Realities.' In Henrik G. Jensen and Torben Agersnap, eds., *Crime, Law and Justice in Greenland*. Copenhagen: New Social Science Monographs.

Jensen, Mette Uldall. 2004. 'Greenland.' *Indigenous World* 27.

Johansen, Lars Emil. 1992. 'Greenland and the European Community.' 16:1–2 *Études/Inuit/Studies* 33.

Johnston, Douglas. 2002. 'The Northwest Passage Revisited.' 33 *Ocean Development and International Law* 145.

Jull, Peter. 1991. *The Politics of Northern Frontiers in Australia, Canada and Other 'First World' Countries*. Darwin: North Australia Research Unit, Australian National University.

– 1995. 'Indigenous Territories and Mega Constitutional Change.' Unpublished paper, 25 June.

– 1998a. *Indigenous Autonomy in Nunavut: Canada's Present and Australia's Possibilities*. Brisbane: Centre for Democracy, Department of Government, University of Queensland.

– 1998b. '"First World" Indigenous Internationalism after Twenty-five Years.' 4:9 *Indigenous Law Bulletin* 8.

– 1999. 'Indigenous Internationalism: What Should We Do Next?' 1 *Indigenous Affairs* 12.

– 2000. 'Inuit and Nunavut: Renewing the New World.' In Jens Dahl, Jack Hicks, and Peter Jull, eds., *Nunavut: Inuit Regain Control of Their Lands and Their Lives*. IWGIA Doc. 102. Copenhagen: IWGIA.

– 2001a. 'Nations with Whom We Are Connected: Indigenous Peoples and Canada's Political System.' In Kathrin Wessendorf, ed., *Challenging Politics: Indigenous Peoples' Experiences with Political Parties and Elections*. IWGIA Doc. 104. Copenhagen: IWGIA.

– 2001b. 'Negotiating Nationhood, Renegotiating Nationhood: Canada's Nunavut and Nunavut's Canada.' 3 *Balayi: Culture, Law and Colonialism*: 67. (Paper for Re-thinking Indigenous Self-Determination: An International Conference on the Theory and Practice of Indigenous Self-Determination. School of Political Science and International Studies University of Queensland, Australia, 25–28 September).

Kersey, Alexandra. 1994. 'The Nunavut Agreement: A Model for Preserving Indigenous Rights.' 11:2 *Arizona Journal of International and Comparative Law* 429.

Keskitalo, Eva C.H. 2004. *Negotiating the Arctic: The Construction of an International Region*. New York and London: Routledge.

Kirton, John, and Don Munton. 1987. 'The Manhattan Voyages and Their Aftermath.' In Franklyn Grffiths, ed., *Politics of the Northwest Passage*. Montreal and Kingston: McGill-Queen's University Press.

Kleist, Mininnguaq. 2004. 'The Status of the Greenlandic Inuit: Are the Greenlandic Inuit a People, an Indigenous People, a Minority, or a Nation? A Practical, Philosophical and Conceptual Investigation.' In Sjúrður Skaale, ed. *The Right to National Self-Determination: The Faroe Islands and Greenland.* Nijhoff Law Specials, vol. 60. Leiden and Boston: Martinus Nijhoff.

Kleivan, Inge. 1971. 'Song Duels in West Greenland: Joking Relationships and Avoidance.' 13 *Folk* 9.

– 1992. 'The Arctic Peoples' Conference in Copenhagen, November 22–25, 1973.' 16:1–2 *Études/Inuit/Studies* 227.

Koivurova, Timo. 2002. *Environmental Impact Assessment in the Arctic: A Study of International Legal Norms.* Aldershot, UK, and Burlington, VT: Ashgate.

Koivurova, Timo, and Leena Heinämäki. 2006. 'The Participation of Indigenous Peoples in International Norm-making in the Arctic.' 42:2 *Polar Record* 101.

Krämer, Hans R. 1982. 'Greenland's European Community (EC): Referendum, Background and Consequences.' 18:25 *German Yearbook of International Law* 273.

Kusugak, Jose. 2000. 'The Tide Has Shifted: Nunavut Works for Us, and It Offers a Lesson to the Broader Global Community.' In Jens Dahl, Jack Hicks, and Peter Jull et al., eds., *Nunavut: Inuit Regain Control of Their Lands and Their Lives.* IWGIA Doc. 102. Copenhagen: IWGIA.

Lachmann, Per. 1983. 'The Negotiations for Greenland's Withdrawal from the Community and Its Inclusion in the OCT-Arrangement.' In Hjalte Rasmussen, ed., *Greenland in the Process of Leaving the European Communities.* Copenhagen: Forlaget Europa.

Langlais, Richard. 1995. 'Reformulating Security. A Case Study from Arctic Canada.' PhD diss., Göteborg University.

Lapidoth, Ruth. 1997. *Autonomy: Flexible Solutions to Ethnic Conflicts.* Washington, DC: United States Institute of Peace Press.

Larsen, Joan Nymand. 2002. 'Economic Development in Greenland: A Time Series Analysis of Dependency, Growth, And Instability.' PhD diss., University of Manitoba.

– 2004. 'External Dependency in Greenland: Implication for Growth and Instability.' In *Northern Veche: Proceedings of the Second Northern Research Forum Open Meeting, September 19–22, 2002, Veliky Novgorod, Russia.* Akureyri, Iceland: Stefansson Arctic Institute and University of Akureyri.

Legaré, André. 1998. 'An Assessment of Recent Political Development in Nunavut: The Challenges and Dilemmas of Inuit Self-Government.' 18:2 *Canadian Journal of Native Studies* 271.

– 2003. 'The Nunavut Tunngavik Inc.: An Examination of Its Mode of Operations and Its Activities.' In Robert B. Anderson and Robert M. Bone, eds., *Natural Resources and Aboriginal People in Canada.* Concord, ON: Captus Press.

Lenarcic, David, and Robert Reford. 1989. 'Sovereignty versus Defence: The Arctic in Canadian-American Relations.' In Edgar J. Dosman, ed., *Sovereignty and Security in the Arctic*. London and New York: Routledge.

Lester, Geoffrey S. 1979. 'Aboriginal Land Rights: The Significance of Inuit Place-Naming.' 3:1 *Études/Inuit/Studies* 53.

– 1981. 'The Territorial Rights of the Inuit of the Canadian Northwest Territories: A Legal Argument.' D.Jur. diss., York University.

Levesque, Francis. 2002. '"Today Inuit Tradition Is Changing": The Concept of *Inuit Qaujimajatuqangit* (Inuit Traditional Knowledge) and Its Introduction into Government Institutions in Nunavut.' Paper presented at the First IPS-SAS PhD seminar. Nuuk, 28 May–8 June.

Lewington, Jennifer. 1987. 'Lessons of the Arctic Pilot Project.' In Franklyn Griffiths, ed., *Politics of the Northwest Passage*. Montreal and Kingston: McGill-Queen's University Press.

Lindholm, Göran. 1985. 'The Right of Autonomous Regions to Participate in Nordic Co-operation.' 54:1–2 *Nordisk Tidsskrift for International Law* 79.

Lindley, Richard. 1969. *Autonomy*. Atlantic Highlights, NJ: Humanities Press.

Loukacheva, Natalia. 2005. 'On Autonomy and Law.' Working Paper. Hamilton: Institute on Globalization and the Human Condition.

Lyche, Ingeborg. 1974. *Nordic Cultural Co-operation: Joint Ventures, 1946–1972*. Oslo, Bergen, and Tromsø: Universitetsforlaget.

Lyck, Lise. 1988. 'Natural Resources in Greenland: Economic Possibilities and Restraints.' 57(3) *Nordic Journal of International Law* 345.

– 1995. 'Lessons to Be Learned on Autonomy and Human Rights from the Faeroese Situation since 1992.' 64:3 *Nordic Journal of International Law* 481.

– ed. 1997. *Socio-Economic Developments in Greenland and in Other Small Nordic Jurisdictions*. Copenhagen: New Social Science Monographs.

– 1999. *Arctic International Trade: A Study Focused on the Greenlandic International Trade Regime*. Copenhagen: New Social Science Monographs.

– 2000. 'Politics and Elections in Greenland with a Focus on Economic and Sustainable Development.' In Lise Lyck, ed., *Greenland and Arctic Economic and Political Issues*. Copenhagen: Nordic Press.

Lynge, Aqqaluk. 2002. *The Right to Return: Fifty Years of Struggle by Relocated Inughuit in Greenland*. Nuuk: Forlaget Atuagkat.

Lynge, Aviâja Egede. 2006. 'The Best Colony in the World.' Paper for Rethinking Nordic Colonialism conference. Nuuk, 22 April.

Lynge, Finn. 1989. 'How Danish Are the Greenlanders, Really?' In Jens Dahl, ed., *Keynote Speeches from the Sixth Inuit Studies Conference*. Copenhagen: Institut for Eskimologi.

Lytthans, Kaspar. 1999. 'Perspectives in the Development of Greenlandic Administration.' In Hanne Petersen and Birger Poppel, eds., *Dependency, Autonomy, Sustainability in the Arctic.* Aldershot, UK, and Brookfield, VT: Ashgate.

Macklem, Patrick. 1992. 'Aboriginal Peoples, Criminal Justice Initiatives and the Constitution.' 26 *U.B.C. Law Review* 280 (special issue on Aboriginal justice).

– 1993. 'Aboriginal Justice, the Distribution of Legislative Authority, and the Judicature Provisions of the *Constitution Act, 1867.*' In *Aboriginal Peoples and the Justice System: Report of the National Round Table on Aboriginal Justice Issues.* Ottawa: Royal Commission on Aboriginal Peoples, Minister of Supply and Services Canada.

– 2001. *Indigenous Difference and the Constitution of Canada.* Toronto: University of Toronto Press.

MacNeil, Gillian. 2006. 'The Northwest Passage: Sovereign Seaway or International Strait? A Reassessment of the Legal Status.' 15 *Dalhousie Journal of Legal Studies* 204.

Marcus, Alan Rudolph. 1992. *Out in the Cold: The Legacy of Canada's Inuit Relocation Experiment in the High Arctic.* Doc. 71. Copenhagen: IWGIA.

– 1995. *Relocating Eden: The Image and Politics of Inuit Exile in the Canadian Arctic.* Hanover, NH, and London: University Press of New England.

Marecic, Charles. 2000. 'Nunavut Territory: Aboriginal Governing in the Canadian Regime of Governance.' 24:2 *American Indian Law Review* 275.

Martens, Gunnar. 1988. 'Administration in Greenland: A Limitation to Autonomy.' 57 *Nordic Journal of International Law* 358.

Mason, Kevin. 1983. 'European Communities Commission: Greenland-EC Commission Draft Approves Withdrawal of Greenland from the European Community and Proposes Terms for Economic Reassociation.' 13:3 *Georgia Journal of International and Comparative Law* 865.

Matthiasson, John Stephen. 1967. 'Eskimo Legal Acculturation: The Adjustment of Baffin Island Eskimos to Canadian Law.' PhD diss., Cornell University.

– 1992. *Living on the Land: Change among the Inuit of Baffin Island.* Peterborough, ON: Broadview Press.

McCready, Catherine M. 2003. '*Inuit Qaujimajatuqangit:* "Living Policy" and the Development of Responsible Governance in Nunavut.' MA thesis, Trent University.

McNeil, Kent. 1982. *Native Rights and the Boundaries of Rupert's Land and the North-Western Territory.* Studies in Aboriginal Rights No. 4. Saskatoon: University of Saskatchewan Native Law Centre.

McPherson, Robert. 2003. *New Owners in Their Own Land: Minerals and Inuit Land Claims.* Calgary: University of Calgary Press.

McRae, Donald M. 1994–5. 'Arctic Sovereignty: Loss by Dereliction?' 22:4 *Northern Perspectives* 8.

Merryman, John Henry. 1998. 'Comparative Law Scholarship.' 21 Hastings International and Comparative Law Review 771.

Mikkelsen, Peter Schmidt. 2005. *One Thousand Days with Sirius: The Greenland Sledge Patrol.* Cawdor, Scotland: Steading Workshop.

Mitchell, Marybelle, and Pat Tobin. 1999. 'Nunavut: The Newest Member of Confederation.' 14:2 *Inuit Quarterly* 18.

Morrow, W.H., ed. 1995. *Northern Justice: The Memoirs of Mr. Justice William G. Morrow.* Toronto: University of Toronto Press.

Morse, Bradford Wilmot. 1988. 'Indigenous Law and State Legal Systems: Conflict and Compatibility.' In Bradford W. Morse and Gordon R. Woodman, eds., *Indigenous Law and the State.* Dordrecht, The Netherlands, and Providence, RI: Foris Publications.

Moss, Wendy. 1995. 'Inuit Perspectives on Treaty Rights and Governance Issues.' In Patrick Macklem et al., eds., *Aboriginal Self-Government: Legal and Constitutional Issues.* Ottawa: Royal Commission on Aboriginal Peoples, Minister of Supply and Services Canada.

Moyels, Robert Gordon. 1979. *British Law and Arctic Men: The Celebrated 1917 Murder Trials of Sinnisiak and Uluksuk, First Inuit Tried under White Man's Law.* Saskatoon: Western Producer Prairie Books.

Myers, Heather. 2000. 'Options for Appropriate Development in Nunavut Communities.' 24:1 *Études/Inuit/Studies* 25.

Myers, Heather, and Don Munton. 2000. 'Cold War, Frozen Wastes: Cleaning up the DEW Line.' 4 *Environment and Security* 119.

Nash, Michael L. 1996. 'The Greenland Option.' 146:6752 *New Law Journal* 1019.

Nauclér, Elisabeth. 2005. 'The Status of Autonomous Territories in International Organizations: Experiences in Nordic and Continental European Cooperation.' In Zelim A. Skurbaty, ed., *Beyond a One-Dimensional State: An Emerging Right to Autonomy?* Raoul Wallenberg Institute Human Rights Library, vol. 19. Leiden and Boston: Martinus Nijhoff.

Neumann, Iver B. 2000. 'State to Region: Nordic Co-operation and the Winds of Change.' In Lars Hedegaard and Bjarne Lindström, eds., *The NEBI Yearbook 2000: North European and Baltic Sea Integration.* Berlin: Springer-Verlag; Nordregio: Nordic Centre for Spatial Development.

Nielsen, Jens Kaalhauge. 2001. *Greenland's Geopolitical Reality and Its Political–Economic Consequences.* DUPI Working Paper 6. Copenhagen: Danish Institute of International Affairs.

Nielsen, Jørn Berglund. 2000. 'Inuit Socio-Cultural Values across the Arctic.' 24:1 *Études/Inuit/Studies* 149.

Nielsen, Lars Nordskov. 1986. 'Greenland: Thule Inughuit Moved by Force.' 45

IWGIA Newsletter 73.

Nowlan-Card, Laureen. 1996. 'Public Government and Regulatory Participation in Nunavut: Effective Self-Government for the Inuit.' 5 *Dalhousie Journal of Legal Studies* 31.

Nungak, Zebedee. 1993. 'Fundamental Values, Norms, and Concepts of Justice.' In *Aboriginal Peoples and the Justice System: Report of the National Round Table on Aboriginal Justice Issues*. Ottawa: Royal Commission on Aboriginal Peoples, Minister of Supply and Services Canada.

– 1999. 'Zebedee Nungaq on Nunavut.' 85 *Inuktitut* 19.

Nuttall, Mark. 1994. 'Greenland: Emergence of an Inuit Homeland.' In Minority Rights Group, ed., *Polar Peoples: Self-Determination and Development*. London: Minority Rights Group.

O'Brien, Kevin. 2003–4. 'Some Thoughts on Consensus Government in Nunavut.' 26:4 *Canadian Parliamentary Review* 6.

Ollivier, Maurice, annotator. 1962. *British North America Acts and Selected Statutes, 1867–1962*. Ottawa: Roger Duhamel Queen's Printer and Controller of Stationery.

Olsen, Moses. 1983. 'Perspectives beyond Greenland's Secession from the EEC.' In Hjalte Rasmussen, ed., *Greenland in the Process of Leaving the European Communities*. Copenhagen: Forlaget Europa.

'On Thinning Ice.' 2002. 27:2 *Northern Perspectives* 1.

Oosten, Jarich. 2000. 'The Notion of *Inua* and the Dynamics of Inuit Knowledge.' *Working Papers from the Symposium on Inuit Philosophy, 3–4 May*. Nuuk: University of Greenland.

Oosten, Jarich, Frédérik Laugrand, and Wim Rasing, eds. 1999. *Interviewing Inuit Elders: Perspectives on Traditional Law*. Vol. 2. Iqaluit: Nunavut Arctic College.

Ørebech, Peter, et al. 2006. *The Role of Customary Law in Sustainable Development*. Cambridge: Cambridge University Press.

Oreskov, Claus. 1995. 'Ultima Thule?' 3 *Indigenous Affairs* 51.

Østreng, Willy. 1992. 'Political-Military Relations among the Ice States: The Conceptual Basis of State Behaviour.' In Franklyn Griffiths, ed., *Arctic Alternatives: Civility or Militarism in the Circumpolar North*. Toronto: Science for Peace/Samuel Stevens Canadian Papers in Peace Studies.

– 1999. 'Danish Security Policy: The Role of the Arctic, the Environment and Arctic Navigation.' In Willy Østreng, ed., *National Security and International Environmental Cooperation in the Arctic: The Case of the Northern Sea Route*. Environment and Policy Series, vol. 16. Dordrecht: Kluwer Academic Publishers.

Patenaude, Allan L. 1985. 'The Concepts of Capital Crime and Punishment Among the Inuit of Eastern Arctic and Greenland.' Unpublished paper, Frobisher Bay, NWT.

– 1989. 'Whose Law? Whose Justice? Two Conflicting Systems of Law and Justice in Canada's Northwest Territories.' BA (Honours) essay, Simon Fraser University.

Pauktuutit: Inuit Women of Canada. 1991. *Arnait: The Views of Inuit Women on Contemporary Issues*. Ottawa: Pauktuutit.

– 1993. *Suvaguuq – National Newsletter on Inuit Social and Cultural Issues* 8:1. Special Issue on Justice.

– 1995. *Inuit Women and Justice. Progress Report 1*. Ottawa: Pauktuutit.

– 2006a. *The Inuit Way: A Guide to Inuit Culture*. Ottawa: Pauktuutit.

– 2006b. *National Strategy to Prevent Abuse in Inuit Communities and Sharing Knowledge, Sharing Wisdom: A Guide to the National Strategy*. Ottawa: Pauktuutit.

Pedersen, Mille Søvndahl. 1999. 'The Historical Development of the Greenlandic Judicial System.' In Hanne Petersen and Birger Poppel, eds., *Dependency, Autonomy, Sustainability in the Arctic*. Aldershot, UK, and Brookfield, VT: Ashgate.

Petersen, Hanne. 1998. 'On Law and Music: From Song Duels to Rhythmic Legal Orders?' 41 *Journal of Legal Pluralism* 75.

– 1999 'Performing Mimetic Administrative Law under Home Rule.' In Hanne Petersen and Birger Poppel, eds. *Dependency, Autonomy, Sustainability in the Arctic*. Aldershot, UK, and Brookfield, VT: Ashgate.

– 2000. 'The Lion King and the Lady Unicorn: Jurisprudential Considerations on Visual Normativity.' *European Yearbook in the Sociology of Law* 173.

– 2001. 'Legal Cultures in the Danish Realm: Greenland in Focus.' In Kirsten Hastrup, ed., *Legal Cultures and Human Rights: The Challenge of Diversity*. The Hague and New York: Kluwer Law International.

– ed. 2006. *Greenland in the Global Society: Development and Change of Norms and Practices* [translation of Danish title]. Nuuk: Atuagkat Publishing/Ilisimatusarfik.

Petersen, Hanne, and Birger Poppel, eds. 1999. *Dependency, Autonomy, Sustainability in the Arctic*. Aldershot, UK, and Brookfield, VT: Ashgate.

Petersen, Nikolaj. 1988. 'Denmark, Greenland, and Arctic Security.' In Kari Möttölä, ed., *The Arctic Challenge: Nordic and Canadian Approaches to Security and Cooperation in an Emerging International Region*. Boulder, CO, and London: Westview.

Petersen, Robert. 1984. 'The Pan-Eskimo Movement.' In David Damas, ed., *Handbook of North American Indians*. Volume 5. Washington: Smithsonian Institute.

– 1992. 'Kolonialisme set fra en tidligere koloniseret' [Colonialism seen from the perspective of those formerly colonized]. In *Grønlandsk Kultur – og Sam-*

fundsforskning [Cultural and social research in Greenland]. Nuuk: University of Greenland Ilisimatusarfik/Atuakkiorfik.
– 1995. 'Colonialism as Seen from a Former Colonized Area.' 32:2 *Arctic Anthropology* 118.
– 1996. 'Administration of Justice in the Traditional Greenlandic Community.' In Guðmundur Alfreðsson and Peter Macalister-Smith, eds., *The Living Law of Nations: Essays on Refugees, Minorities, Indigenous Peoples and the Human Rights of Other Vulnerable Groups in Memory of Alte Grahl-Madsen.* Strasbourg, and Arlington, VA: N.P. Engel.
– 2000. 'On the Background of the Traditional Greenland Organization and Production.' *Working Papers from the Symposium on Inuit Philosophy, 3–4 May.* Nuuk: University of Greenland.
Petersen, Robert, Petrussen, Amandus, and H.C.Petersen. 1991. 'Østgrønlœnderne kommer med' [The Eastgreenlanders and the Northgreenlanders are joining]. In H.C. Petersen, ed., *Grønlœndernes historie før 1925* [The history of Greenlanders before 1925]. Nuuk: Namminersornerullutik and Atuakkiorfik.
Petersson, Olof. 1994. *The Government and Politics of the Nordic Countries.* Trans. Frank Gabriel Perry. Stockholm: Nordstedts Juridik and Publica.
Pharand, Donat. 1981. 'Canada's Jurisdiction in the Arctic.' In Morris Zaslow, ed., *A Century of Canada's Arctic Islands, 1880–1980.* Ottawa: Royal Society of Canada.
– 1984. 'The Legal Regime of the Arctic: Some Outstanding Issues.' 39 *International Journal* 742.
– 1988. *Canada's Arctic Waters in International Law.* Cambridge: Cambridge University Press.
– 1989. 'Sovereignty in the Arctic: The International Legal Context.' In Edgar J. Dosman, ed., *Sovereignty and Security in the Arctic.* London and New York: Routledge.
– 1992. 'The Case for an Arctic Region Council and a Treaty Proposal.' 23 *Revue générale de droit* 163.
Pharand, Donat, with Leonard Legault. 1984. *The Northwest Passage: Arctic Straits.* International Straits of the World, Vol. 7. Dordrecht: Martinus Nijhoff.
Poelzer, Gregory M. 1996. 'Towards a Theory of Native Self-Government: Canada and Russia in Comparative Perspective.' PhD diss., University of Alberta.
Polar Peoples: Self-Determination and Development. 1994. Ed. Minority Rights Group. London: Minority Rights Group.
Pospisil, Leopold J. 1964. 'Law and Societal Structure among the Nunamiut Eskimo.' In Ward H. Goodenough, ed., *Explorations in Cultural Anthropology: Essays in Honour of George Peter Murdock.* New York: McGraw-Hill.

Preuss, Lawrence. 1932 'The Dispute between Denmark and Norway over the Sovereignty of East Greenland.' 26:3 *American Journal of International Law* 469.

Price, Graham. 1986. 'Remote Justice: The Stipendiary Magistrates Court of the Northwest Territories.' LLM thesis, University of Manitoba.

Purich, Donald J. 1992. *The Inuit and Their Land: The Story of Nunavut.* Toronto: Lorimer.

Rasing, Willem C.E. 1984. 'On Conflict Management with Nomadic Inuit: An Ethnological Essay.' PhD diss., Catholic University of Nijmegen.

– 1989. *Crime, Socio-legal Control and Problems of Change: A Legal Anthropological Study of Igloolik, NWT.* Report. Ottawa: Department of Indian Affairs and Northern Development.

– 1993. 'The Case of Kolitalik on the Encounter of Iglulingmiut Culture and Canadian Justice.' In Buijs Cunera, ed., *Continuity and Discontinuity in Arctic Cultures: Essays in Honour of Gerti Nooter, Curator at the National Museum of Ethnology, 1970–1990.* Leiden: Centre of Non-Western Studies.

– 1994. *'Too Many People': Order and Nonconformity in Iglulingmiut Social Process.* Nijmegen, The Netherlands: Katholieke Universiteit Faculteit der Rechtsgeleerdheid.

Rasmussen, Henriette. 1995. 'Greenland: Current Concerns of the Inuit People.' 3 *Indigenous Affairs* 48.

– 1998. 'Greenland's Women Want to Take the Lead.' In Diana Vinding, ed., *Indigenous Women: The Right to Voice.* IWGIA Doc. 88. Copenhagen: IWGIA.

– 2001. 'Greenland, the Inuit and NMD.' 2:2 *Pugwash Occasional Papers* 76.

– 2004. 'Women in Greenland.' Speech at a Nordic Conference 'Women's Movements Inspiration, Intervention and Irritation.' Reykjavik, Iceland, 10–12 June.

Rasmussen, Knud. 1929. *Intellectual Culture of the Iglulik Eskimos.* Report of the Fifth Thule Expedition 1921–4. 7:1. Copenhagen: Nordisk Forlag.

Rasmussen, Lars Toft. 1983a. 'ICC's New Status with United Nations.' 2 *Inuit Arctic Policy Review* 3.

– 1983b. 'Europe's Reluctant Farewell to Greenland.' 2 Inuit Arctic Policy Rev.: 18.

– 1987. 'Greenlandic and Danish Attitudes to Canadian Arctic Shipping.' In Franklyn Griffiths, ed., *The Politics of the Northwest Passage.* Montreal and Kingston: McGill-Queen's University Press.

Rasmussen, Rasmus Ole. 2000. 'Formal Economy, Renewable Resources and Structural Change in West Greenland.' 24:1 *Études/Inuit/Studies* 41.

– 2002. 'Perspectives on Sustainable Development in Greenland.' Paper presented at the International Seminar on International Identity: Possibilities and Choices between Home Rule and Free Arrangements. Nuuk, 14–15 February.

– 2006. 'Oil Exploration in Greenland.' 2–3 *Indigenous Affairs* 40.

Rasmussen, Rasmus Ole, and Lawrence C. Hamilton. 2001. *The Development of Fisheries in Greenland with Focus on Paamiut/Frederikshåb and Sisimiut/Holsteinsborg.* NORS Research Paper 53. Roskilde, Denmark: Roskilde University.

Reitz, John C. 1998. 'How to Do Comparative Law.' 46:4 *American Journal of Comparative Law* 617.

Richstone, Jeffrey. 1983. 'The Inuit and Customary Law: Constitutional Perspectives.' In Harald W. Finkler, ed., *Papers of the Symposia on Folk Law and Legal Pluralism, XIth International Congress of Anthropological and Ethnological Sciences.* Vancouver: Commission on Folk Law and Legal Pluralism.

Rigby Bruce, John MacDonald, and Leah Otak. 2000. 'The Inuit of Nunavut, Canada.' In Milton M.R. Freeman, ed., *Endangered Peoples of the Arctic: Struggles to Survive and Thrive.* Westport, CT: Greenwood Press.

Robertson, Gordon. 2000. *Memoirs of a Very Civil Servant: Mackenzie King to Pierre Trudeau.* Toronto: University of Toronto Press.

Rodon, Thierry. 1998. 'Co-management and Self-Determination in Nunavut.' 22:2 *Polar Geography* 119.

Rógvi, Kári á. 2004. 'The Land of Maybe: A Survey of Faroese Constitutional History.' In Sjúrður Skaale, ed., *The Right to National Self-Determination: The Faroe Islands and Greenland.* Nijhoff Law Specials, vol. 60. Leiden and Boston: Martinus Nijhoff.

Rothwell, Donald R. 1996. *The Polar Regions and the Development of International Law.* Cambridge: Cambridge University Press.

Rotman, Leonard I. 1996. *Parallel Paths: Fiduciary Doctrine and the Crown-Native Relationship in Canada.* Toronto: University of Toronto Press.

Rouland, Norbert. 1978. 'Ethnologie juridique des Inuits: Approche bibliographique critique.' 2:1 *Études/Inuit/Studies* 120.

1979a [1976]. 'Legal Sanctions among Some Inuit Populations: Theoretical Problems and Ways of Intervening for the Community in the Process of Settling Disputes.' Reprint in 3 *Études/Inuit/Studies* 1.

– 1979b. Les modes juridique de solution des conflits chez les Inuits. Special issue 3 *Études/Inuit/Studies.*

Rousseau, Pierre. 1994. 'Les systèmes judiciaires au Nunavut et au Groenland.' 18:1–2 *Études/Inuit/Studies* 155.

– 1995. 'La justice canadienne chez les Inuit de la région de Baffin Territoires du Nord-Ouest.' In Anne-Victoire Charrin, Jean-Michel Lacroix, and Michèle Therrien, eds., *Peuples des Grands Nords: Traditions et transitions.* Paris: Sorbonne.

Rowe, Andrea W. 1990. 'Assimilation through Accommodation: Practice, Rhetoric and Decisions in the Territorial Court of the Northwest Territories 1955–1972.' LLM thesis, University of Toronto.

Russell, Peter H. 1996. 'Aboriginal Nationalism: Prospects for Decolonisation.' 18:2 *Pasifica Review* 57.

– 2004. *Constitutional Odyssey: Can Canadians Become a Sovereign People?* 3rd ed. Toronto: University of Toronto Press.

– 2005. 'Indigenous Self-Determination: Is Canada as Good as It Gets?' In Barbara Ann Hocking, ed., *Unfinished Constitutional Business? Rethinking Indigenous Self-Determination.* Canberra: Aboriginal Studies Press.

Saladin d'Anglure, Bernard, and F. Morin. 1991. *The Inuit and the Internationalization of Aboriginal Powers.* Ottawa: Royal Commission on Aboriginal Peoples.

Sambo, Dalee Dorough. 1992. 'Indigenous Human Rights: The Role of Inuit at the United Nations Working Group on Indigenous Peoples.' 16:1–2 *Études/Inuit/Studies* 27.

– 1993 'Sustainable Security: An Inuit Perspective.' In Jyrki Käkönen, ed. *Politics and Sustainable Growth in the Arctic.* Aldershot, UK, and Brookfield, VT: Dartmouth Publishing.

Sanders, Nora. 2007. 'Trial Court Unification in Nunavut.' In Peter H. Russell ed. *Canada's Trial Courts: Two Tiers or One.* Toronto: University of Toronto Press.

Schechter, Elaine J. 1983. 'The Greenland Criminal Code and the Limits to Legal Pluralism.' 7:2 *Études/Inuit/Studies* 79.

Schledermann, Peter. 2003. 'The Muskox Patrol: High Arctic Sovereignty Revisited.' 56:1 *Arctic* 101.

Schuurman, Hubert J.C. 1976. *Canada's Eastern Neighbour: A View on Change in Greenland.* Ottawa: Minister of Supply and Services Canada.

Scrivener, David. 1996. *Environmental Cooperation in the Arctic: From Strategy to Council.* Oslo: Norwegian Atlantic Committee.

Simon, Mary May. 1985. 'The Role of Inuit in International Affairs.' 9:2 *Études/Inuit/Studies* 33.

– 1989. 'Security, Peace and the Native Peoples of the Arctic.' In Thomas R. Berger et al. *The Arctic Choices for Peace and Security: A Public Inquiry.* The True North Strong and Free Inquiry Society. Vancouver and Seattle: Gordon Soules Book Publishers.

– 1997. *Inuit: One Future – One Arctic.* Peterborough, ON: Cider Press.

Sissons, Jack H. 1968. *Judge of the Far North: The Memoirs of Jack Sissons.* Toronto: McClelland and Stewart.

Skaale, Sjúrður, ed. 2004. *The Right to National Self-Determination: The Faroe Islands and Greenland.* Nijhoff Law Specials, vol. 60. Leiden and Boston: Martinus Nijhoff.

Skeie, John. 1933. *Greenland: The Dispute between Norway and Denmark*. London and Toronto: J.M. Dent and Sons.

Skurbaty, Zelim A., ed. 2005. *Beyond One-Dimensional State: An Emerging Right to Autonomy?* The Raoul Wallenberg Institute Human Rights Library, Vol. 19. Leiden and Boston: Martinus Nijhoff.

Smith, Derek G. 1993. 'The Emergence of "Eskimo Status": An Examination of the Eskimo Disc List System and Its Social Consequences, 1925–1970.' In Noel Dyck and James B. Waldram, eds. *Anthropology, Public Policy, and Native Peoples in Canada*. Montreal and Kingston: McGill-Queen's University Press.

Smith, Gordon W. 1952. 'The Historical and Legal Background of Canada's Arctic Claims.' PhD diss., Columbia University.

Solem, Erik. 1977. *The Nordic Council and Scandinavian Integration*. New York and London: Praeger.

Sonne, Birgitte. 1982. 'The Ideology and Practice of Blood Feuds in East and West Greenland.' 6:2 *Études/Inuit/Studies* 21.

Sørensen, Axel K. 1995. 'Greenland: From Colony to Home Rule.' In Sven Tägil, ed., *Ethnicity and Nation Building in the Nordic World*. London: Hurst and Company.

Spakowski, Mark. 2001. 'Administrative Agencies in Nunavut: A Survey and Recommendations.' LLM thesis, Osgoode Hall Law School, York University.

Statistics Greenland. 2001. *Greenland, 2000–2001 Kalaallit Nunaat Statistical Yearbook*. Nuuk: Greenland Home Rule Government.

Stevens, Samuel. 1993. 'Northwest Territories Community Justice of the Peace Program.' In *Aboriginal Peoples and the Justice System. Report of the National Round Table on Aboriginal Justice Issues*. Ottawa: Royal Commission on Aboriginal Peoples, Minister of Supply and Services Canada.

Stevenson, Mark G. 1993. 'Traditional Inuit Decision-Making Structures and the Administration of Nunavut.' Paper prepared for the Royal Commission on Aboriginal Peoples. September.

Suksi, Markku, ed. 1998. *Autonomy: Applications and Implications*. The Hague and London: Kluwer Law International.

Sutherland, R. 1966. 'The Strategic Significance in the Canadian Arctic.' In Ronald MacDonald, ed., *The Arctic Frontier*. Toronto: University of Toronto Press.

Taagholt, Jørgen, and Jens Claus Hansen. 2001. *Greenland: Security Perspectives*. Trans. Daniel Lufkin. Fairbanks, AK: Arctic Research Consortium of the United States.

Tennberg, Monica. 1996. 'Indigenous Peoples' Involvement in the Arctic Council.' 4 *Northern Notes* 21.

– 2000. *Arctic Environmental Cooperation: A Study in Governmentality.* Aldershot, UK, and Burlington, VT: Ashgate.

Tester, Frank J., and Peter Kulchyski. 1994. *Tammarniit (Mistakes): Inuit Relocation in the Eastern Arctic, 1939–63.* Vancouver: UBC Press.

Thomsen, Marianne Lykke. 1988. 'The Role of the Inuit Women with Regard to Development of Self-Government in the Canadian Arctic.' 30 *Folk* 85.

– 1990. 'Inuit Women in Greenland and Canada: Awareness and Involvement in Political Development.' In Mary Crnkovich, ed., *'Gossip': A Spoken History of Women in the North.* Ottawa: Canadian Arctic Resources Committee.

– 1994–5. 'Greenland.' *Indigenous World 25.*

– 1995–6. 'Greenland.' *Indigenous World 30.*

– 1998–9. 'Greenland.' *Indigenous World 26.*

Timpson, Annis May. 2005. 'The Challenges of Intergovernmental Relations for Nunavut.' In Michael Murphy, ed., *Reconfiguring Aboriginal–State Relations. Canada: The State of the Federation 2003.* Montreal and Kingston: McGill-Queen's University Press.

– 2006. 'Stretching the Concept of Representative Bureaucracy: the Case of Nunavut.' 72:4 *International Review of Administrative Sciences* 517.

Tip of the Iceberg: A Summary of Contacts, Cooperation and Agreements between Greenland and Canada. 2001. Nuuk: Greenland Home Rule Government.

Tomaszewski, E. Andreas. 1995. 'Rethinking Crime and Criminal Justice in Nunavut.' MA thesis, Carleton University.

Vahl, M., et al., eds. 1929. *Greenland.* Vol. 3. *The Colonization of Greenland and Its History until 1929.* Copenhagen: C.A. Reitzel; London: Humphrey Milford, Oxford University Press.

Van Den Steenhoven, Geert. 1956a. *Research Report on Caribou Eskimo Law.* Ottawa: Department of Northern Affairs and National Resources.

– 1956b. *Report to the Department of Northern Affairs and National Resources on a field-research journey for the Study of Legal Concepts among the Eskimos in some parts of the Keewatin District, N.W.T., in the summer of 1955.* Ottawa: Department of Northern Affairs and National Resources.

– 1959. *Legal Concepts among the Netsilik Eskimos of Pelly Bay, N.W.T. Report.* Ottawa: Department of Northern Affairs and National Resources.

– 1962. *Leadership and Law among the Eskimos of the Keewatin District, Northwest Territories.* Report. N.p.

– 1966. 'The Law Trough Eskimo Eyes.' In Maja Van Steensel, ed., *People of Light and Dark.* Ottawa: Department of Indian and Northern Affairs.

VanderZwaag, David L., and Donat Pharand. 1983. 'Inuit and the Ice: Implications for Canadian Arctic Waters.' 21 *Canadian Yearbook of International Law* 53.

Vertes, John Z. 2002. 'Jury Trials in Inuit and other Aboriginal Communities.' Paper prepared in conjunction with a presentation to the Joint Meeting of the Canadian Law and Society Association and the Law and Society Association in Vancouver, 1 June.

Wacker, Jens, and Jens Henrik Hojbjerg. 1992. 'Policing in Greenland.' In Curt Taylor Griffiths, ed., *Self-Sufficiency in Northern Justice Issues.* Burnaby: Simon Fraser University for the Northern Justice Society.

Ward, Elaine. 1993. *Indigenous Peoples between Human Rights and Environmental Protection Based on an Empirical Study of Greenland.* Copenhagen: Danish Centre for Human Rights.

Wareham, Timothy M. 1993. 'Greenland and the Legacy of Colonialism: The Politics and Economy of a Danish Dependency.' Essay, University of Greenland.

Weaver, Sally M. 1980. *Making Canadian Indian Policy: The Hidden Agenda, 1968–1970.* Toronto: University of Toronto Press.

Weiss, Friedl. 1985. 'Greenland's Withdrawal from the European Communities.' 10:3 *European Law Review* 173.

Welhengama, Gnanapala. 2000. *Minorities' Claims: From Autonomy to Secession. International Law and State Practice.* Aldershot, UK, and Burlington, VT: Ashgate.

Wendt, Frantz Wilhelm. 1959. *The Nordic Council and Cooperation in Scandinavia.* Copenhagen: Munksgaard.

– 1981. *Cooperation in the Nordic Countries: Achievements and Obstacles.* Stockholm: Almqvist and Wiksell.

White, Graham. 1991. 'Westminster in the Arctic: The Adaptation of British Parliamentarism in the Northwest Territories.' 24:3 *Canadian Journal of Political Science* 499.

– 1993a. 'Structure and Culture in a Non-Partisan Westminster Parliament: Canada's Northwest Territories.' 28:2 *Australian Journal of Political Science* 322.

– 1993b. 'Northern Distinctiveness, Representation by Population and the Charter: The Politics of Redistribution in the Northwest Territories.' 28:3 *Journal of Canadian Studies* 5.

– 2002. 'Treaty Federalism in Northern Canada: Aboriginal-Government Land Claims Boards.' 32:3 *Publius* 89.

– 2005. *Cabinets and First Ministers.* Vancouver: UBC Press.

– 2006a. 'Traditional Aboriginal Values in a Westminster Parliament: The Legislative Assembly of Nunavut.' 12:1 *Journal of Legislative Studies* 8.

– 2006b. 'Cultures in Collision: Traditional Knowledge and Euro-Canadian Governance Processes in Northern Land–Claim Boards.' 59:4 *Arctic* 401.

Williamson, R.G. 1986. 'International Combinations, Present and Possible, between Circumpolar Inuit National Groups, Politics, Problems and Potentials.' 1–2 *Nordic Journal of International Law* 68.

Wilman, Mary Ekho. 2002. 'Governance through Inuit Qaujimajatuqangit: Changing the Paradigm for the Future of Inuit Society.' In Murielle Nagy, ed., *The Power of Traditions: Identities, Politics and Social Sciences.* Topics in Arctic Social Sciences 4. Quebec City: International Arctic Social Sciences Association.

Wilson, Elana T. 2002. 'Gender, Political Power, and Nationalism in the Circumpolar North: A Case Study of Nunavut, Canada.' M.Phil. thesis, University of Cambridge.

Wutzke, Jeffrey. 1997–8. 'Dependent Independence: Application of the Nunavut Model to Native Hawaiian Sovereignty and Self-Determination Claims.' 22:2 *American Indian Law Review* 509.

Young, Lisa. 1997. 'Gender Equal Legislatures: Evaluating the Proposed Nunavut Electoral System.' 23:3 *Canadian Public Policy* 306.

Young, Oran R. 1996. *The Arctic Council: Making a New Era in International Relations.* New York: Twentieth Century Fund.

– 1997. 'Sustainable Development in the Arctic: Operationalizing the Arctic Council.' In Lassi Heininen and Richard Langlais, eds., *Europe's Northern Dimension: The BEAR Meets the South.* Rovaniemi: University of Lapland Press.

– 2000. 'The Structure of Arctic Cooperation: Solving Problems/Seizing Opportunities.' In *Conference Report: Fourth Conference of Parliamentarians of the Arctic Region.* Helsinki: Edita.

– 2005. 'Governing the Arctic: From Cold War Theater to Mosaic of Cooperation.' 11:1 *Global Governance* 9.

Zaslow, Morris. 1981. 'Administering the Arctic Islands, 1880–1940: Policemen, Missionaries, Fur Traders,' In Morris Zaslow, ed., *A Century of Canada's Arctic Islands: 1880–1980.* Ottawa: Royal Society of Canada.

Zimmerman, Peter. 1987 'The Thule, Fylingdales, and Krasnoyarsk Radars: Innocents Abroad?' 17:2 *Arms Control Today* 9.

Index

Aboriginal rights, recognition of under Canadian constitution, 47, 151
Aboriginal title, surrender of with creation of Nunavut, 41, 49
affirmative action, 70, 71
Akitsiraq, 49, 86, 101
Alaska, 5, 21, 23, 25, 28, 124, 125, 126, 137
Alfreðsson, Guðmundur, 26
Amagoalik, John, 39, 40, 53
Anawak, Jack, 41, 67
Arctic cooperation, 11, 121, 121–4, 127. *See also* Nordic cooperation
Arctic Council, 111, 112, 121, 122, 123; Indigenous Peoples Secretariat, 123
Arctic Peace Model, 95
Arctic Window, 120
Ashlee, Jette E., 18, 19
Atassut (Solidarity) Party, 55, 57, 58, 59, 61
Atuagagdliutit, 11
Aupilaarjuk, Mariano, 81
Authorization Act (2005), 104, 106, 107–8, 109, 127, 129

autonomy, 3, 12, 52, 72, 104, 129, 145–6, 149, 151; definitions of, 6, 15; Inuit/indigenous right to, 4, 5, 147

Bathurst Mandate. *See Pinasuaqtavut*
Bentzon, Agnete Weis, 90
Bergen Trading Company, 18
Birket-Smith, Kaj, 82
Boards of Guardians (Greenland), 22, 89
Breinholt-Larsen, Finn, 44, 85
British North America Act, 1867, 18
Brody, Hugh, 31
Brøndsted, Henning, 92
Bush, George W., 133

Canada: federal government, 67, 142; indigenous internationalism in, 124, 125; legal system, 13, 87; participation in Arctic Council, 122; partnership agreement with EU, 121; sovereignty over the Canadian North, 19, 130, 141, 142
Canadian Charter of Rights and Freedoms, 99

Canadian Forces Northern Area
(CFNA), 139
Chukotka, 5, 124, 125, 126
Citizenship Act, 1947 (Canada), 27
class stratification, 66
climate change, 125, 127, 131, 140,
141
Cold War, 25, 128, 131, 132, 133,
140
colonization, impact on Greenland
and Nunavut/Canadian North: 10,
11–24, 26, 31, 86. *See also* voluntary
colonialism
Commission on Greenland's Judicial
System (2004), 91, 92, 95, 96, 98
Commission on Home Rule for
Greenland (1975–8), 30, 38, 43, 46,
48, 54, 107
Commission on Self-Governance
(Greenland, 1999), 6, 31; Report
and recommendations of (2003),
43, 48, 54, 59, 70, 73, 76, 104, 110,
129, 131, 139, 143, 150
Conference Board of Canada, 76
conflict resolution, in Inuit traditional law, 82–5
constitution: Canadian, 36, 45, *see also*
Constitution Act, 1867, Constitution Act, 1982; Danish, 19–20, 26,
43, 44, 47, 48, 98, 106–7
Constitution Act, 1867 (Canada), 45,
99
Constitution Act, 1982 (Canada), 47,
68, 99
constitutional status of Greenland/
Greenlanders, 7, 19–20, 31–2, 43–5,
47–9
corporate governance in Nunavut,
60–2
correctional facilities, 93, 96–7

courts: in Canadian Arctic, 89–90, 92–
4; in Greenland, 91–2, 95–6, 98–9
Curran, Vivian G., 13

Dacks, Gurston, 68
Dahl, Jens, 20, 23, 30, 54, 55, 57, 59
Danish Administration of Justice Act,
91
Danish-Greenlandic Self-Governance
Commission (2004), 7, 31
Danish Instructions of 1782 (the
Instrux), 19–20, 21
decolonization, 11, 20–1, 24–32
Defence Agreement (U.S.–Denmark,
1951), 129, 132, 133, 134, 136,
137
defence policy, 103, 128, 129; Greenland's interest in, 129–36; Nunavut's
interest in, 129–32, 136–40
Democrats (political party in Greenland), 55, 57, 58, 61
Denmark: jurisdiction in international affairs, 105–7; legal system,
12–13, 87; and Nordic cooperation,
112; participation in Arctic Council, 122; sovereignty over Greenland, 18–19, 21; as unitary state,
43–4
Distant Early Warning (DEW) Line,
25, 136, 137
domestic violence, 100

early warning radar system, 133. *See
also* Distant Early Warning (DEW)
Line
economic development, 76, 77, 110;
sustainable, 117–18, 147
economic sustainability, of Green-
land/Nunavut, 42, 55, 75–6, 149
Egede, Hans, 18

elders, role in legal system, 80, 81, 93, 100, 101, 102
electoral structure: in Greenland, 57–9; in Nunavut, 59–60
Eliasen, Bogi, 44, 127
Engell, Mikaela, 136
Enoksen, Hans, 58
Enoogoo, Piujuq, 100
environment: concern for, 59, 141; impact of military bases on, 135, 137
European Development Fund, 118
European Economic Community (EEC), 30, 116; Greenland's withdrawal from, 115
European Union (EU), 44, 108–9, 111, 114, 123; fisheries agreements with Greenland and Denmark, 119; Greenland and, 115–21, see also overseas countries and territories; Northern Dimension of, 119–21; partnership agreement with Canada, 121
Eyre, Kenneth, 136

family, Inuit extended, 17, 147
Family Abuse Intervention Act (Nunavut, 2006), 100
Faroe Islands, 44, 113, 114
financial dependency of Greenland and Nunavut, 75–7
Finkler, Harald W., 87
Finland, 112, 122
fisheries: Greenland's relations with EU on, 118–19; sustainable management of, 119
Fisheries Partnership Agreement, 118, 119
Fisheries Protocol, 119

foreign affairs. See international relations
Fossett, Renée, 80
Frobisher, Martin, 18

Gallagher-Mackay, Kelly, 16, 47, 68
global warming. See climate change
globalization, 42, 104, 147, 150
Goldschmidt, Verner, 94
Gordon, Mark R., 34
governance in Greenland, 35, 38–40; institutions of, 64–72; problems with, 69–70. See also home rule in Greenland
governance in Nunavut, 38–40; commissioner for Nunavut, 68–9; co-management with federal government, 67, 68; decentralization of, 63–4; institutions of, 64–72; Inuit values and, 65–6; problems associated with, 74–5. See also public governance
Graburn, Nelson, 81, 82, 83
Gray, Kevin, 47, 50
Great Britain, 18, 19
Greenland Administration of Justice Act (1951), 90, 91, 92
Greenland Criminal Code (1954), 15, 90, 94, 95
Greenland Home Rule Act (1978), 7, 30, 31, 38, 40, 41–5, 46, 47–8, 50, 51, 52, 53, 54, 73, 103, 106, 147, 148, 150; constitutional recognition of, 47–8; and international relations/defence policy, 107, 108, 140; political system created by, 54, 59
Greenlanders, definition of, 6
Greenland's commando force (GLK), 139

Griffiths, Franklyn, 140, 141, 142
Gulløv, Hans C., 38

Hallendy, Norman, 80
Hans Island (Tartupaluk), dispute
    between Canada and Denmark
    over, 138
Harhoff, Frederik, 44, 46, 47, 48, 98,
    108
Hedtoft, Hans, 25
Helsinki Treaty, 112
Hendrik, Hans, 138
Hicks, Jack, 56
Hingitaq 53, 134–5
Hoebel, E. Adamson, 80, 81, 82, 84
home rule in Greenland, 6, 30, 31,
    35, 38–9, 43–4, 50–1, 66, 107; evo-
    lution of, 147, 148, 149–50; and
    security policy, 142. See also gover-
    nance in Greenland
Hudson's Bay Company (HBC), 18,
    19, 20, 89

Iceland, 112, 114, 120, 122,
indigenous internationalism, Inuit
    and, 124–7
International Labour Organization
    (ILO), 135; Convention (No. 169)
    Concerning Indigenous and Tribal
    Peoples in Independent Countries
    (1989), 135
international relations, jurisdiction
    over: in Canada, 105, 109; in Den-
    mark, 104, 105–9; in Greenland,
    103–9; in Nunavut, 109; transfer-
    ability of, 126–7, 143
Inuaraq, Susan, 80
Inuit: colonization of, 10, 17–24, 33;
    concept of rights, 33–4, 36; custom-
    ary law, 13, 78–87, 95, 97, see also

law-ways; demography, 10; prior to
    European contact, 17, 33, 36, 80–1,
    147; religious conversion of, 18;
    relocation of, 28, 134–5, 137; tradi-
    tional values, 71, 76–7, 83, 97, 147–
    8. See also indigenous international-
    ism
Inuit Ataqatigiit (Inuit Community)
    Party, 38, 55, 57, 58, 59, 61
Inuit Circumpolar Conference
    (ICC), 34, 62, 103, 110, 111, 112,
    122–3, 124–5, 131; petition to
    Inter-American Commission on
    Human Rights, 125
Inuit Circumpolar Council. See Inuit
    Circumpolar Conference
Inuit Committee on National Issues,
    37
Inuit Impact and Benefit Agree-
    ments, 42
Inuit Qaujimajatuqangit (IQ), 61–2,
    63, 65, 66, 77, 98, 101, 147–8
Inuit Rangers, 139
Inuit Tapirisat of Canada (ITC), 28,
    29, 34, 36
Inuktitut, 71, 93, 100, 101, 102; prob-
    lems of translation of Western legal
    concepts into, 42, 146
Inussuk, 55
Inutiq, Sandra, 101
Iqaluit Restorative Justice Society,
    101, 102
Iqaqrialu, David, 61
Isaac, Thomas, 45, 47, 50

Jensen, Henrik Garlic, 89
Johansen, Lars-Emil, 38, 41
Jull, Peter, 25, 30, 37, 44, 124
Juridical Expedition (Jurex), 89, 90
justice, administration of, in Green-

land, 87, 88–9, 90–2, 94–6, 102; problems with, 97. *See also* courts
justice, administration of, in Nunavut, 87–8, 92–4, 96–7, 100–2; problems with, 93–4, 97–8, 100. *See also* courts

Katimajiit, 66
Kilukishak, Gamailie, 100
King, William Lyon Mackenzie, 136
Kitikmeot Inuit Association, 59, 101
Kivalliq Inuit Association, 59
Kleist, Mininnguaq, 47
Kleivan, Inge, 85
Kublu, Alexina, 93
Kuptana, Rosemarie, 36
Kusugak, Jose, 29, 39

Landsting (parliament of Greenland), 54, 58, 59, 60, 62, 63, 69, 71, 108, 113
Law Reform Committee (1951), 90
law-ways, 79, 80, 82, 83, 85, 86, 89, 94, 97, 100, 102
lay judges, 91–2, 95–6
legal order: Greenlandic customary law, 88–9; impact of colonization on, 86–7; Inuit traditional, 78–87; Western, 86
legal status: of Greenland, 45–6; of Nunavut, 45–7
Legaré, André, 56
lex loci, 79, 86, 97, 102
Lund, Henrik, 130
Lyberth, Jens, 58
Lyck, Lise, 46
Lynge, Aqqaluk, 134, 135
Lynge, Aviâja Egede, 51
Lynge, Finn, 57

Maastricht Treaty, 117
Macklem, Patrick, 99
Marecic, Charles J., 51
Matthiasson, John S., 87
Memorandum of Understanding on Cooperation (2000), 124
militarization of the North, 130, 131, 136, 137; during the Second World War, 24, 132; during the Cold War, 25, 132–4
military bases. *See* United States
missile defence, 133, 138–9, 140
Motzfeldt, Jonathan, 121

nationalism, indigenous/Inuit, 29, 35
natural resources, 73, 76, 141, 142
Nielsen, J. Berglund, 44, 48
Nielsen, Lars Nordskov, 134
non-transferable jurisdiction, 6, 8, 73, 75, 104, 144, 151
Nordic Committee for Cooperation, 114
Nordic cooperation, 111, 112–14, 120–1, 127
Nordic Council, 111, 112–13, 114, 123
Nordic Council of Ministers, 111, 112, 113–14, 121, 123
North American Air/Aerospace Defence (NORAD), 136, 138
North Atlantic Treaty Organization (NATO), 24, 130, 132, 136
Northern Dimension (EU policy), 119–21; Arctic Window in, 120
Northern Dimension of Canada's Foreign Policy, 121
Northern Lights coalition (Greenland), 59
North-West Mounted Police, 22, 88, 89

Northwest Passage, 141, 142
Northwest Territories (NWT), 18, 39, 40, 56, 60, 74, 90, 94, 130
Norway, 19, 112, 120, 122
Nowlan-Card, Laureen, 46
nuclear weapons, 135
Nunavut Act, 8, 11, 38, 39, 40, 41, 42–3, 45, 46, 49, 50, 51, 52, 53, 67, 99, 103, 109, 140, 148
Nunavut Agreement-in-Principle, 47
Nunavut Economic Forum, 76
Nunavut Electoral Boundaries Commission, 62
Nunavut Human Rights Act, 78–9
Nunavut Impact Review Board, 109
Nunavut Implementation Commission (NIC), 54, 56, 61, 62, 63, 92
Nunavut Land Claims Agreement (NLCA), 5, 8, 11, 29, 31, 35, 36, 38, 39, 40, 42–3, 50, 51–2, 53, 74, 103, 130, 139, 142, 148, 151; affirmative action clause in, 70; constitutional recognition of, 41, 45, 46, 47, 49, 74; on international relations/defence policy, 109, 140; limitations of, 146–7; system of governance established by, 59–60, 67, 150.
Nunavut Legislative Assembly, 54, 60, 62–3
Nunavut Political Accord, 39, 40, 47
Nunavut Settlement Area, 49, 70, 109
Nunavut Tunngavik Incorporated (NTI), 42, 59–60, 62, 70, 138, 151
Nungaq, Zebedee, 80
Nuttall, Mark, 27

oil. See natural resources
Okalik, Paul, 139, 142

Østreng, Willy, 130
overseas countries and territories (OCT): Greenland as OCT with EU, 116–18

parliament: Canadian, 40, 41, 46; Danish (the Folketing), 40, 46, 47, 57, 108, 134; Greenland, see Landsting
Parliamentary Committee on Foreign and Security Policy, 143
Patenaude, Allan, 84
Pauktuutit, 62
Pedersen, Mille S., 96
Petersen, Hanne, 86, 97
Petersen, Robert, 22, 81, 83
Pinasuaqtavut, 65, 147
Piugatuk, Frances, 101
Poelzer, Greg, 16
political parties: in Greenland, 54–6, 57–9, 64; lack of in Nunavut, 54, 55
public governance, in Nunavut, 10–11, 31, 32, 35, 39, 40, 49, 54, 67, 73, 148–9; devolution of powers from Ottawa, 73, 77, 142, 151. See also governance in Nunavut
punishment, and Inuit traditional law, 82–3, 85, 94

Qikiqtani Inuit Association, 59
Quassa, Paul, 67

Rasing, Willem, 83
Rasmussen, Henriette, 133
relocation. See Inuit, relocation
Robinson, Qajaq, 101
Rodon, Thierry, 68
Roosevelt, Franklin D., 132
Rouland, Norbert, 80, 82, 83
Rousseau, Pierre, 100

Royal Canadian Mounted Police
(RCMP), 88. *See also* North-West
Mounted Police
Royal Commission on Greenland, 25,
90
Royal Greenland Trading Company
(KGH), 19
Royal Proclamation of 1763, 20
Rupert's Land, 18, 20
Russian Federation, 10, 119, 120,
122

security policy, 103, 140–4
self-governance, Inuit: 4, 29, 32, 39,
49, 65, 67–8, 71, 145–6, 148; Inuit
perspectives on, 33–7; right to, 43,
74, 110, 127
shaman, 80, 81, 82
Sirius Patrol, 139
Sissons, Jack H., 90
Siumut, 54–5, 57–8, 61
song duels, 84–5
strategic importance of Greenland
and Nunavut, 128, 129–30
Sweden, 112, 122

Thule air base/radar system, 129,
132–6, 137, 138, 140, 143; relocation of Inughuit to build, 28, 134–5
trade policy, 110, 127, 141
training programs in Nunavut, 70
treaties, international, 107, 109
treaty rights, recognition of under
Canadian constitution, 47, 151

Tungavik Federation of Nunavut, 39,
67

United Nations: Charter, 26; Draft
Declaration on the Rights of Indig-
enous Peoples, 126; Economic and
Social Council (ECOSOC), 125–6;
Permanent Forum on Indigenous
Issues, 126
United States, 10, 115, 122, 125, 130,
143; military bases in the Canadian
Arctic, 25, 136–7; military bases in
Greenland, 24, 28, 134–6
Uummannaq, relocation of Inughuit
from, 134–5

Van Den Steenhoven, Geert, 80, 81
voluntary colonialism, 41, 52, 148

Ward, Elaine, 48
welfare state, 27, 31
Westminister parliamentary system,
57, 60
White, Graham, 56, 67
Wildlife Act (Nunavut), 66
Wilson, Elana, 29
women, representation of in Greenland and Nunavut legislatures, 62
Women's Party (Greenland), 58, 62
women's rights, 42, 147

Yukon, 45, 57, 74, 94